Language and Culture Pedagogy

D1248126

LANGUAGES FOR INTERCULTURAL COMMUNICATION AND EDUCATION
Editors: Michael Byram, *University of Durham, UK*
Alison Phipps, *University of Glasgow, UK*

The overall aim of this series is to publish books which will ultimately inform learning and teaching, but whose primary focus is on the analysis of intercultural relationships, whether in textual form or in people's experience. There will also be books which deal directly with pedagogy, with the relationships between language learning and cultural learning, between processes inside the classroom and beyond. They will all have in common a concern with the relationship between language and culture, and the development of intercultural communicative competence.

Other Books in the Series
Developing Intercultural Competence in Practice
  Michael Byram, Adam Nichols and David Stevens (eds)
Intercultural Experience and Education
  Geof Alred, Michael Byram and Mike Fleming (eds)
Critical Citizens for an Intercultural World: Foreign Language Education as Cultural Politics
  Manuela Guilherme
How Different Are We? Spoken Discourse in Intercultural Communication
  Helen Fitzgerald
Audible Difference: ESL and Social Identity in Schools
  Jennifer Miller
Context and Culture in Language Teaching and Learning
  Michael Byram and Peter Grundy (eds)
An Intercultural Approach to English language Teaching
  John Corbett
Critical Pedagogy: Political Approaches to Language and Intercultural Communication
  Alison Phipps and Manuela Guilherme (eds)
Vernacular Palaver: Imaginations of the Local and Non-native Languages in West Africa
  Moradewun Adejunmobi
Foreign Language Teachers and Intercultural Competence: An International Investigation
  Lies Sercu with Ewa Bandura, Paloma Castro, Leah Davcheva, Chryssa Laskaridou, Ulla Lundgren, María del Carmen Méndez García and Phyllis Ryan
Language and Culture: Global Flows and Local Complexity
  Karen Risager
Living and Studying Abroad: Research and Practice
  Michael Byram and Anwei Feng (eds)
Education for Intercultural Citizenship: Concepts and Comparisons
  Geof Alred, Mike Byram and Mike Fleming (eds)

Other Books of Interest
Language Teachers, Politics and Cultures
  Michael Byram and Karen Risager

For more details of these or any other of our publications, please contact:
Multilingual Matters, Frankfurt Lodge, Clevedon Hall,
Victoria Road, Clevedon, BS21 7HH, England
http://www.multilingual-matters.com

LANGUAGES FOR INTERCULTURAL COMMUNICATION AND EDUCATION 14
Series Editors: Michael Byram and Alison Phipps

Language and Culture Pedagogy
From a National to a Transnational Paradigm

Karen Risager

MULTILINGUAL MATTERS LTD
Clevedon • Buffalo • Toronto

Library of Congress Cataloging in Publication Data
Risager, Karen
Language and Culture Pedagogy: From a National to a Transnational
Paradigm/Karen Risager.
Languages for Intercultural Communication and Education: 14
Includes bibliographical references and index.
1.Language and languages–Study and teaching. 2. Multicultural education.
3. Language and culture–Study and teaching. I. Title.
P53.45.R57 2007
407.1–dc22   2006022562

British Library Cataloguing in Publication Data
A catalogue entry for this book is available from the British Library.

ISBN-13: 978-1-85359-960-6 (hbk)
ISBN-13: 978-1-85359-959-0 (pbk)

Multilingual Matters Ltd
UK: Frankfurt Lodge, Clevedon Hall, Victoria Road, Clevedon BS21 7HH.
USA: UTP, 2250 Military Road, Tonawanda, NY 14150, USA.
Canada: UTP, 5201 Dufferin Street, North York, Ontario M3H 5T8, Canada.

The policy of Multilingual Matters/Channel View Publications is to use papers that
are natural, renewable and recyclable products, made from wood grown in
sustainable forests. In the manufacturing process of our books, and to further support
our policy, preference is given to printers that have FSC and PEFC Chain of Custody
certification. The FSC and/or PEFC logos will appear on those books where full
certification has been granted to the printer concerned.

Typeset by Saxon Graphics.
Printed and bound in Great Britain by MPG Books Ltd.

Contents

Acknowledgements

This book has been developed from my Danish-language book entitled *Det nationale dilemma i sprog- og kulturpædagogikken: Et studie i forholdet mellem sprog og kultur* [The National Dilemma in Language and Culture Pedagogy: A Study of the Relationship between Language and Culture]. This was published by Akademisk Forlag, Copenhagen, in 2003.

The present volume, *Language and Culture Pedagogy: From a National to a Transnational Paradigm*, is based on Parts II and IV of that volume, revised by myself, and translated into English by Dr John Irons, to whom I am most grateful.

The rest of the original text (Parts I and III) has already been published by Multilingual Matters Ltd as *Language and Culture: Global Flows and Local Complexity*.

I want to thank the Danish Research Council for the Humanities for supporting me throughout my work. They offered me research leave in the years 1998–2000, they supported the publication of the Danish book at Akademisk Forlag, and they financed the translation into English. I also want to thank the Department of Language and Culture, Roskilde University, for their backing and inspiration.

During the elaboration of the original text I received constructive criticism, encouragement and suggestions from many colleagues, friends and family members, not least Ulrich Ammon, Flemming Gorm Andersen, Michael Byram, Inger M. Clausen, Anette Danbæk, Uwe Geist, Annette S. Gregersen, Frans Gregersen, Hartmut Haberland, Jesper Hermann, Anne Holmen, Christian Horst, Karen Sonne Jakobsen, Bent Johansen, Susanne Kjærbeck, Ebbe Klitgaard, Claire Kramsch, Karen Lund, Arne Thing Mortensen, Michael Svendsen Pedersen, Kirsten Holst Petersen, Robert Phillipson, Bent Preisler, Kasper Risager, Elsebeth Rise, Klaus Schulte, Lotte M. Vandel and Johannes Wagner. I am most grateful to them all.

Karen Risager

Foreword

This is the second book derived from Karen Risager's original *Det nationale dilemma i sprog- og kulturpædagogikken. Et studie i forholdet mellem sprog og kultur* (The National Dilemma in Language and Culture Pedagogy. A Study of the Relationship between Language and Culture) published in Danish in 2003 by Akademisk Forlag, Copenhagen. It stands independently of the first book, also published in the series Languages for Intercultural Communication and Education, and can be read in its own right as a major analysis of the history and current development of culture pedagogy, to use Risager's phrase. It can also be read in conjunction with the first book, *Language and Culture. Global Flows and Local Complexity* (Multilingual Matters 2006), since together the two show how language teachers can and should reflect on the relationship between language and culture and plan changes in their own practice.

Here, the author presents her principal aim – and it is one that is also part of the first book – as creating a basis for a change from a national to a transnational paradigm in language and culture pedagogy, but there is much else too.

It is important for any discipline, particularly in its early phases, that its historical evolution should be well understood by those involved. Language and culture pedagogy, and foreign language teaching as a specific and major component, is carried out by professionals, by teachers with a professional training. Training involves acquiring the accepted wisdom and current knowledge and understanding of a discipline, and the practical skills to carry it out, whether this is teaching medicine, law or whatever. Those who are entrusted to professionals, and who put their trust in professionals, do so because they know that they are trained. Training for law and medicine has long been located in universities, whereas it is in most countries only in relatively recent times that teacher training has been moved there from institutions that specialised in teacher training and did not have the functions of a university.

Some people like to mark this development by referring to teacher *education* rather than *training*, but the important point is that universities are places where people acquire professional knowledge and skills and also a *critical* understanding of their profession. This is particularly important when, as is frequently and perhaps increasingly the case in teaching, there is centralised political control of the profession, and an attempt to make teachers follow the 'guidelines' of central authorities.

A critical understanding presupposes awareness of the origins of current knowledge and skills, of the evolution of the discipline and of how what might seem inevitable and taken for granted is in fact the consequence of historical change. Risager provides such an understanding of culture pedagogy and its relationship to language teaching since its beginnings. I hope that all teachers, not least those in pre-service training/ education, who recognise the importance of a cultural dimension in language teaching will learn from the first part of this book.

The book is not, however, simply a history, and even the first part deals with Risager's second purpose: to analyse and question the relationship between language teaching in a national paradigm, which sees a specific language as related to a specific national culture, and to propose a transnational perspective, which denies that any such connection is necessary and inevitable, and which places language teaching firmly within a global social context.

It is at this point that I have to declare a personal interest, as Karen, with whom I have worked for many years, takes a critical look at my model of intercultural competence and improves on it by emphasising the global and transnational, rather than the national perspective that I had assumed. Karen has a long-term vision for language teaching and culture pedagogy to contribute to the education and upbringing of world citizens in an age when nations are no longer as significant. Her vision coincides with that of the great historian of nationalism, Eric Hobsbawm. Contemporary history, he says:

> will inevitably have to be written as the history of a world which can no longer be contained within the limits of nations and nation states as these used to be defined, either politically, or economically, or culturally, *or even linguistically*. It will be largely supranational and infranational, but even infranationality, whether or not it dresses itself up in the costume of some mini-nationalism, will reflect the decline of the old nation state as an operational entity. (…)
> Hobsbawm, E. 1992, *Nations and Nationalism since 1780*. Cambridge University Press, pp. 191–2 (my emphasis)

If he is right, and I suspect and hope he is, then Karen Risager's vision of language teaching and the competence of the world citizen, which language teachers should take as the guideline for their long-term aims, goes further than what I wrote ten years ago.

Karen Risager has thus written a book that is not only a major scholarly analysis of the history of culture pedagogy, but one which points us forward to what language and culture teachers must assess for themselves as the world changes. She provides them with the critical base on which to make their professional judgements, and has thus made a significant contribution to our work into the future.

Michael Byram
April 2006

Chapter 1

Modern Language Studies: Language, Culture, Nation

Introduction

Today, modern language studies take place in a world increasingly influenced by internationalisation and globalisation. Although the main focus of this book is foreign-language studies and foreign-language teaching, it has to be said that all language studies, whether the language in question is a first or second language, a foreign language or a community/heritage language, are social and cultural practices embedded in comprehensive and potentially global processes: transnational communication and migration, transnational cooperation of many types and at many levels, etc.

So language and culture pedagogy must learn to understand their field of reference from a transnational and global perspective. Language teaching can no longer make do with focusing on the target language and target countries – and on cultures as territorially defined phenomena. This applies not only to English as the most widespread international language at present but also to teaching in all languages, no matter how many native speakers there are. Apart from developing the students' communicative (dialogic) competence in the target language, language teaching ought also as far as possible to enable students to develop into multilingually and multiculturally aware world citizens.

This is not synonymous with ceasing to take an interest in national and ethnic identities. Language teaching can deal with many kinds of identities, including national and ethnic ones, but it has to understand them as processes that take place between particular players under particular historical and geographical circumstances in multicultural communities that form and develop across existing national boundaries. Modern language studies therefore have to break with the traditional national paradigm and start to define a transnational paradigm that places language teaching in a transnational and global context.

A prerequisite for making such a change is that language subjects also break with the traditional view that 'language' and 'culture' constitute an inseparable whole, and that language teaching must therefore work for maximum integration between teaching the target language and teaching in the target language culture (or, in other words, culture and society in the target language countries). Language subjects must work on the theory that the relation between language and culture is complex and multidimensional, and that linguistic practice and other cultural practice are parts of more or less comprehensive processes – also transnational and potentially global processes.

The aim of this book

The aim of this book is to establish a basis for a change from a national to a transnational paradigm in language and culture pedagogy. The most fruitful point of departure for such an analysis is *theoretical culture peda-gogy*, i.e. the discipline that deals with the cultural dimension of language teaching, primarily understood as the development of insight into culture and society in the target-language countries. It is precisely in this disci-pline that many statements can be found concerning the relation between language and culture, and that between language teaching and culture teaching. At the same time, it is a discipline that has dealt to an astonish-ingly limited extent with the question of the national. When the analysis of culture pedagogy has been completed, I will, however, return to language and culture pedagogy as a whole, in order to retain the inner cohesion of the field.

The book comprises two sections: *firstly*, there is a critical analysis of the international culture pedagogy discourse concerning language, culture and nation since the 1880s, where it had its beginnings in the newly consti-tuted German Reich. In the analysis, I give an account of a number of the most characteristic positions on the relation between language, culture and nation. This is the first time an attempt has been made to present culture pedagogy as a whole – both geographically and historically – and in a discussion of the possible transition from a national to a transnational paradigm it is important to know how strongly the national paradigm has influenced the culture pedagogy discourse in various ways, depending on such features as theoretical academic position and national background.[1]

Secondly, I present the theory of the multi dimensional relationship between language and culture in a transnational and global perspective (cf. Risager, 2003 and 2006), and I formulate a number of proposals for a new transnational paradigm that deals with how one can work in language teaching with transnational connections and subnational locali-sations. Finally, I list 10 competence areas as comprising the intercultural competence of the world citizen, including languacultural, interpretative and ethnographic competences as well as knowledge of the world.

A transnational language and culture pedagogy must see itself as being interdisciplinary and thereby be interested in language, culture, society and the individual (the subject). This means that, apart from dealing with the complex relation between language and culture, it also deals with the social organisation of language and culture in a broad sense: national and transnational social structures and processes, national and international political relations, etc. It is thus also interested in national and ethnic issues, not only in the sense of national and ethnic communities, identities and discourses but also the societal and political structures that form frameworks and conditions for identity constructions. It places the national and the ethnic in a larger global perspective, and deals with the multilingual and multicultural subject as a world citizen.

This position can be termed postnational and postethnic, i.e. it does not operate with 'the national' and 'the ethnic' as essentialistic entities but as composite historical constructions that are constantly changing their nature by virtue of players' constant strategic use of them. That I in the following prefer nevertheless to use the concept of 'transnational' rather than 'postnational' is because I feel that the concept of 'transnational' points more specifically to processes in the real world, at both micro- and macro-level, including transnational migration flows and transnational flows of information in the media and the Internet. It is important to focus on these flows in order to reach an understanding of the complex relationship between language and culture, or, in other words, between linguistic practice and other forms of cultural practice. Later in this chapter, I will deal in more detail with this conception – and also return to the subject in Chapter 7.

The national paradigm in language studies is not that old

Modern language studies do not have to be nationally shaped. The present national shaping took place in a particular historical period, in connection with the establishment of nations in Europe and the rest of the world, particularly in the course of the 19th and 20th centuries. Not until the latter half of the 19th century did language subjects acquire the aim of conveying a uniform image of the various national states, of the language, the literature, the country and the people.

The national formation of language subjects becomes clear when compared with how they were conceived in the previous period. Before the national idea had a profound impact on language studies, they were more universal and encyclopaedic in orientation. For example, the philosopher and educationalist J.A. Comenius (1592–1670) wrote his Latin primer _Janua linguarum reserata_ (The Messe of Tongues) (1649) with an encyclopaedic content divided into 100 chapters – about the elements, the earth, the body, the economy, grammar, music, geography, history and angels. It was extremely popular, was translated into several languages and also appeared in multilingual editions with reading passages divided into, for example, a Latin, Greek and French column. Another example of this exceptionally broad thematic approach is the Danish reader by Peter Hjort: _Den Danske Børneven. En Læsebog for Borger- og Almue-Skoler [The Danish Children's Friend. A Reader for Primary and Board Schools]_ (sixth edition 1852), which is a reader designed for teaching Danish as a first language. It contains many reading passages of a slightly more practical nature, although still broad and encyclopaedic, e.g. about the globe and its surface, trees, Africa, Peter the Great, law and order and the human soul (cf. Risager, 2003; Risager, 2006; Hüllen, 2005).

The language subjects, however, gradually became nationalised and included in the general educating of populations towards a nationally structured view of the world. A geographical division of labour developed between the language subjects which involved a narrowing and focusing with regard to content: the subject English looked towards England, the English and the English language; the subject French looked towards France, the French and the French language, etc.

Culture Pedagogy: A Presentation

Culture pedagogy arose as a subject for debate and theoretical reflection in the last decades of the 19th century. Language teaching has admittedly always had a cultural dimension in terms of content, either universal / encyclopaedic or national. Reading pieces have been studied that have been written for the occasion, or taken from unadapted literature, and conversational exercises have been constructed on the basis of conversational examples and translated texts – some with a cohesive content, others strongly fragmented in character ('compositional exercises') (cf. the critical presentation in Jespersen, 1901). The whole philological tradition represents a relatively integrated approach to language, texts and history, if the teaching of grammar at elementary level is excluded (cf. Svanholt, 1968).

But not until the last decades of the 19th century did an interest develop in certain places in parts of the content of language teaching that go beyond literary education as such, and from the 1960s onwards culture pedagogy began to crystallise out as a more or less independent discipline. Culture pedagogy first arose, then, in the national phase of the history of language teaching. Language pedagogy, on the other hand, has roots that stretch back at least as far as 500 BC (Kelly, 1969).

Language pedagogy and culture pedagogy did not, however, have much to do with each other until the 1990s, when it was possible to see signs of a burgeoning awareness of each other's work and perspectives – in some respects also a rapprochement, especially under the banner of 'intercultural learning'. The expression 'language and culture pedagogy' captures precisely the point that the theoretical field is at one and the same time a unity and a duality.

The plethora of terminology

There are many terms for what I here refer to as culture pedagogy. In English, the title can, for example, be 'background studies' (now being abandoned) or 'cultural studies' (UK) or 'the teaching of culture' (US), in German *Landeskunde*, *Kulturkunde* (both more or less abandoned) or in recent years: *interkulturelles Lernen*, in French *civilisation*, *culture étrangère* or *l'interculturel*, in Russian *stranovedenie*, in Swedish formerly *realia* and *kulturorientering*, now more usually *interkulturell förståelse*, in Danish *kulturpædagogik* or *kulturforståelse*, in Norwegian *kulturkunnskap*, etc. This is by no means an exhaustive list, simply examples. The plethora of terminology reflects the difficulties in conceptualising the area and is also an expression of the diversity of national traditions. It would seem, however, that a common title is beginning to establish itself around 'the intercultural'.[2]

Already at this early juncture, I must point out that 'culture pedagogy' is a category that 'pulls', to use an expression from the world of libraries: all approaches that in some way or other have cultural relevance I call 'culture pedagogical', even though their representatives might not do so themselves. Something similar applies to my use of the word 'culture educationalist' for theorists in the field.

The primary focus of culture pedagogy: General foreign and second language teaching

Culture pedagogy normally refers to language teaching with a general purpose, since it is here that 'language and culture' occur as a combined object for teaching.[3] That language teaching with a general purpose ought to deal with both language and culture is something about which a broad consensus has gradually been established in most of the world, though more in theory (statements of intent) than in practice. It is mostly taken to mean that language teaching is to include teaching in cultural and social relations in the target-language countries. General language teaching thus has a dual syllabus. It is the basis for the fundamental pedagogical challenge of language teaching, i.e. the integration between the linguistic and the cultural dimension.

Furthermore, culture pedagogy has traditionally focused on foreign- and second-language teaching, with the main emphasis on foreign-language teaching. i.e. the teaching of languages that are primarily spoken in other countries than the country in which the teaching takes place.[4] In both forms of teaching, great demands are made on the teacher to be a *generalist* who has an overview of the entire subject area, including language, literature, culture and society. On the other hand, teaching in the first language (as majority or official language) normally has a narrower linguistic–literary aim, since this teaching is supplemented by other subjects with special responsibility for (national) history, geography, social studies, etc. That foreign- rather than second-language teaching has been the main focus has presumably something to do with the fact that foreign-language teaching has the longest and most institutionalised history in the school systems. As far as teaching in the first language when it is a minority language (community/heritage language) is concerned, there has not been, as far as I know, any real theoretical debate or research on the cultural dimension.

As regards the level of teaching, culture pedagogy has gradually been introduced at all levels, from primary education to education and independent cultural learning in higher education.

Literature pedagogy as culture pedagogy

I do not intend to deal with the more specialised form of literature pedagogy that has an academic study of literature as its point of departure and focuses on such areas as literary critical competence and the development of insight into trends of literary history. When I include teaching by means of fictional literature, it is when thinking of the relevance of working with literature for linguistic and cultural learning, including the development of the ability to empathise with various cultural and societal conditions and undertake a shift of perspective between various types of experience.

In the language and culture pedagogy context, the work with written and oral forms of literature is an important portal to what some people refer to as 'foreign experiences': other ways of living, other ways of seeing the world, other perceptions, perspectives and states of mind. At the same time, it is also an important means for becoming aware of the fact that other people in other cultural, social and historical contexts can have universally human experiences that are very similar to one's own. Reading literature and literature-pedagogical activities can help learners apprehend differences and similarities.

I intend to operate with an open non-hierarchical concept of literature, as in the Cultural Studies tradition. That means that 'literature' for me refers to both high brow and low brow cultural forms (novellas, feature films, music videos, jokes, etc.). It also means that I do not sharply distinguish between fiction and non-fiction, but am of the opinion that it is best to operate with a continuum between relatively objective non-fiction via various hybrid forms ('faction', etc.) to undisputable fiction with a more or less realistic content.

Language and culture pedagogy is not only relevant for language subjects

Language and culture pedagogy is not only relevant for language subjects proper. All teaching subjects have a language/culture dimension. But the language/culture dimension normally only becomes visible when the language in question is a second language or a foreign language for those involved. When children and young people from linguistic minorities go to school, they typically use the official language of the country as their second language in the various subjects – and the subject teacher in question therefore has the task of helping these students to develop their second language in relation to their own subject. And when a school chooses to teach its students in, for example, English (as a foreign language) in a range of subjects, such as geography, mathematics and physical education, teachers of these subjects acquire a language- and culture-pedagogical task over and above their normal subject-related didactics.[5] In interdisciplinary work, too, teachers from other subjects can be incorporated into language teaching, e.g. in a project where history and French collaborate on certain French texts, or in connection with a study trip to e.g. London, where the civics and history teachers contribute to a greater or lesser extent to English teaching alongside the English teacher. But also when the language in, for example, geography is the first language for all those involved, students also learn there to use the relevant specialised terminology in their first language.

Since all subjects have, then, a language/culture aspect, the horizon of language and culture pedagogy ought not to be restricted to language subjects proper. Apart from being a subject-related didactic area, language and culture pedagogy is thus also a general pedagogical area that deals with issues that belong potentially to all subjects – and thereby to the education system as a whole. It is important to point this out not least in connection with internationalisation, which of course affects all subjects, although in different ways.

In the following, however, in order to retain the empirical focus, I intend to concentrate on language teaching within language subjects proper. This is not synonymous with dealing with the language subjects in isolation. In my opinion, language subjects ought to try out all possibilities for inter-disciplinary cooperation inside and outside the school. Even so, my point of departure is independent language subjects provided with teachers that (ideally) have a training that combines qualifications in the specific language subjects with qualifications in language and culture pedagogy.

The cultural dimension

The cultural dimension of language teaching appears in various guises; broadly speaking, it is possible to distinguish between three types of dimension:

- the content dimension;
- the context dimension;
- the poetic dimension.

The content dimension has to do with the thematic content of teaching, including the cultural and societal relations that are studied in various types of text, film, etc. Here, culture is synonymous with the images of the target-language countries the students are presented with, interpret and work on. This dimension is that best represented in culture pedagogy as regards both breadth and number of publications. It is for that reason that I intend to deal mainly with this dimension in the following.

The context dimension has to do with the social situations in which language use takes place, and the sociocultural knowledge necessary to be able to use language in a situationally adequate way. Here, then, 'culture' is the context of language use – typically the context we find in the coun-tries where the target language is spoken as a first language. This dimen-sion is represented in culture pedagogy by an intercultural pragmatic approach which I will return to later.

The poetic dimension has to do with the poetics of language. Here, then, 'culture' is synonymous with aesthetic, poetic uses of language in both written and spoken form. In relation to this dimension, I will discuss a couple of recent approaches.

In the following, I wish to begin to seek to isolate the culture pedagogy that has its point of departure in the humanities and/or social sciences, after which I will briefly mention a number of different culture-pedagogical approaches that arise out of the language-pedagogy tradition and have a linguistic/sociolinguistic point of departure.[6] Whereas the former approaches focus on the content dimension, the latter, linguistic approaches are broader. Some focus on the content dimension, others on the context dimension, and still others also include the poetic dimension.

Culture pedagogy with a point of departure in the humanities and/or the social sciences

Culture pedagogy with a point of departure in culture and social sciences is the most comprehensive branch, containing approaches inspired by sociology, history, social psychology, anthropology and Cultural Studies.

It could be said that this type of culture pedagogy has from the outset conceived itself as a corrective to language pedagogy, with its traditionally one-sided linguistic focus. It has partially different theoretical and philosophical approaches, including the hermeneutical, which makes it opposed to language pedagogy. It has always had a more holistic view of language learning, as it has been interested in man not only as a language learner but as someone who also develops other facets of the personality in connection with language learning – especially a greater knowledge and understanding of the world. So culture pedagogy can be described as a particular version of humanistic tendencies within language teaching – a version that is relatively cognitive in its orientation.[7] Culture pedagogy has been particularly interested in teaching about cultural and societal conditions in the countries where the target language is spoken as the first language, and thus with what themes, texts (literary and non-literary) and methods can be used in the teaching in order to develop the students' cultural understanding and (inter)cultural competence. The horizon in terms of content and theme is very broad, with an almost endless range of subjects: everyday life in various countries and in various social groups, subcultures, music and art, educational conditions, regional conditions, the environment, market conditions, economics, politics, technology, etc. The subject English as a foreign language has almost experienced an explosion in that direction. On the basis of this potential abundance of material, culture pedagogy has concerned itself not least with discussing relevant aims, selection criteria, perspectives and methods, also in relation to teaching materials.

A shift of emphasis has taken place in culture pedagogy over the past 15–20 years, from a focus on the teaching material to one on cultural learning processes. This has meant, among other things, a greater focus on the individual students – an interest in the development of their consciousness and personality in connection with work on the foreign cultures seen in relation to their own cultural background. There is an emphasis on comparing cultures, reflexiveness and an understanding of 'the other'. The focus is on such concepts as intercultural competence and the intercultural speaker: a person who is able to mediate between various languages and various cultural contexts.

Culture pedagogy with a point of departure in linguistics/ sociolinguistics

During the 1970s and 1980s, and especially the 1990s, an interest in culture has grown out of the language-pedagogy tradition. The precursor is the communicative approach that developed in the 1970s and 1980s, especially in connection with the work done by the Council of Europe to develop communicative skills and mobility within the European Common Market (van Ek, 1975; Wilkins, 1976, etc.). This approach recognises that (linguistic) communication develops best in connection with a meaningful content – and certain people began to discuss what this content could actually be. In this connection, that meant discussing what knowledge language users had to possess in order to communicate effectively with the aid of the target language. One aspect of this was semantic knowledge of the cultural connotations of the lexis.

In the 1980s and 1990s, the communicative approach developed a more intercultural orientation in the light of research into intercultural pragmatics and intercultural communication in general, and it began to show an interest in teaching cultural differences in language use and in using the target language as a lingua franca.

In the 1980s and 1990s, research was also undertaken into linguistic socialisation in various cultures (Ochs, 1988), in addition to research into second-language socialisation in the classroom. And an interest has developed in discourses, cultural understanding and cultural constructions in the classroom – an interest that also addresses the poetic dimension of language.

The concept of language-and-culture

Many statements have been made in culture pedagogy about a close connection between language and culture, and this view is used as an argument for language teaching having to be accompanied by instruction in cultural relations in the countries where the target language is spoken ('the target-language countries'). Byram, for example, talks about 'language-and-culture' (also in the plural: 'language-and-cultures') (Byram, Morgan & colleagues, 1994), Galisson talks about *langue-culture* (language-culture) (1994) and Crozet and Liddicoat talk about 'culture-in-language' (2000). Culture pedagogy can be said to be typified by the idea of culture-bound language. This can be seen in the following quotation, taken from an article by the German culture educationalist P. Doyé:

> The very nature of language forbids the separation of language from culture. If language is considered as a system of signs, and signs are characterized by the fact that they are units of form and meaning, it is impossible to learn a language by simply acquiring the forms without their content. And as the content of a language is always culture-bound, any reasonable foreign-language teaching cannot but include the study of a culture from which the language stems. (Doyé, 1996: 105)

There can be no doubt that there are many links between language and culture, but the question is: What culture or cultural forms is the target language in question 'bound to' – and how? These are questions I will later seek to clarify (Chapter 7).

The conception of culture-bound language can be related to what is called first-language bias or native-language bias within linguistics in general, which means that language is studied without an awareness of only studying it in its capacity of first language for language users. This means that one is unaware of the fact that a close connection, or insepara-bility or 'boundness' between language and culture in practice only has to do with language in its capacity of first language. The national-romantic idea of an inner connection between the national language and the national culture actually has to do with those who have grown up with their first language and 'the first-language culture' (translation from the German expression: *die muttersprachliche Kultur*).

The above expressions 'language-and-culture', *langue-culture*, etc. relate implicitly to this perception. Language and culture pedagogy is therefore in the paradoxical situation that it builds on the first-language bias at the same time as it deals precisely with language as foreign and second language. Possibly, this situation has something to do with the traditional ideal for foreign- and second-language learning: to get close to first-language competence as much as possible. But if the situation of the learner is taken as the point of departure, e.g. if the person involved is learning French, the alleged connection between the French language and French culture does not exist as a reality but as a *norm* – and we are even dealing with a norm that in principle is unattainable as it is impossible to have the same learning history as a first-language speaker, even if the learner gains a very high degree of language proficiency. The idea of inseparability between language and culture in a *descriptive* sense has no immediate meaning when the language functions as a foreign or second language. This will be returned to later (Chapter 7).

A generic and a differential understanding of language and culture

It should be mentioned at this juncture that it is important to distinguish between a generic and a differential understanding of language and culture (see also Risager, 2003 and Risager, 2006).

In a *generic* understanding of language and culture, these phenomena are seen as being universal: language in general (Fr. *langage*) and culture in general (culture as opposed to nature). In the generic understanding, language and culture are under all circumstances inseparable: human language is always embedded in culture – no matter what form it assumes. But in the *differential* understanding, the languages of the world are looked at in their diversity, as are all kinds of cultural diversity. In the differential understanding the question always has to be: What forms of culture actually go with the language in question? And this is an empirical question.

Within the differential understanding a distinction can be made between a general and a specific level. Studies of language contact, multi-lingualism and language teaching in general belong to the general level, while studies related to a particular language, e.g. Arabic, English or Maori, belong to the specific level.

Absence of a discussion of the national in culture pedagogy

Expressions such as language-and-culture (in the differential sense) can be based on a national conception of the national language and the national culture, but they do not have to be so. It can, however, be difficult to decide whether the discourse is national or not. In culture pedagogy, the national is not so often referred to in explicit terms (although it does happen from the 1990s onwards, e.g. Thürmann, 1994 and Altmayer, 1997). This absence can be interpreted as an implicit distancing from nationalism. But it would also seem to be a denial of the national in general in the language-and-culture-pedagogy discourse. One example is the absence of 'nation' or 'national' as a reference word in *Routledge Encyclopedia of Language Teaching and Learning*, ed. by Byram, 2000a. The word 'international', on the other hand, is an index word in the same work. A major discussion of perspectives regarding postnational society or transnationalism has not taken place in the culture-pedagogy discourse prior to my book of 2003 (although it is implicit in the approach found in Guilherme, 2002, see Chapter 8).

Theories of Nationality: Some Central Concepts

Banal nationalism

In order to illustrate the national paradigm in foreign languages, I would include, among others, the British social psychologist Michael Billig's theory of 'banal nationalism' (Billig, 1995). Banal nationalism is 'the ideological means by which nation-states are reproduced' (Billig, 1995: 6), or, defined slightly more fully: 'include(s) the patterns of belief and practice which reproduce the world – "our" world – as a world of nation-states, in which "we" live as citizens of nation-states' (Billig, 1995: 7). Banal nationalism finds expression in the many small everyday things and statements that remind us that the world is divided into national states, and that presupposes that this is common sense – a quite natural thing that could not be otherwise. The flag on official buildings; the political map, where countries are clearly demarcated from each other and in different colours; expressions such as 'Australian weather' or 'German birds'; the expression 'the whole country'; the political deixis that lies in the use of 'us' and 'them' – all these are examples of the apparently innocent things that keep alive our national conception of the world. It is virtually omnipresent, and Billig has analysed it in particular in political speeches and news reports, including the sports pages.

But even though banal nationalism seems to be innocent and a matter of routine, Billig emphasises that it is not harmless. It is an ideology – in fact, one of the most successful in the history of the human race (Billig, 1995: 22), for the belief that the whole world of necessity has to be divided up into national states with precise borders is universal today, despite the fact that nationalism and the establishing of national states is only 200–300 years old.

When we use the word 'nationalism', we are normally referring to a passionate and violent phenomenon. While banal nationalism accompanies us unnoticed in our daily lives, 'nationalism' is something that 'the others' practise: separatists, fascists and guerrillas. This more passionate form of nationalism Billig calls 'hot nationalism', and he stresses the distinction: 'Surely, there is a distinction between the flag waved by Serbian ethnic cleansers and that hanging unobtrusively outside the US post office' (Billig, 1995: 6). (Billig's basic metaphor is the flag, and the distinction between banal and hot nationalism is that between the waved and the unwaved flag). Banal nationalism, however, is not harmless, for it functions as a mental 'warm-up' to hot nationalism and can easily change into this in connection with, for example, war propaganda.

Billig emphasises that the idea of a national language is an important ingredient in banal nationalism and, while referring to B. Anderson's conception of a nation as an 'imagined community' (Anderson, 1991), Billig says that 'national languages also have to be imagined, and this lies at the root of today's common sense belief that discrete languages "naturally" exist' (Billig, 1995: 10). Banal nationalism treats the concept of a national language as an unproblematic entity, which we know it is not, and when it sees the world as equipped with a number of languages that are separate from each other, it is a small step to take to seeing it as being perfectly natural for people that speak the same language wishing to have a common national state.[8]

Banal nationalism finds expression, for example, in national identity, a positive way of speaking about oneself and society, and this identity is generally perceived as being quite crucial, but also natural. Banal nationalism implies that it is impossible to imagine a person who does not have a national identity or does not wish to have one.

Clearly – and Billig also emphasises this – all of us are strongly influenced by banal nationalism, even though we are well aware of it and know that it has had a relatively short history. We are dealing with a habitual mental structure today – one that, not least, characterises language subjects.

A political and an ethnic conception of the national

Within nationality research a distinction is normally made between two different conceptions of the national, and this distinction is very fruitful in connection with an analysis of the national paradigm in language subjects. It has to do with two different conceptions that I will call here a political and an ethnic conception of the national. This is a difference that has been one of the most central points of discussion in nationality research, both the earlier and the more recent. With regard to more recent research, a number of significant monographs have been published since the late 1960s, and especially in the 1980s, on the origins and development of nationalism and nations, including Anderson, 1991 (1983); Gellner, 1983; Smith, 1986 and Hobsbawm, 1990. They treat the subject very differently, although they all emphasise that the phenomena of nations and nationalism first arose in connection with modern developments since the 18th century.[9] These phenomena appear in many different guises. As Hobsbawm emphasises (Hobsbawm, 1990: 7), it is not possible to define the concept of nation in a consistent way, neither with the aid of 'objective' criteria (language, religion, etc.) nor with the aid of 'subjective' ones – either collective, as Ernest Renan's *plébiscite de tous les jours* (the daily referendum) (Renan, 1882) or purely individual, such as those who perceive nationality as the individual's free choice. But a much-used short definition of nationalism is provided by Gellner (1983: 1): 'Nationalism is primarily a principle which holds that the political and the national unit should be congruent.'

This definition builds on a political understanding of a nation. But it is important, as mentioned, to note the differences between a political and an ethnic understanding of a nation. This distinction is described by Anthony Smith, who in his book *The Ethnic Origins of Nations* (1986: 138ff.) distinguishes between two different models for the formation of nations: 'western territorialism' (which corresponds to what I call the political model) and 'eastern ethnicism' (which corresponds to what I call the ethnic model). The former, territorial, model is one that we mainly find represented in the development of the earliest 'ethnic' states in Western Europe since the 13th century: England and France as the first, then Spain, the Netherlands, Sweden and Russia: state formations where a particular territory was defined and politically dominated by a particular 'core ethnie',[10] while there were also other, smaller ethnies represented within the territory. Here, the building up of a nation consisted in creating a common citizenship, based on a common political, legal and economic (state) system, a common culture (including a 'myth-symbol complex'), a common religion and a common language, beginning with a common standard written language. This model spread to large parts of the world, including India.[11]

The second, ethnic, model can be represented by the development in Central and Eastern Europe, where dynasties such as the Habsburgs ruled over a large number of different ethnies. Since these ethnies aspired to becoming nations, they particularly cultivated 'descent, populism, vernacular culture and nativism' (Smith, 1986: 145) and, in particular, language (first language) as identity factors. It is in connection with this national model that fertile ground can be found for ideas about the inseparability of language and (ethnic) culture. The ethnic model[12] also pervades today as an alternative way of conceiving a nation, and it can be seen mixing with the territorial, political model in that certain states can be described as containing nations at two different levels that call for a 'dual loyalty': Spain, for example, can be said to comprise both a Spanish nation (territorially, politically) and a Catalan and Basque nation respectively (ethnic).

German research has also dealt a great deal with nationality theory because it has been of vital interest for an understanding of German identity over the past two centuries. The above distinction between two models for conceiving a nation are often referred to in the recent German tradition as *Staatsnation* (the political variant) and *Kulturnation* (the ethnic variant) respectively. Stevenson provides the following summary of the two concepts:

> *Staatsnation* refers to the bonds of a common political history and so to overtly formal characteristics, *Kulturnation* is based on a shared cultural heritage and will typically incorporate things like language and literature. Each of these phenomena can exist independently of the other, but also each can subsume the other and each may derive from the other. On the one hand, for example, Switzerland could be seen as a single *Staatsnation* containing several distinct *Kulturnationen*, while early nineteenth-century Germany or indeed the post-1949 German states taken collectively could be regarded as a single *Kulturnation* encompassing discrete *Staatsnationen*. (Stevenson, 1993: 340, italics in the original)

This example sticks to a spatial, place-bound conception of both the *Staatsnation* and the *Kulturnation* – and this is not tenable in the transnational understanding I wish to introduce. *Staatsnationen* are today still territorially bound entities,[13] while *Kulturnationen*, as I prefer to call ethnic cultural communities, do not have to be defined in terms of territory/ locality, even though they normally contain a narrative of a local origin some place or other in the world (a homeland). Global diasporas (Cohen, 1997) are examples of non-localised ethnic communities.

If this conceptual division is compared with Billig's description of banal nationalism, it can be said that in general it is probably the political understanding of the national that is apparent in banal nationalism: 'I come from this country, you come from that country, etc.'. But hot nationalism (the waved flag) can, as is known, be based on both forms.

Transnational cultural flows

Within the social sciences, there has been a great interest in transnational theory over the past 10–15 years. Here I wish to present a theory that is particularly fruitful when trying to understand the complex relationship between language and culture in a global perspective. This is a theory of cultural complexity formulated by the Swedish social anthropologist Ulf Hannerz (presented in a comprehensive form in Hannerz,

1992a). He has developed a macro-anthropological theory as to how the cultural flows in the world are organised by cultural diversity or complexity. He defines culture very broadly as meaning and is particularly interested in how various cultural flows are spread via social networks of varying extents – from personal interaction at the micro-level to communication processes, mobility and the transportation of commodities at higher levels: national, transnational, transcontinental and global. An example of a cultural flow can be the routes taken by various musical genres and styles, and the ways in which they are mixed or fuse in various cultural centres around the world.

It could be said that, whereas 'banal nationalism' is an ideology, and the conceptual distinction between a political and an ethnic understanding of the national is a basic distinction within political theory and practice, Hannerz's theory of transnational cultural flows is an attempt to *make visible cultural practices and processes that cut across national structures.*

In Risager 2003 and Risager 2006 I have developed Hannerz's thoughts further in the form of a theory concerning the relation between language and culture in a transnational perspective. Fundamental to this theory is a transnational view of language. An example of this could be the Japanese language: the Japanese language is (naturally) not spoken only in Japan but also around the world in larger or smaller networks of persons and institutions. The Japanese language (or, more correctly, linguistic practice in Japanese) is spread in social networks, many of which are transnational and some even global. This spread takes place via transnational migration of Japanese speakers, but it is also enabled by teaching in Japanese around the world. In the same way, other languages can be seen in a transnational optic and thereby tools can be acquired for understanding language contact, code-switching and code-mixing as results of linguistic spreading processes over larger and smaller distances.

Other forms of culture of Japanese origin follow other routes, e.g. the sushi culture that has spread to many parts of the world, even to contexts where there is no knowledge of the Japanese language. And discourses about Japan and the Japanese are to be found all over the world, not only in Japanese but also in many other languages. Discourses about Japanese cultural and societal conditions spread then across language communities via translation processes and other content transformations. In this way, a picture emerges of more or less global linguistic and cultural processes of spreading and mixing. In Chapter 7 I will deal in more detail with the theory found in Risager 2003 and Risager 2006.

The History of Culture Pedagogy: Method of Analysis

The following contains some information about – and reflections on – the method I use when analysing the culture pedagogy discourse about language, culture and nation.

As already indicated, culture pedagogy is a very heterogeneous area, with many different approaches. The following presentation is not comprehensive and profound enough to constitute a real history of the discipline. It can better be described as a signalling of important lines of development in the 'world history' of the subject, with a special focus on the ideas to do with language, culture and nation that can be derived from the theoretical discourse. The presentation is an internal analysis with a special thematic focus. The text material is large and has not been sufficiently clarified from a sociological point of view to be able, for example, to be subjected to a strict sociological analysis – which would of course be highly interesting.

The theoretical discourse has first and foremost been developed by people who have been or are employed at educational institutions at various levels and who have possibly also participated in producing textbooks or developing curricula in language subjects. Practically all of them have a background in language or literature research.

The discourse-analytical approach

The discourse-analytical approach draws considerably on the 'Duisburg School', especially Siegfried Jäger (1993), who has been directly inspired by Foucault's use of the concepts of discourse, power and knowledge. Jäger's short definition of discourse is: 'a flow of text and speech, or knowledge, through time'[14] (Jäger, 1993: 153). In his opinion, texts and speech (in the following I prefer to talk of written and oral texts) must be treated as discourse fragments that are part of discourse strings which in turn are part of larger discourses (discursive formations) that have to do with and develop particular subjects. The discourses exist at various levels: there are scientific special discourses (e.g. language pedagogy discourse) and various inter-discourses that intertwine discourses from the scientific level and everyday language in various ways. I believe that the culture pedagogy discourse can be described as a type of inter-discourse which has, since the 1970s, developed into a special discourse.

Periodising by decades

The first of the historical chapters deals with developments up to and including the 1960s, with the subsequent chapters dealing with the 1970s, 1980s, 1990s and the present-day situation. Each of these chapters contains a general overview of developments. Occasionally, the overview is interrupted by examples that are treated somewhat more thoroughly: important works, mostly monographs, the contents of which illustrate characteristic ways of handling language, culture and nation. They could be called discourse fragments with a special key status. There is a total of 17 such examples: four in Chapter 3, four in Chapter 4, four in Chapter 5, and five in Chapter 6.[15] The periodising into decades is purely analytical and to aid communication. There are no special 'turning points' at the changing of the decades, and the culture pedagogy discussions in the various language subjects and the various countries have at times differed considerably and therefore show no special synchronisation when it comes to themes, etc. I have used the periodising flexibly – one of the works dealt with, Galisson (1991), for example, is treated under the 1980s despite its date of publication, since it is part of sustained study undertaken throughout that decade.

The national classification

The national classification corresponds partially to reality, insofar as culture pedagogy has very different (national) cultural points of departure and still today is characterised by different accentuations that can be linked to various national educational traditions. But, on the other hand, the explanatory power of the national factor is limited, as there are various competing tendencies in most countries, and this may be due to a whole range of factors: differences in academic institutions and networks, different traditions and profiles in various language subjects, individual preferences, friendships and alliances, etc. Moreover, it is problematic to assume that authors of publications in, for example, Germany are 'German' and represent 'German points of view'. Firstly, it is characteristic of language subjects in particular that some of the teachers and researchers are immigrants (perhaps second-generation) or guest teachers from one of the target-language countries. Secondly, others – whether they are immigrants or not – will gain inspiration from discussions in the target-language countries and introduce these into the country where the teaching takes place. And with the increasing internationalisation that has taken place since the 1980s, influences and collaborations have under all circumstances become more transnational, as will become increasingly obvious in the chapters on the 1990s and the present-day situation.

The chapters could have been structured on the basis of academic position. But that would have produced a somewhat shimmering picture, as there are a great many different positions. This is, among other things, because people have allowed themselves to be inspired by theories of culture and society that are vastly different from each other. So I have preferred to provide an overview of the most important positions in Chapter 6 and then to discuss the main disparities between those that are now most topical.

Foreign- or second-language pedagogy?

The chapters refer most often to foreign-language teaching, as culture pedagogy has mainly dealt with this form. But a difficulty arises here, because in several national traditions it is not always made quite clear whether references are being made to foreign- or second-language pedagogy. This is particularly a problem in the North American discourse about culture pedagogy. It is not uncommon for people in the USA to use the expression 'second-language teaching' as an overall concept and then possibly, at other points in the text, to distinguish between 'foreign-language teaching' and 'second-language teaching' in a narrower sense. Some people, such as Damen (1987), feel that there is no great difference when it comes to the cultural aspect of foreign- and second-language teaching. This, I believe, is something that can be questioned. In the German discussion, too, there is an ambiguous use of the expressions *Deutsch als Fremdsprache (DaF)* (German as a Foreign Language) and *Interkulturelle Germanistik* (Intercultural German Studies). Both refer to German as a foreign language as well as German as a second language (although the former discipline is linguistic in its orientation, and the latter hermeneutic and literary).

Two theoretical levels in language and culture pedagogy: A general and a pedagogical

The language educationalists J.C. Richards and T.S. Rogers emphasise in their book *Approaches and Methods in Language Teaching* (1986) the importance of distinguishing between three levels when analysing language-pedagogy approaches: approach, design and procedure. The first level has to do with which theories of language and language learning/language acquisition underlie the approach. The second level has to do with general conditions concerning the pedagogical approach in question: aims and subaims, selection and organisation of the content of the teaching and the materials involved, pedagogical activities, student roles and teacher roles. And the third level has to do with the practical organisation of the individual teaching session.

The third level will not be dealt with here, but in the following I wish to structure the discussion of culture pedagogy into two levels that correspond to Richards and Rogers' approach and design. These I refer to as the general and the pedagogical levels, respectively.

- The general level deals with language theory and culture theory, including theories concerning the relationship between language and culture. It contains both a practice side (linguistic and cultural practice) and a knowledge side (linguistic and cultural knowledge in the individual and how this develops). A possible belief that language and culture are inseparable belongs to this level.
- The pedagogical level deals with theories about (teaching-controlled) language and culture learning and language and culture teaching. A possible belief that language teaching and culture teaching ought always to be integrated into each other belongs to this level.

Overview of This Book

Apart from the introductory chapter, the chapters of the book fall into two parts: Chapters 2–6 deal with the history of culture pedagogy, focusing in particular on its discourse about language, culture and nation (developments in the national paradigm), and Chapters 7–9 deal with a transnational approach to language and culture, and with how a transnational paradigm for language subjects can begin to be envisaged.

Chapter 2 deals with the development of culture pedagogy from its beginnings in the Germany of the 1880s to the USA of the 1960s.

Chapter 3 deals with culture pedagogy in the 1970s, with special attention being paid to the following theorists: Erdmenger & Istel (1973), Fichou (1979), Seelye 1974 and Vereščagin & Kostomarov (1973).

Chapter 4 deals with culture pedagogy in the 1980s, with special attention being paid to the following theorists: Byram (1989), Galisson (1991), Melde (1987) and Zarate (1986).

Chapter 5 deals with culture pedagogy in the 1980s, with special attention being paid to the following theorists: Brøgger (1992), Byram (1997a), Kramsch (1993) and Starkey (1991a).

Chapter 6 deals with the present-day status of culture pedagogy, with special attention being paid to the following theorists: Burwitz-Melzer (2003), Crozet & Liddicoat (2000), Guilherme (2002), Risager (2003) and Roberts *et al.* (2001).

Chapter 7 provides an account of the structure of the complex relationship between language and culture in a transnational and global perspective.

Chapter 8 deals with how a transnational approach to language and culture pedagogy can be described, ending with a discussion of what can be referred to as the national dilemma of modern language studies.

Chapter 9 is a concluding chapter that summarises the content of the world citizen's intercultural competence.

Notes

1. So far, there are only partial studies of culture pedagogy, especially of the German tradition, e.g. Apelt (1967), Buttjes (1982 and 1991), Melde (1987), Kramer (1997), Wegner (1999), Spantzel (2001), as well as a whole range of literary overviews, especially of developments in USA and Canada, e.g. Morain (1983), Stern (1983), Allen (1985), Lessard-Clouston (1997) and Kramsch (forthcoming a) (cf. also a number of dictionary articles in Byram, 2000a). I have also written a number of short studies (Risager, 1984, 1987a, 1989b and 1994), which are part of the basis for the following presentation (and are part of my more comprehensive book in Danish: Risager, 2003).

2. The terms can also be categorised according to whether they refer to the substance, the activity or the teaching aim: The substance: 'culture' (Eng. and Fr.), civilisation, realia. The activity: 'cultural studies', 'culture teaching', 'intercultural learning', interkulturelles Lernen. The teaching aim: 'intercultural competence', Landeskunde, kulturforsttelse, kulturkunnskap.

3. Language for specific purposes, e.g. teaching the hairdressing profession in French, also has a cultural aspect, but I do not intend to discuss this in the present context.

4. It is also important to problematise the distinction between the concepts foreign language and second language cf. Holmen and Risager, 2003; Risager, 2003 and Risager, 2006.

5. I am thinking here of so-called 'content-based language instruction', cf. Krueger and Ryan, 1993; Brinton and Master, 1997; Snow and Brinton, 1997.

6. I wish to emphasise that I am naturally of the opinion that linguistics/ sociolinguistics are part of the humanities and social sciences. But for analytical reasons, I intend to distinguish between them in the following.

7. The other humanistic approaches are more interested in the affective dimension. Suggestopedia could be mentioned as an example of this (Richards & Rogers, 1986). I would refer here to the traditional socio-psychological distinction between cognitive, affective and conative/behavioural aspects (of, for example, a person's competence).

8. Billig does not use the word/concept 'culture' in the book, so the question of the relation between language and culture is not dealt with.

9. Smith, (1986) differs from the others by arguing that the phenomenon of nation has early ethnic forms.

10. Smith uses the French term 'ethnie' for "the collective cultural units and sentiments of previous eras" (Smith, 1986: 13), and lists the following six components as characterising an ethnie: a collective name, a common myth of descent, a shared history, a distinctive shared culture, an association with a specific territory, a sense of solidarity (Smith, 1986: 22).

11. This model is also called the state-to-nation model or, in French, 'nation par volonté'.
12. This model is also called the nation-to-state model.
13. Experiments have been made on the Internet to establish 'virtual states' (see, for example, Appadurai, 1996).
14. '(ein) Fluss von Text und Rede bzw. von Wissen durch die Zeit'.
15. The 17 are made up of 15 monographs and two articles (Starkey, 1991a and Crozet & Liddicoat, 2000). The 17 monographs have been selected from the approx. 36 monographs published until now specifically within culture pedagogy. These are the following (in chronological order): Verlée, 1973 (1969); Erdmenger and Istel, 1973; Vereščagin and Kostomarov, 1973; Seelye, 1974; Fichou, 1979; Krauskopf, 1985; Robinson, 1985; Meyer, 1986; Zarate, 1986; Melde, 1987; Damen, 1987; Byram, 1989; Kramer, 1990; Baumgratz-Gangl, 1990; Friz, 1991; Galisson, 1991; Byram and Esarte-Sarries, 1991; Byram, Esarte-Sarries and Taylor, 1991; Brøgger, 1992; Kramsch, 1993; Tomalin and Stempleski, 1993; Zarate, 1993; Cain and Briane, 1994; Byram, Morgan and colleagues, 1994; Steele and Suozzi, 1994; Erdmenger, 1996; Byram, 1997a; Kramer, 1997; Byram and Risager, 1999; Wegner, 1999; Sercu, 2000; Morgan and Cain, 2000; Roberts *et al.*, 2001; Guilherme, 2002; Burwitz-Melzer, 2003; Risager, 2003. In addition, there are quite a number of anthologies and a large corpus of articles in journals.

Chapter 2

Culture Pedagogy up to the 1960s

Introduction

In this chapter I provide a description of the history of culture pedagogy up to the 1960s. This history can be divided into two phases:

- earlier culture pedagogy from 1880;
- more recent culture pedagogy from 1960.

Firstly, however, I intend to give a brief account of the concept of 'realia', which goes much further back than 1880 and which is the concept that most clearly links culture pedagogy to earlier traditions in language teaching.

Then I intend to describe earlier culture pedagogy, which began at roughly the same time as the reform movement in language pedagogy, i.e. around 1880. In that connection, I deal in somewhat more detail with the earlier German discussion of culture teaching – a culture-pedagogical discussion that normally goes by the name of the *Kulturkunde* movement (knowledge of culture). The reason for emphasising the German tradition is that it is in (West) Germany that the culture-pedagogical discourse has been and still is most well developed – this is something I will make more explicit and illustrate in ensuing chapters.

Finally, I return to the USA in the 1960s, where more recent culture pedagogy started in the form of a more systematic reflection on the aims and content of culture teaching, including considerations about which cultural and societal references (parent disciplines) were the most relevant.

The Concept of Realia

Many of the types of knowledge that were subjected to more systematic subject-related discussion with the emergence of culture pedagogy from the 1880s – and particularly as an autonomous field in the 1960s – functioned before then as background information for European philological work on language and literature.[1] A central concept in connection with this background material is realia.[2] It is a concept with a long tradition that goes back at least to the latter half of the 17th century, when books began to appear on the geography of the Bible together with editions of classical writers with factual commentaries.[3]

Since factual knowledge is typically relevant in relation to texts or text locations, this is usually unsystematic and dependent on the choice of text. It can appear as actual notes, but it can also take the form of independent reference books for use in language and literature teaching – traditionally in the form of an account of (state) institutions, cf., for example, *A Survey of English Institutions* (Bodelsen, 1942), which was made use of in Denmark.

The concept of realia is thus traditionally linked to the reading of texts in an academic environment. But there have also been other situations in which concrete information was needed about other countries – and here I wish in particular to focus on foreign travel and polite conversation in foreign languages. It is also possible to use the concept of realia in relation to these activities, even in connection with practical oral proficiency – and even at the beginner stage.

Before the age of charter travel, trips abroad normally called for preparation in the form of teaching or self-study, based on phrase books – collections of situation-linked dialogues.[4] Many of these were specially designed for the purposes of travel, and then the conversations were normally supplemented by what could be called 'travel realia', practical information about the country as a travel destination: currency, transport, sights and attractions, climate, etc. The 'realia' we are talking about here are completely practical and geared to the time in question. Independent, systematic presentations can be found in manuals about etiquette in the country in question, e.g. about *savoir-vivre* in France.

Polite conversation in foreign languages has been an important educational aim for upper-class girls for centuries in Europe. This proficiency was typically developed in connection with private instruction using native teachers, and in the last decades of the 19th century at special institutes for young women.[5] Here it was a question of practical oral proficiency that assumed a certain knowledge of housekeeping and everyday and social life in aristocratic or bourgeois homes.

So it is possible to talk about at least three dimensions in connection with the concept of realia: a broad historical dimension, which in particular was relevant in connection with text reading of older and more recent texts: a more locally oriented dimension, which was particularly relevant to travel activities; and an everyday-oriented dimension, which was particularly relevant to social life and working life in the home.

In certain countries, the term 'realia' was used until the 1980s as a term for cultural and social conditions in foreign-language teaching, e.g. in Sweden (Lundgren, 1995 and 2001; Risager, 1991a), and even today it can be said that there is a 'realia' trend in culture pedagogy, which focuses on the background information that is a prerequisite for understanding texts.

Earlier Culture Pedagogy from 1880

An increasing interest in realia knowledge

In the last decades of the 19th century, a practice gradually evolved for teaching oral proficiency within the ordinary school system, in both the public academic system and the growing number of private secondary schools. It was a form of teaching that emphasised conversational language. Here, the linguistic content at the beginner stage was governed by a grammatical progression – a continuation of the earlier language-pedagogical tradition (Svanholt, 1968) – and subjects of conversation were quite general and normally required only a limited knowledge of realia. Those who represented this reform pedagogy in the late 19th century, however, spoke in favour of a more meaningful and down-to-earth language teaching, in both the selection of texts and the subjects of conversation. The Dane Otto Jespersen (cf. Jespersen, 1901) and the German Wilhelm Viëtor were highly active in this connection, and Viëtor spoke of the need for more *Realienkunde* (knowledge of realia) in language teaching (Buttjes, 1991).[6]

In beginner textbooks from the 1940s, 1950s and 1960s, a transition can be observed from pure orientation about realia to a somewhat more systematic teaching of culture: the Belgian-French use of *centres d'intérêt* (fields of interest) in connection with the audio-visual method consisted, for example, of presenting pupils with particular environments (*milieux*) and their vocabulary: harvesting in the fields, the house and workmen, domestic animals, etc., not dissimilar to vocabulary teaching by way of visual instruction in first-language teaching. Here is an example taken from a Finnish-produced textbook in French:

> La maison et les artisans. Les parties de la maison sont: le sous-sol avec la cave, le rez-de-chaussée, les étages et le grenier qui se trouve sous le toit. La maison est construite en pierre ou en bois. Le plan d'une maison a été dessiné par un architecte. Pour construire une maison, il faut… (Sohlberg, 1957, quote from Verlée, 1973: 15)[7]

One procedure continuing this idea – and which paid special attention to the fact that foreign-language teaching was involved – designed the textbooks as travel accounts where young people travelled as tourists in the foreign country, as, for example, a trip to London, taken from an English-produced textbook in English as a foreign language:[8]

Then they walked down Whitehall, which is the street where all the Government offices are. When they were crossing the road to Westminster Abbey, 'Big Ben', the clock on the House of Parliament, struck ten. From Westminster they went down the River Thames by boat to the Tower of London, which is ... (Candlin, 1962, quoted from Verlée, 1973: 22)

From the 1920s up to the 1960s, much work was done on producing word-frequency dictionaries and on drawing up basic, controlled vocabularies that could be used in teaching first and foremost English, but also other languages, and this naturally enough acquired a certain amount of importance for the realia that could be dealt with in the textbook material. Basic vocabularies were drawn up for English: *Basic English* (Ogden, 1930) and for French: *Le français fondamental* (Gougenheim, 1964).[9] After the 1960s, the idea of a regulated vocabulary in beginner teaching was, if not abandoned, modified somewhat, probably as a result of the communicative orientation that started in the 1970s.

Focus on the national: The land-and-people tradition

Apart from more-or-less random knowledge of realia, the reading of literature could also give an impression of broader culture-historical trends and of aspects of everyday life in the other country. This was an interest that was gradually generated as language subjects became nationalised. Interest was generally – though with shifts of emphasis – focused on the national-typical: the national character, historical constants in the national mentality and life patterns. Jespersen was one of those who described the broad cultural aims of language teaching in national terms:

> ...the highest purpose in the teaching of languages may perhaps be said to be the access to the best thoughts and institutions of a foreign nation, its literature, culture – in short, the spirit of the nation in the widest sense of the word. But at the same time we must remember that we cannot reach the goal with one bound, and that there are many other things on the way which are also worth taking in. We do not learn our native tongue merely so as to be able to read Shakespeare and Browning, and neither do we learn it for the sake of giving orders to the shoemaker or making out the washerwoman's bill. (Jespersen, 1904: 9, Danish original edition 1901)

It can be seen from Jespersen's choice of words that his conception of culture is related to the German idealistic tradition ('the spirit of the nation'). But, like the other reformist educationalists, he also stresses that language teaching should promote a practical language with a real content.[10] His conception of culture is explicitly hierarchical, as was typical at the time.[11]

The national-typical orientation was – as we will see below – strongly represented in Germany in the interwar period and up to the 1960s (Apelt, 1967), although teaching in other countries was to a certain extent influenced by it, cf. the much-used (in Denmark) *Deutsche Kultur- und Charakterbilder* (Images of German Culture and Character) (Sigtryggsson, 1933), *On England and the English* (Ring Hansen & Mouridsen, 1955) and *Frankrig. Tekster af kulturelt og socialt indhold* (France. Texts with a Cultural and Social Content) (Blinkenberg & Svanholt, 1932), who promise in their introduction 'to illustrate the development of French society and the permanent characteristics of the nature of the country and the people'. Knowledge about the land-and-people has been widespread – at least as background knowledge – in language teaching[12] both inside and outside Europe.

There is a model still known in the teaching of German as a foreign language (at least among German teachers in Denmark) and which is possibly the result of a symposium in Uppsala in 1971 (Sörensen & Thunander, 1980). It is known as the 'Uppsala Quadrant' and it describes German teaching as lying between two extremes: '*Brötchenkunde*' and

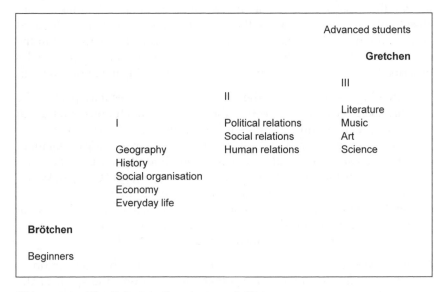

Figure 2.1   The *Brötchen-Gretchen* model[14]

'Gretchenkunde'.[13] I mention it here as a late example of the land-and-people tradition, an example that plays on 'the high' and 'the low', just as in the Jespersen quotation.

The model is intended to be a tool for analysing the image of Germany presented by (Swedish) German textbooks. It is a good example of a differential concept of culture (cf. Chapter 1), understood in hierarchical terms as it is based on the idea of a progression from everyday life, which is seen as simple in content, to literature, which is seen as complex or polysemantic in content. This high–low structuring we also find in the American distinction between 'Culture with a capital C' and 'culture with a small c' (see Chapter 3).

The Belgian Léon Verlée,[15] from whose textbook the quotations have been taken, can be considered as one of the last representatives of the earlier tradition within culture pedagogy (Verlée, 1973, 1st edition 1969). Verlée expresses a hierarchical view of culture, since he is of the opinion that what culture teaching should deal with is:

> ...everything which, in the course of time, has constituted or shaped the actual character of the people who speak the language being instructed in, everything by which this people has enriched the inheritance of humanity, everything that distinguishes this nation from other nations. (Verlée, 1973: 9)

At the same time he has one foot in the new era, as he emphasises that language teaching is to give the students more cultural information than before. But his concrete proposals for how this can be done, however, are in line with the earlier tradition: cultural information is to be communicated via work on historical and cultural relations, e.g. an incident in Cézanne's life.

So it would seem as if a certain consensus had emerged among writers of textbooks since the reform movement at the end of the 19th century that language teaching, also at the elementary level, ought to be accompanied by a cultural colouring that could possibly lead to dealing with life in the target-language country. But it is nevertheless possible to *start* in other ways. And here I cannot resist quoting from an untraditional book for beginners in French from 1967: *Le français sans soucis* (French without Tears), produced in Denmark (Koefoed, 1967). It begins with a little tale based on a grammatical progression (with a different layout, illustrated with drawings and provided with phonetic transcription):

> One frog, two frogs. – A big frog and a small frog. – A lake, two lakes. A big lake and a small lake. The big frog jumps into the small lake. The

small frog also jumps. The small frog also jumps into the small lake. The two frogs jump into the small lake. – The big frog swims. The small frog also swims. The two frogs swim in the small lake. – Two fish. A big fish and a small fish. – The two fish swim in the small lake. The two fish swim after the two frogs. – The two fish eat the two frogs...[16]

The frogs escape, however, since the fish are caught by a little boy and a little girl, who hear the frogs croaking inside the fish. The boy cuts open the stomachs of the fish and frees the frogs. The children take the frogs home to their family and play with them, and after a while they let the frogs loose again. The frogs call a meeting of all the other frogs to tell them about their experiences with the two children. The tale takes a total of 14 lessons.[17] Only then does the book switch to a more traditional description of the everyday life of a wealthy Parisian businessman (although in a special dialogue form where an omniscient narrator/commentator talks to the main character – almost as when an adult reader reads out loud for a child and 'plays along' in the action together with the child).

Earlier culture pedagogy normally resulted, then, in a concrete teaching practice which, among other things, is reflected in the more-or-less scattered references in the textbooks to cultural and social conditions in the target-language countries. There was very little discussion, on the other hand, of didactic issues and perspectives – with a sole exception: the discussion in Germany, which I intend to deal with now.

The earlier German discussion

In the 1880s, when the newly unified German Reich introduced the teaching of modern foreign languages in schools, a discussion started among language teachers of the content dimension of foreign-language teaching – a discussion that was linked both to the realia tradition and to the land-and-people tradition. The discussion was a struggle about the content of language teaching, expressed in such concepts as *Realienkunde* (knowledge of realia), *Landeskunde* (knowledge of society/the country – the most unmarked term), *Kulturkunde* (knowledge of culture) and *Wesenskunde* (knowledge of mentality), each of which placed different politico-ideological emphases on content, ranging from factual information (*Realienkunde*) to the most idealistic folk psychology (*Wesenskunde*). This discussion, which is related to problems in Germany's rapid industrialisation and modernisation – its formation as a nation state, economic growth, geopolitical and colonial ambitions, the Nazi period and the coming to terms with this period – is described in Apelt (1967) and Rülcker (1969). Both, especially the former, contain a critical account of the entire discussion.[18] Apelt's presentation begins in 1886, which was the year when the first *Neuphilologentag* was held (the first convention for teachers of modern languages).

Since the 1880s, there has been a tradition in (especially) German foreign-language teaching for more-or-less systematic instruction in elementary geographical, institutional and social relations in the target-language countries, so-called *Landeskunde*, specified by some as *Realienkunde*. This development coincided with the establishment of 'Realschulen', with a realia content including foreign languages, especially English. In the Weimar Republic from 1919 onwards, this teaching was dominated by the nationalist and idealist[19] *Kulturkunde* movement – one that in principle included all school subjects, although here we are interested only in how it affected foreign-language subjects.

The Weimar Republic resulted from a reaction against the revolutionary uprisings in Germany in the last stages of the First World War, and even though it was led by the Social Democrats it was dominated by the bourgeoisie and the old groupings of officials and the military. Its self-understanding was typified by nationalism and revanchism in the wake of the Treaty of Versailles. This left its mark on foreign-language teaching, which was exploited to consolidate national self-awareness.

Many foreign-language teachers were under the influence of an anti-positivist trend that reacted against *Realienkunde* as being far too superficial and extrinsic. They wanted a more spiritual, intrinsic approach, whereby the pupils understood the mentality of the foreign people in order better to understand themselves. For a seminal concept in *Kulturkunde* was the idea of 'Germanness': the most important mission of foreign-language teaching was to be to contribute to the Germanness of the pupils. The slogan was 'All knowledge of culture is knowledge of Germanness' (*Alle Kulturkunde ist Deutschkunde*). The cultures of foreign countries were to serve as a mirror in which the pupils could confirm their own identity and value as Germans. For that reason, the comparison of cultures was a fundamental method, and the special task of foreign-language teaching was to supply comparative images (*Gegenbilder*), while teaching in German as a first language was to supply model images (*Vorbilder*) (Kroyman & Ostermann, 1977: 147).[20]

The concept of culture was structure-psychological in its orientation and linked to the concept of national or popular character. It was believed that a people's culture, i.e. its language and literature, was an expression of its unchanging mentality (*Wesenskunde*). One psychologist in particular was influential: Eduard Spranger, who attempted '...to construct the absolutely eternal basic forms of individuality in a number of ideal types'. (Spranger,

1925, quoted by Apelt, 1967: 46). By means of structure-psychological research he wanted to attain, by 'the illumination of life-relations and cultural relations' an 'awareness of the nature of the spirit and research into the spirit' (translated from Kroymann & Ostermann, 1977: 146). Here, one was operating within a completely ahistorical folk-psychology, which was by the way also nurtured by the contemporaneous upsurge of interest in *Volkstum*, e.g. folklore, home region and blood ties (Emmerich, 1971). Much effort went into defining the German, English and French national character: *'der Dauerengländer'* (the typical Englishman), *'der Dauerfranzose'* (the typical Frenchman).

From the late 1920s onwards, nationalism changed character. As the community of interest of West European capitalism increased, and fascism and anti-communism grew in strength, Europeanism emerged – a conception of Europe as a cultural unit with autonomous significance. Nationalism, however, survived as a view of German culture as being the most valuable, as a culture that had a historic mission in Europe. At that time, fascist ideology began to appear. It was accompanied by racist-influenced ideas about refinding the Germanic element in English and French culture. In the years immediately preceding and during the war foreign-language teaching was a forum for downright propaganda in the glorification of colonialism and regionalism (*Blut und Boden* – Blood and Soil), the cult of race, the glorification of war and the cult of 'Führer' personalities (Kroymann & Ostermann, 1977: 158ff.). Some people even cultivated linguistic-biological ideas on the relationship between sentence syntax and national character:

> Unlike the strict organisation of the complex Latin sentence, with its hypotaxis and subordination that can be compared to the military discipline of the Roman army and the strict centralisation of Roman government, the parataxis of the English sentence can well be seen as the expression of the self-awareness and pride in freedom of the noble Germanic peasant. (Translated from Bona, 1938: 365)

In the post-war years, as a result of the partition of Germany into West Germany (FRG) and East Germany (GDR), two different culture-pedagogical traditions developed. In West Germany, *Kulturkunde* survived into the 1950s and 1960s, although the strong nationalism that had been turned against England and France was toned down and partially replaced by Western Europeanism turned against the USSR in connection with the cold war. Idealism still existed, although negative national stereotypes were turned into positive ones, cf. these examples quoted from Baur-Langenbucher (1972):

By 'Knowledge of France' we mean general knowledge of the fundamentals of the French nation: people and country, state and church, culture and society, which are indispensable for any profound understanding and interpretation of France and of the French; 'Spoiled by nature, inhabited by cheerful, free, inventive, talented people that understand how to enjoy life, France offers a bright-coloured palette'. (Translated from Schüttler, 1964, quoted Baur-Langenbucher: 8)

Until the end of the 1960s, there was, however, a loud silence in West Germany regarding the content of foreign-language teaching – the subject had been removed from public discussion on account of its ideological 'hot-potato' status. For a more detailed account of developments in West Germany, see Chapter 3.

As far back as the early 1960s, however, a thesis was written in the GDR that dealt with the possible content of *Sowjetkunde* (knowledge of the USSR) in Russian teaching (Süss, 1961), and the above-mentioned history of the subject appeared by Apelt (1967). I will also return to East German and Soviet culture pedagogy in Chapter 3.

More Recent Culture Pedagogy: The USA in the 1960s

The intensification of globalisation from the 1960s onwards led to increasing international communication in the Western world, partly as a result of transnational tourism and labour migration, and partly as a result of transnational communication via TV and other media. It became increasingly important for the labour force to be mobile and flexible – and to be able to communicate and have a minimum of knowledge about the world.

As far as the USA is concerned, it is relevant to mention both the internal conflicts and the external geopolitical situation. The conception of the USA's national cultural 'melting pot', which had enjoyed widespread support until well into the 1960s as a result of the cold war and the material upswing that occurred at the same time, was replaced by a growing recognition of socio-cultural inequalities and conflicts – especially racial ones. This recognition made its impact in the 1960s, when a large number of social and ethnic movements began to manifest themselves. The USA experienced a civil rights movement as well as Black Power, hippy and student movements, the feminist movement and 'the ethnic revival'. At the same time, the Vietnam War and demonstrations in connection with this questioned American politicians' knowledge of other countries and their ability to communicate with the rest of the world. This entire development placed, among other things, the necessity of intercultural communication on the agenda.

Contemporary culture pedagogy began in the USA at the end of the period that, with regard to language pedagogy, had been dominated by the audio-visual method. It could be claimed that culture pedagogy started with the publication of the book *Linguistics across Cultures* (Lado, 1957), which deals with language teaching and concludes with the chapter: 'How to compare two cultures'. Lado defines culture here as 'a structured system of patterned behavior', and he suggests comparing 'units' from the two cultures as regards 'form', 'meaning' and 'distribution', e.g. meals, or more specifically as, for example, 'salads'. Here he was inspired by contemporary cultural anthropology and linguistic anthropology, first and foremost by Pike (1967 [1954]) and Hoijer (1954).[21]

The first important conference on culture pedagogy was held in 1960, when the annual meeting of *Northeast Conference on the Teaching of Foreign Languages* had as its theme *'Culture in Language Learning'*.[22] Nelson Brooks, who, like Lado, is among the earliest representatives of American cultural-anthropological culture pedagogy,[23] published in 1960 a book with the title *Language and Language Learning*, which contained a brief chapter on *'Language and Culture'*. It contains the first example I have found to date of the explicit assertion of the inseparability of language and culture in the differential sense (an assertion that has been implicitly anticipated since the 1930s by, for example, Whorf's work) (cf. Risager, 2006):

> Language is the most typical, the most representative, and the most central element in any culture. Language and culture are not separable; it is better to see the special characteristics of a language as cultural entities and to recognize that language enters into the learning and use of nearly all other cultural elements. (Brooks, 1960: 85)

Taken on their own, the formulations without an article ('language') can be seen as having a generic meaning, i.e. they deal with human language in general. But since the content of the book as a whole points towards a differential concept of language, i.e. deals with the languages of the world (here: the target language in language teaching), it is most natural to read the above as dealing with a particular 'language' and its 'culture'. The intention is precisely to broaden the understanding of what it means to learn and use a specific target language.

In addition, two important articles from the 1960s should be mentioned, one by Brooks (1968), the other by Howard Lee Nostrand (1966), both of which deal with French as a foreign language.

Brooks points out that 'culture' in language teaching is neither geography, history, folklore, sociology, literature nor *civilization*.[24] It is something else, something which, on the other hand, is related to all of these subject areas. He divides his concept of culture into five meanings: Culture 1: biological growth, Culture 2: personal refinement, Culture 3: literature and the fine arts, Culture 4: patterns for living, and Culture 5: the sum total of a way of life. In his opinion, language teaching, especially during the first years, must focus on Culture 4, and never lose sight of the individual:

> Culture 4 refers to the individual's role in the unending kaleidoscope of life situations of every kind and the rules and models for attitude and conduct in them. By reference to these models, every human being, from infancy onward, justifies the world to himself as best he can, associates with those around him, and relates to the social order to which he is attached. (Brooks, 1968: 210)

Brooks, then, has an everyday-oriented, individual-centred view of culture teaching. It ought also to be added that in his opinion it is very important for teaching to include both more and less visible aspects of everyday culture, including kinesics (non-verbal communication). Here, he – like many others – has been inspired by the two popular books of Edward T. Hall: *The Silent Language* (1959) and *The Hidden Dimension* (1966), which deal with invisible or implicit culture: norms and values, the relation to time and space, etc.

Nostrand believes that language teaching must have two goals: intercultural communication and intercultural understanding. Unlike most of the other American cultural educationalists, he was inspired by the American sociologist Parsons' theory of society, which means that in his opinion language teaching is to deal with both the social and the cultural system or, as he puts it, the socio-cultural system. To this end, he has developed a model he calls *the emergent model*, to which references have frequently been made in American culture pedagogy. The model consists of a comprehensive classification of themes[25] (in this case in relation to France) divided into four main groups: the social, the cultural, the individual and the ecological. He is particularly interested in the French system of values and the French national character, i.e. his work has a national-psychological and idealistic slant of which he himself is uncritical.

It is in particular the culture-anthropological culture pedagogy in Brooks' version that set the agenda for the discussion in USA right up until the 1990s, and it has its origins especially in foreign languages such as French and Spanish. This culture-pedagogical tradition is characterised by culture being used as a comprehensive concept, even after this view was being abandoned in cultural anthropology as such (see, for example, Risager, 2006). Societal structures are either underplayed or totally omitted and attention is seldom paid to structures of dominance and more politically coloured issues (with the partial exception of the movement for 'global education', see Chapter 4). Culture-anthropological culture pedagogy, on the other hand, is psychologically and social-psychologically oriented, as is the broader discipline of intercultural communication that a number of the American cultural educationalists refer to and from which they have also borrowed some methods for the developing of cultural awareness (see Chapter 4).

Conclusion

The culture-pedagogical discourse has developed at two moments in time – earlier culture pedagogy since 1880, and the more recent since c.1960. It builds on two earlier traditions: on the one hand, the 'realia' tradition, which is a purely informative tradition, and on the other hand, a much larger complex of a history of ideas, namely the German philosophical and political discussion of the relation between language, nation, people and culture. The two traditions are interwoven in the philosophical conflict between positivism and idealism, which is also a characteristically German problematic.

These assumptions concerning the history of ideas shaped the discussion in the German Reich and the Weimar Republic – a discussion that was based on the hypothesis of the identity between language, nation, people and culture and which comprised a number of positions, ranging from a positivist orientation concerning facts at the one extreme to an idealistic and stereotyping interest in national-psychological traits at the other. This discussion fell almost completely silent in West Germany in the post-war period up until the 1960s, although it returned at full strength in the 1970s.

In the USA of the 1960s a discussion gradually arose of the need to make visible the cultural content of language teaching and to develop the theoretical and pedagogical implications of this. This encouraged the development of more recent culture pedagogy as an academic discipline, and took place in a context characterised by racial, ethnic and political conflicts that caused all sorts of differences to mushroom out of the apparently well-integrated American 'melting pot'. In the USA, the development of more recent culture pedagogy is thus closely linked to the spread of cultural relativism as a value basis for the development of a multicultural society.

Notes

1. Cf. Musumeci (1997), who deals with the language-pedagogical ideas of Guarini (1374–1460), Loyola (1491–1556) and Comenius 1592–1670), also to a certain extent with thematic content in language teaching.
2. This concept of realia must not be confused with another one used elsewhere, e.g. in Tomalin and Stempleski (1993). Here, 'realia' means 'things' or 'requisites', e.g. stamps, menus, signs, etc.
3. In British teaching of classical languages, 'realia' are referred to as 'antiquities'.
4. Cf., for example, Haastrup (1988) and Wagner (1999).
5. Whereas work on literature and realia was reserved, until about 1900, for boys (in secondary and grammar schools and at the universities) (Jakobsen et al., 1984).
6. In 1918, a fairly comprehensive government report was published in Great Britain on the necessity of modern studies in the teaching of modern foreign languages (Leathes Report). It stressed among other things that it had become clear during the war how important it was for the population as a whole to have a knowledge of other European countries.
7. 'The house and the workmen. The parts of the house are: the basement with the cellar, the ground floor, the upper floors and the attic, which is under the roof. The house is made out of stones or wood. The plan of a house has been designed by an architect. To construct a house, one must...'
8. Similar passages are to be found, for example, in the much used Cours de langue et de civilisation françaises from 1953 (Course in French language and civilisation) (see Chapter 3).
9. See Risager and Andersen (1980) for a critical discussion of the use of basic vocabulary in language teaching.
10. This interest is also manifest in his work on developing the artificial language Ido.
11. The modern showdown with the hierarchical concept of culture began with Boas' and a little later Malinowsky's critique of evolutionism, i.e. a few years after Jespersen's book (see, for example, Risager, 2006).
12. In Dutch, the teaching of cultural and social conditions can still be referred to as KLV (= kennis van land en volk) (knowledge of land and people).
13. Knowledge of 'Brötchen' [rolls] (everyday life) and Gretchen [Gretel] (high literature).
14. Redrawn and translated from Sörensen and Thunander (1980: 81).
15. Who was attached to one of the centres for the development of the audio-visual method: AIMAV (Association internationale pour la recherche et la diffusion des méthodes audiovisuelles et structuro-globales), Brussels.
16. 'Une grenouille, deux grenouilles. – Une grande grenouille et une petite grenouille. – Un lac, deux lacs. Un grand lac et un petit lac. – La grande grenouille saute. La grande grenouille saute dans le petit lac. – La petite grenouille saute aussi. La petite grenouille saute aussi dans le petit lac. Les deux grenouilles sautent dans le petit lac. – La grande grenouille nage. La petite grenouille nage aussi. Les deux grenouilles nagent dans le petit lac. – Deux poissons. Un grand poisson et un petit poisson. – Les deux poissons nagent dans le petit lac. Les deux poissons nagent après les deux grenouilles. – Les deux poissons mangent les deux grenouilles...'

17. This story would have some very interesting side effects if it occurred in a British textbook for French, as the commonest pejorative British expression for Frenchmen is 'frogs'.
18. Apelt's book is a valuable presentation, but it should be recalled that it is written on the basis of an East German, Marxist-Leninist view, which means that the framework is to show that foreign-language teaching in the first half of the 20th century became an instrument for imperialist interests, unlike the later East German socialist, 'peace-loving' foreign-language teaching.
19. German idealism was originally humanist, seeing history as a self-realisation of the human spirit. But in the course of the latter half of the 19th century, a nationalistic version developed which focused on the national-cultural spirit or soul, and this version came to occupy a central position in the *Kulturkunde* movement.
20. It is important to have this line of thought at the back of one's mind when speaking in favour of comparative methods in culture pedagogy today. One should be clear as to what the aim of the comparison is – to confirm or problematise national stereotypes?
21. Lado (1957) was translated into German in 1973 and played a certain role in the development of the discipline in Europe as well, especially in West Germany, where Lado's culture-anthropological view of language and culture as analogous to everyday phenomena made its impact. This applies in particular to the cultural educationalist Peter Doyé (see Chapter 3).
22. See Bishop (1960). Brooks also mentions in a four-week seminar in 1953 at the University of Michigan on the subject *'Developing cultural understanding through foreign language study'*. The report was published in PMLA 68, 1953, but there were no other repercussions, as, according to Brooks, the discussion was ahead of its time (Brooks, 1968).
23. He has also been a central figure in the development of the audiolingual method – and he was the one who invented the term 'audio-lingual'.
24. Brooks defines 'civilization' as follows: 'Civilization deals with an advanced state of human society, in which a high level of culture, science, industry, and government has been attained' (Brooks, 1968: 209).
25. Inspired by the anthropologists' archives of cultural terms for comparing cultures. The model has i.a. been published in Nostrand (1967).

Chapter 3

Culture Pedagogy in the 1970s: Knowledge of Society

Introduction

In the 1970s, a number of other countries entered the scene alongside the USA. Culture pedagogy was still a marginal movement that was struggling to make cultural content visible, whether by upgrading an orientation in culture and society in connection with the reading of literary texts in higher education, or by implementing a more meaningful teaching of culture that the existing textbooks at beginner and medium levels could live up to. Early culture pedagogy therefore adopted in general a critical position in relation to contemporary language pedagogy, with its functionally oriented communicative approach (in Europe)/proficiency approach (in the USA).

The development of culture pedagogy in the 1970s coincided with that which is connected to 'the expanded text concept'. This meant that other texts were included in language teaching than literary ones in the traditional sense: so-called authentic texts: non-fiction texts of various kinds, often texts from newspapers and magazines, or texts used in everyday life: menus, signs, tickets, etc. It was typical for an understanding of these texts that a greater knowledge of the outside world was called for than the literary, and so new work on non-fiction texts went hand in hand with an increased orientation to culture and society. At the same time, theme-based language teaching began to develop, the content of which was centred on a theme that could then be illustrated with the aid of a number of texts of various genres: extracts from short stories, newspaper reports, statistics, images, etc.

I intend to start with the developments in the USA, so as to link back to the previous chapter. Then I will move on to Europe, first to the Council of Europe and Great Britain, then to West Germany, the USSR/GDR, France, Denmark and Norway. The four examples specially treated in this chapter are:

- Seelye: *Teaching Culture* (1974).
- Erdmenger and Istel: *Didaktik der Landeskunde* (Didactics of Landeskunde) (1973).

- Vereščagin and Kostomarov: *Jazyk i kul'tura* (Language and Culture) (1973).
- Fichou: *Enseigner les civilisations* (The Teaching of Civilisations) (1979).

As emphasised in Chapter 1, it is important in the analysis of culture-pedagogical approaches to distinguish between two levels: the *general level*, which deals with language theory and culture theory, including the relationship between language and culture both in society and in the single individual, and the *pedagogical level*, which deals with theories about how one learns about and teaches language and culture, including how culture teaching can be incorporated into language teaching.

I therefore intend to organise the specially treated examples in this and the following chapters as follows:

- Presentation.
- The relationship between language and culture.
- The relationship between language teaching and culture teaching.

The approaches differ as regards the prominence of the concept of society. For that reason, I also discuss ideas about the relationship between culture and society at points when it is relevant (and possible) to do so.

The USA in the 1970s

A pragmatic culture-anthropological approach takes shape

In the USA of the 1970s, the interest in an anthropological understanding of culture started to spread in society in general, which also led to an interest in teaching everyday culture in foreign-language teaching. Since – as in Europe – literature, history and geography had for many years been taught in language learning at higher levels, two different concepts of culture were thus brought together, and it became popular to distinguish between on the one hand 'Culture with a big/capital C' (literature and other forms of artistic production, as well as history and geography) and 'culture with a little/small c' (behaviour, norms and values in everyday interaction). So here we are dealing with a hierarchical conception of culture with two poles – similar to the earlier land-and-people tradition mentioned in Chapter 2 (e.g. the *Brötchen-Gretchen* model).[1] American culture pedagogy has particularly focused on 'culture with a little c', starting with such people as Brooks, mentioned in Chapter 2.

The *Northeast Conference* in 1972 had as its theme *'Language-in-Culture'*, and in 1974 the first edition appeared of Ned Seelye's book *Teaching*

Culture, which has had a major influence and which I will deal with in the next section.

In 1975, the anthology *The Cultural Revolution in Foreign Language Teaching* (Lafayette, 1975) appeared. It was a critical publication which drew attention to ethnic and gender differences in the USA and in the foreign-language classroom (Strasheim, 1975). It was one of the first culture-pedagogical publications that explicitly dealt with issues that had become relevant because of 'the ethnic revival' in the USA.

American culture pedagogy stood (and still stands to a certain extent) for a highly practical orientation. This can be seen in the general idea that culture is 'the fifth skill' (after listening, talking, reading and writing) – an idea that is only now being abandoned. Especially in the USA, a whole range of practical methods have developed since the 1960s, and particularly in the 1970s, for teaching about cultural differences in connection with teaching about intercultural communication for out sourced business employees, Peace Corps workers, etc., and a number of these have also been implemented in foreign-language teaching. They are quite well known among language teachers in the USA, and I would like to provide a brief overview of them here (see also, for example, Seelye, 1974 and Morain, 1983). The most important are:

- *Culture capsule*: a short talk about a minimal cultural difference between the target-language culture and the students' own culture, e.g. what main head movements the Americans and the Greeks use when they mean yes and no respectively. The talk can be given by the teacher or by a student who has prepared it at home, possibly via field work. The talk should preferably be illustrated by the use of images of objects ('realia'). All of it should be able to be put into a shoe box for later use ('capsule').
- *Culture cluster*: a number of 'culture capsules' that interconnect in terms of subject and that are worked with in the course of a few days. Finally, a dramatic simulation is made in class of a characteristic situation in the foreign culture, which is afterwards discussed in class. An example of this could be a series of situations to do with a meal in France: laying the table, use of tableware, conversation, etc. Both 'culture capsule' and 'culture cluster' compare cultures for the most part; they are not intercultural in the sense that work is done on intercultural communication situations. This, however, is the case in the next methods:
- *Mini-drama*: Some of the class dramatise an interactive situation in which people from two cultures interact and where misunderstandings

typically occur and thus (communicative) conflicts arise. The action is terminated before the conflict has been solved, and the teacher draws the attention of the class to the parties' possible false expectations of the situation.

- *Culture assimilator*: a kind of test suitable for self-study. It comprises a description, in normally written text, of an intercultural encounter that creates confusion or animosity between the parties involved (a 'critical incident'). The student then has to choose between four apparently plausible explanations of why the difficulty arose, and is finally told what the correct answer is.
- *Micrologue*: the reading aloud by the teacher of a 'culturally valid text' (Morain, 1983: 404). The students listen, talk about the text, retell it, and write it down as a dictation exercise.

These methods are specially designed for beginner teaching and are themselves characterised by a positivist approach in the sense that they are interested in factual information and mainly encourage reproduction. They can, of course, also give rise to more reflective conversations if the teacher and the students are willing to try this – and if the teacher has been trained in how to do so.

The various measures taken to develop culture pedagogy in the USA are to be seen in the light of the fact that there are not many students who follow foreign-language teaching in the USA and that methods are therefore required that retain and motivate those few students there are. Foreign-language teaching is quantitatively speaking quite a small area in the USA. In 1980, a report was published that drew attention to some of the problems linked to the lack of knowledge of foreign languages and cultures in the USA. It was called *Strength Through Wisdom*, and had been written by a commission set up by President Jimmy Carter. It emphasised that US security depended on the country's being able to communicate with its allies. In the wake of this report, a number of projects were implemented to support foreign-language teaching – for example, 12 international high schools were established in major cities around the country that offered extra teaching in foreign-languages and cultures.[2]

Seelye: *Teaching Culture* (1974): Presentation

The above book by Seelye has Spanish as a foreign-language as its point of departure and its target group is in particular teachers at high school and college level. It has been much used in the American context and was republished in 1985 (see Chapter 4). Seelye's starting point is a reaction against traditional culture pedagogy: 'Our objectives are not to learn more art, music, history, and geography, but to learn to communicate more accurately and to understand more completely the effect of culture on man' (Seelye, 1974: 2).

Seelye's scientific frame of reference is much more anthropological than linguistic, so he represents the branch of culture pedagogy that adopts a cultural or social perspective (cf. Chapter 1). His view of culture is sometimes closely allied to cultural anthropology in its most behaviouristic version: 'culture is seen to include everything people learn to do' (Seelye, 1974: 10), while elsewhere he tends to describe culture in holistic terms as a way of life: culture is 'a broad concept that embraces all aspects of the life of man, from folktales to carved whales' (Seelye, 1974: 22). As a guideline for what is most essential in culture he refers to A.H. Maslow's theory of the basic and other needs that motivate human behaviour (Maslow, 1954).[3]

In Seelye, 'culture' often appears as a national culture: 'German culture', 'France', 'Honduras', although there are also examples of other categories than national ones: 'Hispanic culture', 'desert Arabs'. The various cultures are referred to as static (ahistorical) entities; Seelye does not mention examples of culture or language spread such as loan words, etc. On the other hand, Seelye also emphasises the need to arrive at a sociologically differentiated understanding of culture in order to be able to act in a socially and culturally appropriate manner. He stresses that in the course of teaching a cultural awareness should be developed that has an eye for social variation in cultural behaviour – first and foremost variations in everyday behaviour seen in relation to social class, age, gender, etc.

Seelye (1974): The relationship between language and culture

Seelye represents the cultural-anthropological tendency within culture pedagogy and, considering that cultural anthropology itself has been interested in the relationship between language and culture (e.g. Sapir & Whorf, see Carroll, 1956), Seelye might have been expected to analyse the relationship between language and culture in language teaching. However, he focuses only on one aspect of this relationship, one that is of course also important: the cultural connotations of vocabulary. Apart from that, he expresses a view of language that is structural and autonomous, one that is typical for the structural linguistic paradigm he indirectly refers to (via such writers as E.T. Hall):

> Knowledge of the linguistic structure alone does not carry with it any special insight into the political, social, religious, or economic system. While a convenient place to begin learning about the target culture is

in our foreign-language classes, culture must be taught systematically *in addition to* purely linguistic concerns. (Seelye, 1974: 5, italics in the original)

Seelye thus distinguishes between language structure and semantics (he does not, incidentally, use the word 'semantics' at all in his book). In Seelye's approach, the semantics (here: vocabulary) of language becomes something that belongs more to culture than to language. This makes it difficult for him to describe any connection between language and culture. They are portrayed as separate, parallel systems.

Seelye (1974): The relationship between language teaching and culture teaching

At one point, Seelye describes the aim of language teaching simply as to achieve 'target behaviour' (Seelye, 1974: 36), although he also emphasises the cognitive prerequisites for attaining this general objective. He sets up seven parallel goals for teaching culture, beginning with a 'supergoal': 'All students will develop the cultural understandings, attitudes and performance skills needed to function appropriately within a society of the target-language and to communicate with the culture bearer' (Seelye, 1974: 39). The seven goals are as follows:

- The importance or functionality of culturally determined behaviour: 'The student should demonstrate an understanding that people act the way they do because they are using options the society allows for satisfying basic physical and psychological needs.'
- Interaction between language and social variables: 'The student should demonstrate an understanding that such variables as age, sex, social class, and place of residence affect the way people speak and behave.'
- Conventional behaviour in common situations: 'The student should indicate an ability to demonstrate how people conventionally act in the most common mundane and crisis situations in the target culture.'[4]
- Cultural connotations in words and expressions: 'The student should indicate an awareness that culturally conditioned images are associated with even the most common target words and phrases.'
- Evaluation of statements about society: 'The student should demonstrate the ability to evaluate the relative strength of a generality concerning the target culture in terms of the amount of evidence substantiating the statement.'

- Investigation of another culture: 'The student should show that he has developed the skills needed to locate and organise information about the target culture from the library, the mass media, people, and personal observation.'
- Attitudes towards other cultures: 'The student should demonstrate intellectual curiosity about the target culture and empathy towards its people.' (Seelye, 1974: 39–45)

As can be seen, language occurs in connection with an argument about linguistic variation and in connection with an argument about cultural connotations. There is no mention of any analysis of the relationship between the two linguistically oriented goals and the other goals, i.e. there is no analysis of the relationship between teaching language and teaching culture. There is only a list.

The methods Seelye recommends for teaching culture are the methods outlined above (mini-dramas, etc.), and in general he approves of an inter-disciplinary approach to problem-solving whereby the students are placed in situations where they have to find a practical solution to a communication problem.

So Seelye describes a highly practical approach to culture pedagogy that is oriented towards an understanding of the target-language culture seen as a specially differentiated unity. His point of departure is taken from examples of everyday interpersonal interaction, either between members of the indigenous population of the target-language country, or between such members and representatives of the students' own culture. Both linguistic and non-linguistic behaviour is observed. Comparisons are undertaken, but it is very much the target culture that is in focus. No wish is expressed for the students to gain an understanding of their own culture via this encounter. The word 'target' is a key word that is often used, e.g. in expressions such as 'target behaviour', 'target people', 'target culture' and 'target words'. Seelye warns against exaggerated overgeneralisations in a conception of the target-language countries, and yet he nevertheless uncritically refers to studies of national character.[5] Seelye expresses a culture-determinist understanding of human behaviour ('the culture bearer') and his approach is mainly behaviouristic and ahistorical, although the wish is also expressed that students should develop their cultural understanding and their attitudes towards other cultures.

Europe in the 1970s

In the 1970s, Europe – as in previous decades – was characterised by being divided into two blocs, each facing its own direction: Western

Europe towards the USA and Eastern Europe towards the Soviet Union. In Western Europe, as in the USA, many social movements arose in the 1960s and 1970s, and there was increasing immigration of labour. At the same time the European Common Market was in the making, and that development created a need for an increased knowledge of other countries in Western Europe. Thus foreign-language teaching expanded in Western Europe specifically as part of the construction of the European Common Market – and this trend, which also gradually changed (some of the) language subjects from being elitist to subjects for everyone in schools, brought about a need for a more motivating and down-to-earth content that was able to provide insight into the cultural and social conditions of (the major) European countries. This in turn led to negative national stereotypes being problematised and relativised – stereotypes that had played a large role in Europe's conflict-ridden history over the previous two centuries.

In this context, West Germany occupied a special position, most obviously because of its relation to the GDR but also because of the country's geopolitical position in European history in general and its always potentially difficult relationship to neighbouring states. For this reason, culture pedagogy in West Germany – and later in the reunified Germany – has been a battleground to a greater extent than in other countries. And this continues to apply today.

For the GDR and the USSR, teaching culture in language subjects was, among other things, a matter of legitimising their particular societal structure to (among others) students from abroad and immigrant workers, and of building up 'the socialist personality'.

The Council of Europe and Great Britain in the 1970s

In 1971, the Council of Europe took the initiative of developing language teaching in Europe via a project about a common 'unit-credit system' for language teaching for adults, the focus being on a fairly elementary level ('threshold level').[6] An important platform was thereby established for developing the communicative approach, and some of those active within this approach also dealt with subjects and subject areas in language teaching. J.A. van Ek (1975) and D. Coste *et al.* (1976) represent two slightly differing views of how an overview can be gained of various language functions, domains of language use and communicative needs. Within these areas, they propose a large number of subjects and subject areas that students ought to be able to use language in relation to. The overall subject areas in van Ek, for example, are: personal identification, house and home, trade and industry, leisure and entertainment, travel, interpersonal relations, health and welfare, education, shopping, food and drink, service, locations, foreign languages, the weather. This is a quite pragmatic and contemporary list, and it is akin to the approach we find in the cultural educationalists Erdmenger and Istel, to be dealt with later in this chapter. It should, however, be emphasised at this juncture that we are dealing here with extremely general categories that have been explicitly conceived as being pan-European, cf. the following passage in van Ek:

> The model also satisfies the requirement of a European system... Functions such as *apologizing*, general notions such as *past/present* and specific notions such as *house* and *meat* are likely to be needed, if not in all languages, at least in all the languages for which the system is designed, the languages spoken in the member countries of the Council of Europe. (van Ek, 1975: 6, italics in the original)[7]

So it is not being proposed that more local cultural contexts be considered – and there is thus no intention of developing any cultural understanding in such an approach. So I do not intend to deal further with the approach of the Council of Europe in the 1970s.

Something similar can be said about the Englishman D.A. Wilkins' *Notional Syllabuses* from 1976. It takes the work of the Council of Europe further to develop a communicative approach and focuses on what components there ought to be in a syllabus that organises language teaching on the basis of communicative criteria. In Wilkins' opinion, this involves structuring teaching according to semantic and functional categories, and he operates with three such categories: *Semantico-grammatical categories* (ways in which it is possible in the target-language to express time, space, quantity, deixis and such semantic roles as 'agent', 'beneficiary' etc.); *Categories of modal meaning* (ways in which it is possible to express various types of modality); and *Categories of communicative function* (ways in which it is possible to express various linguistic acts such as information, evaluation, promises, requests, etc.). This approach is suitable for thematising language differences in semantics and pragmatics, but it does not link these language differences to other cultural relations. By focusing on general categories, it is implicitly linked to a universalistic (or pan-European) understanding of culture, as was the case in van Ek.

West Germany in the 1970s

English teaching

A violent discussion flared up in West Germany in the 1970s as a reaction against the idealistic and at times Nazi-influenced content that culture pedagogy had had since the time of the First World War. The subjects of English and, especially, French were involved in this debate, with a number of anthologies being published, including Arndt and Weller (1978), Baumgratz and Picht (1978), Kramer (1976a), Olbert (1977), Picht (1974) and Weber (1976). The debate began with the publication of a critical treatment of the *Kulturkunde* movement (Apelt, 1967) and it had a common basis – a broad agreement that it was important to deideologise the teaching of *Landeskunde/Kulturkunde*. The term *Kulturkunde* was perceived as being far too charged and, with a few exceptions, everyone stopped using it. There was, however, considerable disagreement on what was to replace it. Here it is possible to distinguish between three main positions (cf. Buttjes, 1982): a literary, hermeneutic position; a socially oriented position; and a language-pedagogical (communicative) position.

I do not intend to deal with the first-mentioned position here, as its orientation was mostly literary and did not have very much to say about a broader knowledge of culture and society. There is, however, one person who is normally associated with this wing and who occupies a special position in the German debate: Gottfried Keller, who ever since the 1970s has worked on national stereotypes seen from a social-psychological perspective that is more traditionally positivist in nature (Keller, 1970, 1983, 1987, 1996). Throughout the 1970s and 1980s, Keller retained the term *Kulturkunde*, in an attempt to reinterpret it. He was particularly interested in the links between the various types of national stereotype that occur in connection with foreign-language teaching: partly the students' stereotypes regarding the countries and peoples they come into contact with (heterostereotypes), partly their stereotypes about themselves (autostereotypes) and partly the stereotypes the foreign students have about them (autoheterostereotypes). He has not dealt with the relationship between language and culture, although he does express a system-oriented and essentialist view of culture within a national paradigm, i.e. he draws on the old holistic tradition within culture research.

The socially oriented position represented a more realist and objectivising approach to an understanding of society, emphasising that language teaching should educate students to be critical and independent (*mündig*) citizens in a representative democracy, both as state citizens and world citizens. They wanted foreign-language teaching to actively contribute to an overriding educational goal of *politische Bildung* (political education/ education for citizenship). Jürgen Langer and Manfred Schurig wrote, for example:

> As soon as students learn a foreign language, social norms are conveyed at the same time. We need to free this statement from its abstract nature and, in accordance with its claim, to consider the practical consequences for teaching. For this reason, we wish in the following to examine certain approaches that deal with the relationship between foreign language learning and politics and to ask the question as to what political ideas are connected to foreign language teaching and to what extent the discussions offer an opportunity via foreign language teaching to contribute to the education of critical, i.e. independent state citizens. (Translated from Langer & Schurig, 1972: 5)

Langer and Schurig, then, emphasise socially realistic communication that enables the students to adopt not an affirmative but a critical attitude towards society.

Buttjes and Kane emphasised the need for an empirical and systematic societal approach. In an article from 1978 they say:

> This article assumes that it is only possible to convey an objective picture of a target culture via socially and scientifically based *Landeskunde*. Understood in this way, such a *Landeskunde* would have to take both instrumental and humanistic learning goals into account. If solely interested in instrumental purposes, it would only register those aspects of the target culture that are usable in language practice, whereas a humanistic *Landeskunde* would be able to include a political goal as well. (Buttjes & Kane, 1978: 51)

They are advocating an autonomous, scientific and interdisciplinary *Landeskunde* that makes use of exemplary and comparative methods. According to them, *Landeskunde* exists in a tension between two aims: 'instrumental language learning' and 'political affective learning' and, correspondingly, between two levels in a description of society: the micro- and the macro-levels. They believe that teacher education ought to comprise knowledge in three areas: (1) the scientific basis of *Landeskunde*, (2) everyday life as a social field, and (3) institutional and social framework conditions for the individual.

The socially oriented wing within the subject of English generally chose to lean towards the British critical Cultural Studies tradition (Kramer, 1976b, Buttjes, 1981 and later Kramer, 1990 and 1997), which favoured society-related and critical studies of both literary and non-literary texts in language teaching. Kramer argued in favour of completely scrapping the German terms *Landeskunde* and *Kulturkunde* and of replacing them by Cultural Studies.

The language-pedagogical, communicative position stood for a semantically and pragmatically oriented *Landeskunde*, in which it was the communicative needs that determined the cultural content. This approach, which thematised more directly the relationship between language and culture/society in language teaching, had its most important representation in a book by Erdmenger and Istel.

Erdmenger and Istel: *Didaktik der Landeskunde* (Didactics of Landeskunde) (1973): Presentation

Manfred Erdmenger and Hans-Wolf Istel are West German language educationalists within English as a foreign language and are two of the earliest and best-known representatives of the so-called pragmatic position in West Germany. Their book *Didaktik der Landeskunde* is the only comprehensive presentation to date of (a special version of) culture pedagogy that discusses all stages of education.

Erdmenger and Istel represent the wing of culture pedagogy that has linguistics as its point of departure. They wrote their book during the period when the Council of Europe was initiating the above-mentioned project on 'threshold levels' in foreign languages, so the book can therefore be said to represent a culture-pedagogical extension of the early phase of the communicative approach. Erdmenger and Istel perceive communication as comprising aspects that have to do with both content and the affective. They wish to develop students' understanding of 'the other (person)', emphasising both *verstehen* (to understand) and *Verständnis* (to arrive at an understanding with each other, to communicate).

So they view the aim of *Landeskunde* as being a double one: to develop (linguistic) communicative competences and to strengthen understanding between peoples (*Völkerverständigung*). They emphasise that there must be no one single affirmative picture of the foreign country: 'Everyday conversational language, which is mainly used for communicative purposes, happens to contain all conventional clichés. This danger must be realised and correctly assessed' (Erdmenger & Istel, 1973: 9). This must be seen in the light of their wish to distance themselves from the earlier *Kulturkunde* and therefore to support a communication of facts about the target country that is as objective as possible.

Erdmenger and Istel describe *Landeskunde* as an interdisciplinary field that has relations to such neighbouring sciences as geography,[8] history, political science, sociology, anthropology and *Volkskunde* (folklore). What they are dealing with could be described as area studies that can be characterised as having an anthropogenous point of departure – one based on the life and (communicative) needs of the individual (cf. Brooks' insistence on having the individual at the centre, Chapter 2). The authors offer the following diagram which indicates certain differences between knowledge of the subject and *Landeskunde* (see Figure 3.1).

Knowledge of the subject (*Fachwissenschaft*)	Knowledge of the country (*Landeskunde*)

Point of departure:
  Facts about the country
Aim:
  Generalisation
 	
Method:
  Comparison with other countries
  similar facts
	Point of departure:
	  Anthropogenous points of view
	Aim:
	  Specialisation
	  (in *one* country and its inhabitants)
	Method:
	  Comparison with one's own
	  country

Figure 3.1 Erdmenger and Istel: Knowledge of the subject and *Landeskunde*[9]

Landeskunde, then, is a cross-section of a number of sciences with a special anthropogenous point of departure, with a specific orientation towards the individual target-language country, and characterised by a (solely bilateral) comparative method.

The model talks of *'one country and its inhabitants'*, but because of this political-national demarcation the authors are also operating with a model that indicates that they feel certain societal and cultural characteristics are universal, others more limited, and yet others locally specific – a static, 'spatial', geographical model (see Figure 3.2).

Universal facts (*Tatbestand*)						
	Facts in Western civilisation					
		Facts in the Anglo-Saxon area				
			Facts in Great Britain			
				Facts in England		
					Facts in Somerset	
						Facts in Bath

Figure 3.2 Erdmenger and Istel: The universal and the specific in *Landeskunde*[10]

So Erdmenger and Istel do not represent the view that there is a homogeneous culture within the framework of a country / state. The country is seen as a place where phenomena of major or minor geographical extent are mixed. But the model is unsatisfying because it is static and constructed of boxes inside each other, which conceals crossing (cross-national etc.) processes and relationships.

Erdmenger and Istel (1973): The relationship between language and culture

Occasionally, Erdmenger and Istel make use of the concept of culture, but in an ambiguous and obscure way. They sometimes refer to an aesthetic and hierarchical concept of culture that comprises, among other things, literature and art. In addition, they refer to a view that is strongly influenced by anthropology and is more or less holistic, also referring to Lado (1957) at this point. As regards the relationship between language and culture, they refer to Doyé (whom I cited in Chapter 1, and to whom I will return in this chapter), who throughout the period from the 1960s to the 1990s stressed the idea of the inseparable link between language, culture, country and people.[11] Doyé writes in 1966 that language teaching:

> ...has a twofold teaching subject: the foreign language and the culture expressed by means of that language... It is impossible to study a language separately from the contents it designates, and any foreign language teaching that is sensibly conducted will eventually inevitably communicate knowledge of the other country and the

people that speaks the language. (Translated from Doyé, 1966: 270, quoted from Erdmenger & Istel, 1973: 11)

Erdmenger and Istel themselves – using slightly different words from Doyé – emphasise that the linguistic sign is inextricably connected to the non-linguistic and to the language users (where it would seem they are implicitly building on Peirce's tripartite sign theory: sign, object and interpretant):

> It is important to note in connection with the *Landeskunde* aspect that linguistic signs are inextricably linked to non-linguistic facts (also ones relevant to *Landeskunde*) and to the people (who make use of these linguistic signs). Whoever learns a language, immediately learns aspects of *Landeskunde* at the same time. (Erdmenger & Istel, 1973: 14)

Moreover, Erdmenger and Istel do not have much to say explicitly about the relationship between language and culture, and the few statements above only function as an underlying justification for the rest of the work. It can be noted that there is a strong emphasis on the interconnection between the individual language and the individual culture – an emphasis not to be found in, for example, Seelye. Furthermore, semantics is treated by Erdmenger and Istel as part of linguistics, as we see below.

Erdmenger and Istel (1973): The relationship between language teaching and culture teaching

Erdmenger and Istel represent a so-called language-immanent or language-inherent approach to the teaching of culture, i.e. an approach in which knowledge of the target-language country has a 'servicing' ('*dienende*') function in relation to the communicative aims of language teaching:

> *Landeskunde* within the framework of foreign-language teaching gains … its aims and content from its being embedded in language teaching. Language teaching with the aim of communicative competence supplies the point of reference for the selection of *Landeskunde* content. Here, the servicing function of *Landeskunde* is obvious. Its aims are thus grounded in the language itself, principally within the field of semantics. (Translated from Erdmenger & Istel, 1973: 12)

Erdmenger and Istel thus stress the central role of semantics. They say about *Landeskunde* that in relation to linguistics it is an implied discipline that provides semantic aid (Erdmenger & Istel, 1973: 37). This function is realised when teaching provides information about the culture-specific meaning of such words as 'school inspector', 'Speech Day', 'public school', 'cricket', 'plum pudding', 'fudge', 'sports club', 'Christmas', 'mantlepiece', etc. *Landeskunde* can thus give the semantic description a culture-comparative dimension.

So that the interdisciplinary study of *Landeskunde* (geography, history, etc.) does not become too unwieldy, the authors emphasise that certain social roles and certain types of communication situation that the teaching is in particular to prepare the students for, must be described. They describe these central roles as: (1) to be a future user; (2) to be a future traveller abroad; and (3) to be a future host for foreigners in one's own country. Erdmenger and Istel give, for example, the following summary of what they believe should be the aims of teaching *Landeskunde* at *Grundstufe* and *Sekundarstufe I* levels, i.e. 8–15 years:

> It is the global aim of foreign-language teaching in terms of the *Landeskunde* aspect… to help the student attain communicative competence in the situations arising from his future roles as consumer of real and ideal products of the foreign country, as a traveller abroad and as someone who has contact with foreigners in his own country, and to awaken in him a willingness to adopt an attitude and to negotiate. (Erdmenger & Istel, 1973: 40)

This practical thinking about needs sends *Landeskunde* teaching in a particular direction. It is oriented towards what seems relevant for students to be able to cope, mainly orally, in everyday situations that are typical of the above-mentioned social roles – later also in writing, both receptively and productively. In practice, this understanding of *Landeskunde* is very closely aligned to teaching that is geared to the future needs of tourists (students, business travellers, etc.), and this is also obvious from many beginner's books in foreign languages from the 1970s onwards, which are even more travel-oriented than textbooks from the preceding years (cf. Chapter 2). The students are prepared to find their bearings in foreign surroundings, make contacts, manage the necessities of everyday life, etc. That is why there is also quite of lot of travel realia in the teaching materials: transport conditions, campsites and hotels, sights and attractions. This can be compared with the understanding of needs on which Seelye bases himself – one that gains its inspiration from Maslow's pyramid of needs.

The *Landeskunde* teaching that is implied here is not based on texts but on topics. Logically speaking, determining the social role comes first, followed by the communication situation that has been selected and then the knowledge which is necessary to be able to communicate in the given situation. This knowledge is formulated in the teaching topic. Only then are the texts and other materials (linguistic and possibly visual) decided on that are to be used to illustrate the topic.

Erdmenger and Istel are of the opinion that teaching in the younger classes should have the universal (cf. Figure 3.2) as its point of departure and then gradually move towards the specific. At the same time, it should increasingly make use of comparisons with the student's own country – although comparisons as such are not given high priority in their view of teaching, which should mainly be oriented towards the target-language country / countries.

The necessary societal and cultural knowledge naturally increases to keep abreast of the levels of teaching and the required communicative skills – and at higher levels there is a need for more systematic orientation about various areas of practical relevance. Regarding education at *Sekundarstufe II* level (16–19), Erdmenger and Istel write that the aim ought to be understood as communicative proficiency in general and specific situations. They suggest that the following aspects be dealt with: general philosophical and humanistic aspects, geographical, historical, politico-sociological and ecological aspects, more specialised aspects such as scientific, psychological aspects and also the history of knowledge and special occupationally related aspects (Erdmenger & Istel, 1973: 44). They also suggest that at the upper-secondary level education should rather be called *Kulturwissenschaft* (knowledge of / studies of culture) than *Landeskunde*, and that at university level only the term *Kulturwissenschaft* be used – here with a research dimension oriented towards area studies with special regard to their historical, societal and cultural dimensions. *Kulturwissenschaft* could feature alongside *Sprachwissenschaft* (knowledge of / studies of language, linguistics) and *Literaturwissenschaft* (knowledge of / studies of literature, comparative literary history). This has subsequently been adopted at a number of German universities.

By talking about *'die Sprachinhärenz der Landeskunde'* (the language inherence of *Landeskunde*), Erdmenger and Istel represent a predominantly functional and instrumental understanding of knowledge. On the basis of this communicative needs orientation, we are dealing with a knowledge that is limited by the everyday perspective of the student and the future consumer, or tourist. The position is cognitive (in respect of knowledge) and positivist in its orientation towards realia. There is no encouragement of an analysis or adoption of a critical attitude towards cultural and societal conditions or to a historical understanding. This view finds only that knowledge relevant which is thought to be necessary for the future communicative needs of that particular student or group of students. A topic on the history of the Indians in the colonial period in North America, for example, would be superfluous or highly peripheral.

The position of Erdmenger and Istel is interesting as an early communicative approach which emphasises a broad orientation about the societal conditions in the target countries but which places this entire orientation under the communicative (linguistic) goal – whereas Seelye, for example, is aiming at 'appropriate target behavior', with just as much emphasis being placed on non-linguistic as on linguistic behaviour.

French teaching in West Germany

Within the teaching of French in West Germany, Gisela Baumgratz, Wilma Melde and Klaus Schüle were among the most active critics of the teaching of culture at the time. Together, they wrote an article (Baumgratz, Melde & Schüle, 1980) which stated that the content of French teaching ought to derive from interdisciplinary social sciences (*Sozialwissenschaft*). They described their position as being socio-critical, the overall aim for foreign-language teaching being *'transnationale Kommunikationsfähigkeit'* ('transnational communicative proficiency') – a concept that is part of a wider conception of transnational political practice which comprises the whole school. They say the following about transnational communicative ability:

> Alongside scientific and epistemological premises and subject-related bases from the realm of social sciences and those of language and communication, this concept also contains normative scales of values conveyed by the idea of peaceful co-existence with equal rights, achieved by the dismantling of barriers of perception and communication and the removal of discrimination and suppression, since the possibility is created for establishing new transnational group solidarities. (Baumgratz, Melde & Schüle, 1980: 90)

This definition, which strongly stresses tolerance and cooperation, is a radical version of a goal often mentioned in connection with *politische Bildung* (political education), i.e. *'Partnerfähigkeit'* ('partner capacity'), which contains the concrete idea of the integration of West Germany into Western Europe and of the raising of German children and young people to participate in parliamentary democracy. Baumgratz, Melde and Schüle believe it is important to have a socio-critical objective that has social and political problems as its point of departure:

> Corresponding to emancipatory socio-critical objective, themes and methods should preferably be chosen that are important for the recognition of functional problems and developmental trends in contempo-

rary France. The specific task of *Landeskunde* consists of bringing out national peculiarities in the assessment, treatment and effects of in principle comparable problems in both countries. (Translated from Baumgratz, Melde & Schüle, 1980: 81)

They come up with quite a few ideas and requirements for such teaching: student focus, project work, group work and, first and foremost: a teacher education that provides both scientific, subject-related and subject-teaching qualifications.

Baumgratz helped produce an important educational document that was published in 1982, but which, with regard to content, is a further development of trends found in the 1970s: *Stuttgarter Thesen*. Its full name is *Fremdsprachenunterricht und Internationale Beziehungen – Stuttgarter Thesen zur Rolle der Landeskunde im Französischunterricht* (Foreign Language Teaching and International Relations – Stuttgart Theses on the Role of *Landeskunde* in French Teaching), and it was written in connection with efforts to develop educational collaboration between West Germany and France as a part of European integration. This collaboration took the form of comprehensive exchange programmes organised not least by the German-French institute in Ludwigsburg. The booklet is built up around the concept of transnational communicative proficiency as the most important learning goal for foreign-language teaching (French teaching) and it is described here as being based on the assumption:

> ...that the individual is always strongly influenced by his national society and its history and by his position in this society. Foreign-language teaching must therefore deal intensively with attitudes and patterns of perception and behaviour regarding people of other languages and cultures at home and abroad. (Translated from Baumgratz *et al.*, 1982: 8)

All in all, the subject of French in (West) Germany is probably the forum in which the most politically conscious efforts have been made in culture pedagogy seen as a whole (cf., for example, Buttjes, 1982), which, among other things, can be ascribed to the great importance the Franco-German axis has had in the process of European integration – an importance that is expressed in the exchange programmes mentioned above for schoolchildren on both sides of the border.

The social orientation of both English and French teaching in West Germany could also be seen in the critique of textbooks, including critical analyses of the societal content of textbooks, including sex roles.[12] This attention to the picture of society in the materials had an important institutional background in West Germany, where there was (and is) public censure of schoolbooks, and where textbook commissions undertake regular evaluations of schoolbooks on the basis of certain catalogues of criteria (see, for example, the textbook evaluations in Engel, 1979).

It should also be mentioned that within French as a foreign language, not only in West Germany but also in other countries and in France itself, there is a comparatively strong tradition of being interested in teaching the semantics of vocabulary, especially at beginner level. One of the very first articles concerning vocabulary and culture in French teaching's beginner stage in West Germany was, for example, an article by Baur-Langenbucher from 1972: *Frankreichkunde und Sprachunterricht* (Knowledge of France and Language Teaching). It is emphasised in that article that 'There exists an inseparable connection between language and culture, account of which must absolutely be taken in foreign language teaching' (Baur-Langenbucher: 7). This inseparable connection between language and culture has specifically to do with the vocabulary, and here Baur-Langenbucher agrees with A. Martinet's statement that 'culture is shared connotations' (*la culture, c'est les connotations partagées*). So *Landeskunde* about France must, from the outset, deal with how ordinary Frenchmen view their own lives and how they perceive their own history – and this is to be achieved via working with the vocabulary of the French language. An important method here is comparing cultures, which in this connection means the comparison of words that have partially the same denotation but different connotations: English 'breakfast' v. French 'petit déjeuner' German 'Frühstück', etc. Baur-Langenbucher calls this approach the cultural-linguistic view[13] (cf. below on *sprachbezogene Landeskunde* – linguistically oriented *Landeskunde*).

The USSR and the GDR in the 1970s

Vereščagin and Kostomarov: *Jazyk i kul'tura* (1973) (Language and Culture): Presentation

This book deals with Russian as a foreign language. Apart from having importance in the USSR, it also made an impact in the GDR. E.M. Vereščagin and V.G. Kostomarov are lexicologists and language educationalists and are both particularly interested in teaching Soviet society via work on the vocabulary of the Russian language.[14] They came to have a profound influence on culture pedagogy in the USSR because of their book, whose full title is *Jazyk i kul'tura – lingvostranovedenie v prepodavanii russkogo jazyka kak innostrannogo* (Language and Culture – Knowledge of Language and Country in the Teaching of Russian as a Foreign Language). The authors have had a number of subsequent publications, but this book

– until 1988 at least (Munck, 1988a) – was their only complete presentation of culture pedagogy.[15]

The book, which was thoroughly reviewed by Herrde *et al.* in 1975, deals in particular with vocabulary studies as an important aspect of language teaching. The authors have also published two articles in German: Vereščagin und Kostomarov (1972) and (1974).[16]

Vereščagin and Kostomarov adopt a linguistic point of departure in relation to culture pedagogy. They do not claim (as do Erdmenger and Istel) that their theory covers all of culture pedagogy (*stranovedenie*) but only part of it – that part which ought to have an integral place in foreign-language teaching (Russian as a foreign language): *lingvostranovedenie* – or their preferred term in German: *sprachbezogene Landeskunde* (linguistically oriented *Landeskunde*). They believe that linguistically oriented *Landeskunde* should be the fifth aspect of teaching, alongside the four others: the lexical, the grammatical, the phonetic and the stylistic aspects.

This view of culture pedagogy is linked to a 'Marxist-Leninist theory of culture', and culture (in the reviewers' translation) is defined as follows: 'Culture – is the product of social activity of human collectives: it has a historical genesis and ultimately plays a determining role in the development of the individual human personality' (translated from Herrde *et al.*, 1975: 242).

In the GDR, where the teaching of Russian had a strong position, Vereščagin and Kostomarov's book was also of great importance. Herrde *et al.* (1975) translated the Russian word *lingvostranovedenie* by *Linguolandeskunde*,[17] and this concept became a specialist term in East German foreign-language methodology[18] alongside the more usual *sprachbezogene Landeskunde*.

Gudrun Fischer is one of those who has written about *Landeskunde* and *Linguolandeskunde* in the GDR (Fischer, 1979). She distinguishes between *Landeskunde als Prinzip* (*Landeskunde* as a principle) throughout the educational process (we are dealing here with German as a foreign language), *Landeskunde als selbständiges Lehrfach* (*Landeskunde* as an independent subject), i.e. lectures, seminars, excursions, etc., possibly in the students' first language, and *Linguolandeskunde* (linguistically oriented *Landeskunde*) as an integral part of language teaching. She finds *Linguolandeskunde* important because it deals with ideology-relevant vocabulary, unlike 'bourgeois' language pedagogy, which considers itself free of ideology. So Fischer distinguishes between a linguistic *Landeskunde*, and, a non-linguistic *Landeskunde* and even though she says that the two are inseparable, they actually take place in practice as separate activities / subjects.[19]

Although Vereščagin and Kostomarov's theory has been developed in relation to a social system that has now virtually disappeared, the actual idea of teaching about society via the language is still relevant, and it still survives in Russian teaching as a special method. As an example, an article by Dobrynine (1991) could be mentioned, which deals with teaching Russian in France, and which is interested in *les mots porteurs de civilisation* (cultural words): words that are used in connection with such thematic areas as everyday life, including sport, eating habits and work, and man and his surroundings, including man and nature, man and the city, and man and the immediate environment (the home, the family, etc.).[20]

Vereščagin and Kostomarov 1973: The relationship between language and culture

The authors do not say much about the relationship between language and culture, although they make a comment which reveals that culture in their opinion is reflected in language: 'The subject of language-related teaching in *Landeskunde* is basically the culture of the country whose language is being learned. The teaching should demonstrate how this culture is reflected in the language' (Vereščagin & Kostomarov, 1974: 309). They do not have the difficult relationship to the concept of culture that their German contemporaries had, and generally refer to Humboldt, to the neo-Humboldtian Weisgerber and to Sapir and Whorf. How culture and society – and thereby also language and society – are interrelated is not clear. Vereščagin and Kostomarov do not deal with sociolinguistic issues.

As regards the attitude of the authors to the question of the national, it must be mentioned that there are certain indications of a view of the national that are to be expected within orthodox Marxism-Leninism: 'Just as any other language, Russian reflects the two cultures of every national culture', i.e. the democratic and socialist culture and the bourgeois culture (translated from Vereščagin & Kostomarov, 1972: 74). In spite of this division, they are referred to in Herrde *et al.*'s review (Herrde *et al.*, 1975) as saying that there can be both something national and something international in a culture, so that cultures, e.g. that of the target-language and that of the students, will contain both specific and common elements. It is unclear, however, what an understanding of these different layers of culture mean for the practical teaching of culture.

Kostomarov and Vereščagin distinguish between two main approaches to vocabulary: the linguistic and the 'languacultural' (German: *linguolandeskundliche*). The linguistic approach deals with the words and expressions (lexical units) that are equivalent in relation to the students' first language, i.e. have roughly the same meaning, while the languacultural approach deals with the words and expressions that are non-equivalent, i.e. there is no corresponding word or expression in the students' first language. There are (were) many non-equivalent words within the area of society in Russian (in relation to 'Western' languages). So it is assumed that the first language is involved in work on the vocabulary, and explicit work on translation is carried out. This is only an initial division, for there is a comprehensive system in the book concerning various types of words and the types of languacultural commentaries they must be provided with for the students to gain a better understanding of them and, by means of this, of the text/conversation. Words without equivalents are divided, for example, into seven groups (but it is emphasised that they do not exhaust the vocabulary that could be thought relevant) – the following has been taken from 1988, but is also presented in Vereščagin und Kostomarov (1972 and 1973):

* Sovietisms, e.g. *kolchoz*;
* words from modern everyday life, e.g. *udarnik*: a worker who always stands out as the best in his group and works far more than prescribed by the norms;
* words from traditional everyday life, e.g. *boršč*: beetroot soup;
* historicisms, e.g. *dvor'anin*: nobleman, not found after the 1917 Revolution;
* phrasal expressions, e.g. *načat' s azov*: to begin from the beginning, lit. to begin from A;
* words from folklore, e.g. *baba-jaga*: a witch, from children's fairytales;
* loan words, e.g. *bazar.*

It is only the first-mentioned group, Sovietisms, that can be said to deal directly with the social system, but it is mentioned first, and is also the one that is most typical of their approach. This approach would also give high priority in non-Soviet contexts to words that deal with societal institutions: the education system, the political system, etc. The other groups are more usual, but it is characteristic that loan words are also included; this is not a group usually seen in culture pedagogy, which traditionally has a preference for the 'culture specific' in the sense 'indigenous'.[21] But I feel that loan words are a very important group, because they are an indicator of language spread across language communities.

Vereščagin and Kostomarov (1973): The relationship between language teaching and culture teaching

Vereščagin and Kostomarov distinguish between two methods of explaining or demonstrating how language reflects culture and society: the system commentary and the complex commentary. The system commentary has as its starting point the individual word or expression, and explains the semantic field ('system') in which this occurs. For example, it is impossible to understand the expression *junger Pionier* (young pioneer) without knowing something about the Soviet system of children and youth organisations and that young pioneers are (were) a particular age group. The system commentary corresponds to an entry in an encyclopedia.

The starting point for a complex commentary is a text that is worked with in teaching, e.g. a short story. It contains certain expression to do with schooling that need an explanation, e.g. 'a rural state school' (1) and further on in the text 'a teacher's room' (7) etc. The complex commentary, then, is a non-literary prose text that places all the expression involved together in a continuous narrative presentation, for example:

> In the USSR, children learn in urban or rural state schools (1). School buildings normally contain the following rooms: a classroom (3), an assembly hall, a gymnasium, a dining hall and a teachers' room (7) (a special room for the teachers). The teaching system consists of... (Translated from Vereščagin & Kostomarov, 1972: 76)

Presumably, Kostomarov and Vereščagin imagine that complex commentaries are written by textbook writers, not by teachers.[22]

The learning objective in Vereščagin and Kostomarov is mainly to understand written texts that refer to Russia and the Soviet Union. They operate with an extremely factual, knowledge-oriented learning objective. A means of acquiring this understanding is translation and work on the above-mentioned system and complex commentaries. The approach is an extension of the realia tradition,[23] which is also implied by the term 'commentary'.

This approach is also characterised by the authors distinguishing between a language-oriented culture pedagogy and a non-language-oriented culture pedagogy, unlike both Seelye and Erdmenger and Istel; they do not deal with the relationship between the two forms of culture pedagogy. I will return to this division in Chapter 7 in connection with a presentation and discussion of the concept of languaculture.

Vereščagin and Kostomarov's approach is interesting as a position that cultivates a semantic, society-oriented culture pedagogy, though admittedly in a highly traditional pedagogical form. Modernised and updated to a present-day communicative understanding of language teaching, this approach contains an important aspect that is otherwise underexposed in today's culture pedagogy: an interest in how various societal, institutional and ideological relations can be reflected in the vocabulary of the language – an interest that could be developed further if culture pedagogy began, for example, to a greater extent to include methods taken from critical discourse analysis.

France in the 1970s

Civilisation and a new concept of *culture*

There was a sporadic discussion of the cultural side of language teaching in France before the 1970s, especially in connection with the audio-visual method, which involved working with dialogues in situations illustrated by drawings, etc.[24] One of the first to start the discussion in its more modern form was Albert Barrera-Vidal, who taught French in West Germany and referred to the discussion there. He was particularly interested in the stereotype picture of France in West Germany, and pleaded for a more realistic transmission of culture based on empirical sociological surveys (*enquêtes*) (Barrera-Vidal, 1972).

Barrera-Vidal used two concepts about the cultural side of teaching: *connaissance de la France* (knowledge of France), presumably a translation of the German *Frankreichkunde*, and *civilisation française* (French civilisation). This latter concept is the traditional concept that everyone else also used at the time and which is still used today to a great extent. It broadly covers society and culture, including technological and economic development. The concept is an all-inclusive one that can be both very broad and in the singular: *civilisation universelle*, and can also comprise large cultural areas *les grandes civilisations* (major civilisations). Lastly, it can also mean cultural and societal relations in a single state, e.g. *la civilisation britannique*. The concept of civilisation further has a clear historical dimension: *civilisation* is something that develops over time, and the concept thus has an evolutionist tinge that can be traced back at least to the classical evolutionist phase of culture research in the latter half of the 19th century, but probably also further back to the idea of progress in the Enlightenment period.[25]

So the central concept of culture pedagogy in France, *civilisation*, had a completely different nature from its contemporary German *Landeskunde*, the meaning of which was much more limited and full of pre-scientific connotations because of the word *Kunde* (knowledge). But in West Germany (and the GDR) the concept of *Landeskunde* was needed in the 1970s as a progressive concept in relation to the controversial concept of *Kulturkunde*, so the actual *Landeskunde* concept was hardly a subject of debate in the 1970s. It became so only in the 1980s. On the other hand, the

French *civilisation* was already being challenged by the concept of culture in the 1970s – in the American anthropological sense.

The *'grand old man'* of culture pedagogy in France, André Reboullet, published in 1973 the first anthology on culture pedagogy, focusing in particular on the teaching of French culture and society (*L'enseignement de la civilisation française*) (The teaching of French civilisation). It appeared in connection with an international symposium in Santiago in Chile in 1970 on university teaching of French culture and society. The Latin-American connection forms perhaps an important basis for Reboullet and some of the other authors pleading for the introduction of the American anthropological conception of culture (which also had a strong position in Spanish-speaking America) into the French context.[26]

In the introduction to the above anthology there is a proposal for systematising culture pedagogy, which has become quite well known in France. This was *le rapport langue-civilisation* (the relationship between language and civilisation),[27] which begins with a remark that here *civilisation* is to be understood as synonymous with *culture*, as understood by Anglo-Saxon and Spanish-speaking anthropologists and sociologists. The model distinguishes between *réalités de civilisation, manifestations culturelles* and *système culturel*. By *réalités de civilisation* is meant the physical and social reality in which language develops, that which is built into the lexical and morphosyntactic categories of language. This refers to such fields as climate, flora and fauna in the area involved, and to the technology and social structure that has developed locally. These *réalités* can be studied via work on *mots de civilisation* (cultural words), e.g. within such subjects as housing, food and drink, the family, etc.

By *manifestations culturelles* is meant the use of language in varied contexts: in everyday communication, in factual and subject-related communication and in poetic (literary) communication. Via these cultural manifestations links are established with the aid of varied language use between *les réalités de civilisation* and a more abstract level which is called *le système culturel*.

Le système culturel is a more or less unconscious or latent system of values that the writers feel characterises the individual *civilisation*. Here we have an idealistic (value-oriented) version of the 'classical' or 'functionalist' concept of culture found in cultural anthropologists in the 1950s, e.g. Lado, E.T. Hall and Kluckhohn, whom Reboullet refers to, and all of whom stand for various versions of a holistic concept of culture that includes explicit and implicit patterns of action and systems of values.

It is important to add that *culture* otherwise refers to *enrichissement de l'esprit* (enrichment of the mind), i.e. to a development of the personality that makes the person more cultivated (an individual concept of culture). With the introduction of an 'anthropological' concept of culture, i.e. a collective, non-hierarchical concept of culture, the word *culture* has had two main meanings in French culture pedagogy since the 1970s.

Alongside the cultural-anthropological position there is also a society-oriented and encyclopedic position in France which emphasises the need to communicate a cohesive view of society as a whole. The most important representative of this position in the 1970s is Jean-Pierre Fichou, who in his book *Enseigner les civilisations* (Teaching Civilisations) (1979) describes an approach based on analysis, synthesis and reflection, and who in addition stresses the importance of an understanding of historical continuity in the development of civilisation – here British civilisation. I intend to deal with this in more detail in the next section.

It is remarkable that culture pedagogy as a theoretical discipline is strongest in France in the environments that deal with French as a foreign language – though the subject English is well represented – whereas in West Germany it was not people linked to German as a foreign language who were active but people involved in teaching English and French. This has possibly something to do with the very different self-images that existed in France and West Germany at the time: the French self-understanding could draw on its revolutionary history, republican ideals and a democratic tradition (the Vichy period was bracketed out), and it was natural to portray a positive picture of French social life at all levels. Post-war West Germany was not in such a position, which might explain why culture pedagogy within German as a foreign and second language was for a long time more oriented towards literature than it was in other language subjects in (West) Germany.

Fichou: *Enseigner les civilisations* (1979) (Teaching Civilisations): Presentation

Fichou works within the subject of English, and his book is mainly for teachers at university and upper-secondary levels. He discusses the possibility of developing teaching *civilisation* as an independent subject, with its own objectives and method. Those teaching *civilisation* he calls *civilisationnistes* – a term coined by French germanists in 1971 (Fichou, 1979: 10).

The overall objective of teaching is to 'convey a picture that is as human and complete as possible' (Fichou, 1979: 38). The idea of a whole, a synthesis and *globalité*, is very central, with the subject of history as the main reference. But in addition there are an impressive number of disciplines as potential references (which in an English context would be referred to as *parent disciplines*): economics, sociology, demography, (socio)linguistics, geography, literature, art, ethnology and psychoanalysis.

Fichou distinguishes between civilisation and culture by saying that *civilisation* is a broader, more historically oriented concept than *culture*. He refers here to Lahbabi (1961), who wrote:

> National culture can be defined as the concretisation of the genius of a people in its work, its vision of the world and its behaviour, whereas civilisation would be (...) the objectivisation of the geniuses of all peoples in their combined efforts in the course of human history: a common inheritance ... diversity in unity – that is what cultures are; the mixing of the diverse in unity – that is what civilisation is. (Translated from the quote in Fichou, 1979: 26)

So here he places national cultures in a larger civilisation-historical context – a holistic and evolutionist view. He is particularly interested in the *idées-forces* that characterise societies, quoting as examples for the USA: 'optimism, dynamism, movement, pluralism, puritanism, liberalism, proselytism', and for Great Britain: 'pragmatism, insularism, Protestantism, heritage, humour, decentralisation' (Fichou, 1979: 86). This blend of idea-historical trends and stereotypes is Fichou's suggestion for a holistic culture pedagogy – one that is very idealistic even though he repeatedly stresses the sociological basis of his views.

Fichou (1973): The relationship between language and culture

With regard to his view of language, Fichou prefers a general sociolinguistic and language-historical approach, referring here to Labov, Fishman and Sauvageot.[28] He favours dealing with foreign societies as multilingual and possibly diglossic societies, unlike Seelye, Erdmenger and Istel and Vereščagin and Kostomarov.

As a result of this fundamentally sociolinguistic approach, Fichou is cautious when it comes to talking about the relationship between language and culture. He mentions the Whorf hypothesis, concluding (after quite a brief discussion) by saying that 'One can affirm with complete peace of mind that language reflects the civilisation of which it is the vehicle'. And he adds a language-historical remark about, for example, the USA:

> The environment (geographical names, names of plants and animals (...) industrialisation, urbanisation, the contributions made by pre-existing groups (Indians, French, Spanish, etc...) shape without a doubt the present language, in the same way as upheavals in the history of the group. (Fichou, 1979: 17)

This is the only comment Fichou makes about the relationship between language and culture. With his sociologically based attitude, it would have been much more obvious to investigate linguistic and cultural complexity in relation to each other, but he does not do so – perhaps because he is actually more interested in the above-mentioned highly abstract idea-historical comparisons: optimism, pragmatism, etc. In practice, there is often a kind of identification of language and culture in his discourse, in the form of an identification of language and society: the expression *'la société dont on étudie la langue'* (the society whose language one is studying) is one he frequently uses throughout the book.

Fichou (1973): The relationship between language teaching and culture teaching

Fichou's idea of teaching culture is very intellectual in its orientation, with emphasis being placed on analysis and synthesis, on an understanding of generalities. The aim is also for students to gain a reflective understanding of their own society. Fichou calls this approach *civilisation appliquée* (applied civilisation), stressing that it is a comparative approach.

To prevent fragmentation of the image of society, he feels that it is important to organise teaching thematically around various types of *documents* (written texts, speech, visual material). At the same time, he maintains that the students' first language should at all costs be avoided, even when working with relatively complex subjects in connection with social relations.

Fichou's main purpose is to strengthen the teaching of civics in France. That is why he has included in his book the outline of a reform of the teaching of *instruction civique* (civics) in French schools, developed into a larger understanding of French society in its structure and history. Beginning at Class 6 level with topics connected with the municipality (institutions, school, environment, transport, leisure), he continues in Class 7 with topics related to the département, in Class 8 with topics to do with the region, and in the higher classes with a range of topics about French society in general. Civics, strengthened in this way, can, among other things, help to make the comparisons in foreign-language teaching more accurate.[29]

The approaches of both Fichou and Erdmenger and Istel are very ambitious in the subject-related spectrum indicated, but while Erdmenger and Istel's topics are chosen more *ad hoc* in relation to communicative needs, Fichou's is highly structured in a systematic progression that does not allow much freedom to either teacher or students. As a result of this high level of ambition, both approaches also attempt to address the problem of the lack of a scientific approach to culture pedagogy, something that was particularly felt to be a problem in the 1970s, when culture pedagogy was still in its infancy: how can one prevent the area becoming a field for amateur historians, amateur sociologists, etc.; how does one avoid becoming pure mediators of other disciplines?

Fichou's position also contrasts strongly with Seelye's practical, behaviourist-influenced position, and if Fichou's position is related to that of Vereščagin and Kostomarov, it must be said that Fichou does not devote much space to more linguistically oriented, semantic studies: Fichou is interested in the larger contexts. So it could be said to sum up that he is one of the most consistent representatives of the French rationalist tradition in culture pedagogy, with an emphasis on the factual, encyclopedic and historical overview.

Denmark and Norway in the 1970s

In *Denmark*, the traditional term for the area was *kulturformidling* (the transmission of culture), and it mainly referred to the literary content of language teaching and to its general introduction to land-and-people in the target-language country/countries. It was in particular as a result of Helga Andersen's and my work from 1976 that the area was introduced into Denmark. The approach in our[30] first article on culture pedagogy *Samfunds- og kulturformidling* (The Teaching of Society and Culture) (Andersen & Risager, 1977), had been inspired by the German discussion, especially the positions represented by people within French teaching in West Germany: Baumgratz, Melde and Schüle. We analysed the ideological content of foreign-language teaching at beginner level and discussed the 'hidden socialisation' of foreign-language teaching. The aim was to develop the content side of foreign-language teaching, particularly in textbooks, so it became more representative in a sociological sense and comprised both the interactional situations of the micro-level and the various institutions and other societal structures of the macro-level. We wanted to use as our point of departure the societal topics and social issues that could encourage students to adopt an independent position as regards societal questions and give them a higher level of sociological and political awareness. As was common in social sciences at the time, we did not use the term 'culture' all that much – and seldom as an all-inclusive term.

In *Norway* there was a debate in the late 1970s and early 1980s about *kulturkunnskap* (cultural knowledge) within English which had to do with the content of the teaching of culture at university level and its relation to the teaching of language and literature. Representatives that could be mentioned are Skårdal (1979) and Oakland (1984), both of whom advocated a broad orientation, starting with present-day institutions in the broad sense, and Gulliksen (1978), who advocated a more idea-historical approach. Brøgger distanced himself from a society-oriented approach and proposed an anthropological[31] concept of culture, the emphasis being on the norm sets of social groups (Brøgger, 1979, 1980).[32] The debate later led to Brøgger's book *Culture, Language, Text* (1992), which I will look at more closely in Chapter 5.

Conclusion

The 1970s was a time of upheaval within the area of culture pedagogy, especially in West Germany although also in France. If the situation in the USA, West Germany / GDR and France is compared, it is clear that developments within culture pedagogy had widely differing points of departure: in the USA a cultural-anthropological, behaviourist oriented mode of thought, in West Germany and the GDR a politically tainted *Kulturkunde* that had to be resisted and neutralised via a concept of *Landeskunde* that was unsatisfactory in many ways, and in France a historical and holistic way of thinking via a concept of *civilisation* that called for both a historical and societal overview rooted in the encyclopedic tradition of the Enlightenment. With the importation of the American anthropological concept of culture into French culture pedagogy in the 1970s, two different concepts developed: a new collective concept of culture alongside the old concept, which referred to the process of cultivation in the individual.

The four examples of culture-pedagogical viewpoints can be divided into two that have a linguistic point of departure, and two that start from the humanities and / or social sciences – and within both groups there are also clear distinctions:

Point of departure in linguistics:
* Erdmenger and Istel: a communicative, pragmatic, socially oriented approach.
* Vereščagin and Kostomarov: a semantic, socially oriented approach.

Point of departure in the humanities and/or the social sciences:
* Seelye: a cultural-anthropological, psychological approach.
* Fichou: a historical, social sciences approach.

While the American tradition in the 1970s emphasised the connection with cultural anthropology, the tendencies in European culture pedagogy were more oriented towards studies of society. Some in a more fact-oriented, positivist direction (Erdmenger & Istel, Vereščagin & Kostomarov), others in a rationalistic, emancipatory direction (Baumgratz, Kramer, Melde – the latter I will return to in Chapter 4).

As regards the relationship between language and culture, the overall tendency is an unclear and in many cases relatively cautious claim of a link between language and culture/society. Erdmenger and Istel go furthest here, referring to Doyé and stating that language and culture are inseparable. At the same time, their box model concerning universal and local cultural features (Figure 3.2) implies that it is not possible simply to talk about clearly demarcated national cultural spaces. The importance of this idea for the interpretation of the relationship between language and culture apparently does not occur to them.

As regards the relationship between teaching language and teaching culture, all four approaches represent to varying degrees the view that teaching culture has first and foremost to do with the thematic content of the teaching. They mainly represent *the content-oriented culture pedagogy* mentioned in Chapter 1, which focuses on the content dimension: the relationship between linguistic practice and its cultural content. Erdmenger and Istel emphasise the content (*landeskundliche Inhalte*) at the levels of both the word (the semantics of vocabulary) and the text (texts about cultural and societal relations in the target country). Vereščagin and Kostomarov particularly stress lexical semantic information. Seelye is interested in knowledge of the target countries, but also in how adequate linguistic and non-linguistic behaviour can be developed. Seelye's approach thus addresses both content-oriented culture pedagogy and *context-oriented culture pedagogy* (Chapter 1), which focuses on the context dimension: the relationship between linguistic practice and its cultural context. Fichou is clearly interested in the content of texts in language teaching and outlines a content-oriented culture pedagogy that involves quite a lot of work on the cultural and societal relations of the target countries, including their linguistic diversity.

It can generally be said that all the cultural educationalists mentioned above agree about being interested in the target-languages and the 'target-language countries' involved, no matter whether a linguistic or a culture-and-society point of departure is chosen, and no matter whether cultural terms or societal terms are used. But none of them makes any real effort to define language v. culture, or to discuss the concept of the nation in relation to those of language and culture – either generally or in relation to language teaching. Despite all the lack of clarity, however, it is possible to say that there is an unspoken national paradigm of a political nature underlying the culture-pedagogical discourse of the 1970s.

Notes

1. Notice, however, that we are dealing with two different hierarchies: in the *Brötchen-Gretchen* model geography and history are at the low end of the scale – a reflection of German idealism?
2. See also President Bush's initiative referred to in Chapter 6.
3. In which Maslow describes his well-known hierarchy of needs, ranging from physiological needs via security needs and love and appreciation needs to self-realisation needs.
4. As examples of critical situations Seelye mentions those where one is to console someone who has been exposed to a divorce or a serious illness.
5. He refers here to such researchers as the anthropologist M. Mead and the social psychologist Harry C. Triandis.
6. The interest of the Council of Europe in language teaching in Europe began as early as 1964, with the project *'Major Project – Modern Languages'*.
7. A passus that reveals that the universalism of the communicative approach was actually a Europeanism.
8. *Landeskunde* (knowledge of the country), which is an old term in German foreign language teaching, can be contrasted with *Länderkunde* (knowledge of countries), which is or has been an important regional discipline within geography.
9. Translated from Erdmengel & Istel, 1973: 25.
10. Translated from Erdmengel & Istel, 1973: 29.
11. Which Melde (1987) calls the 'thesis of identity' in the German tradition, see Chapter 4.
12. Cf. an anthology edited by Freudenstein, 1978.
13. With a reference to Sapir and Whorf as 'cultural linguists'. Cf. the more recent English term 'cultural linguistics' (i.a. Palmer, 1996).
14. Since I do not know enough Russian to have an overview of the authors' production in Russian, I am mainly relying on their articles in German, together with the sources mentioned below: Herrde *et al.* (1975) and Munck (1988a and b).
15. It appeared in the second edition in 1976 and in the 3rd edition in 1983. I have not, however, seen these editions.
16. In the 1970s, Kostomarov was leader of the Pushkin Institute in Moscow and Vereščagin worked at the same institute, which stood, among other things, for the preparation of a Russian *Landeskunde-Wörterbuch* (mentioned in Vereščagin & Kostomarov, 1974).
17. *Stranovedenie*, on the other hand, is a loan translation of the German *Landeskunde*.
18. A German working translation of Vereščagin and Kostomarov's book is also said to exist, but I have been unable to get hold of it.
19. The discussion in the GDR has, by the way, been dealt with in Kramer (1997) and in a dissertation, Spantzel (2001).
20. It is possible to view K. Jonas and Hans-Otto Rosenbohm's *Kleines Wörterbuch zur Landeskunde* (1994) (Small *Landeskunde* Dictionary) as an example of this lexicographical approach to realia.
21. With important exceptions in the loan words in the students' first language that come from the target-language (e.g. the French word *garage* in Danish) and vice versa (e.g. the Danish word *koekenmoeding* in French).

22. Bearing complex commentary in mind, it can be seen that the above-mentioned article by Dobrynine assumes the form of a complex commentary in long passages, including a section on words for typical Russian dishes.
23. The word *realii* is also used in Russian.
24. Cf. the system *Voix et Images de la France* (Voices and Images of France) (Gauvenet *et al.*, 1960). There was also a much-used French system in the 1950s, mainly in l'Alliance Française. It was called *Cours de langue et de civilisation françaises* (Course of French language and civilisation) (Mauger, 1953). As the name implies, it also included an introduction to French culture and society.
25. The French word *civilisation* is said to go back to the mid-18th century (cf. Fichou, 1979: 20).
26. They were not the very first, e.g. Darbelnet (1971) suggested the same thing.
27. Cf. also the discussion in Debyser (1973).
28. Sauvageot (1964). Sauvageot is part of the French tradition of research into the cultural history of the vocabulary.
29. Note that in Erdmenger and Istel the progression goes the opposite way: from the universal to the local.
30. I wrote about culture pedagogy with Helga Andersen until 1981, after which I pursued the subject on my own.
31. Brøgger refers to the use of 'the anthropological concept of culture' to be found in American Studies.
32. Risager (1991a) is a short article on the culture-pedagogical debate in Denmark, Norway and Sweden.

Chapter 4

Culture Pedagogy in the 1980s: The Marriage of Language and Culture

Introduction

Taking into account the highly different national starting points for culture pedagogy, one could say that in the 1980s a parallel though still relatively separate history grew up that revolved around 'the anthropological concept of culture' as a common reference, especially in its interpretive variant (Cl. Geertz).

Alongside the interpretive aspect, the visual aspect of cultural teaching was also strengthened in the course of the 1980s. This was due to the development of video technology, which made it possible to record films, etc. from television and use them directly in teaching, and which meant *inter alia* a much more realistic and detailed mediation of the situational context for language communication. It also led to a greater opportunity to work with concrete, visible aspects of language, culture, society and nature: non-verbal communication (gestures, proxemics, etc.), clothing, interiors, street environments, landscapes, flora and fauna, etc. It was a development that could be made use of both for a more surface-focused observation of culture and for meaning-oriented work on sign systems and semiotics in general.

The examples of culture-pedagogical approaches dealt with in particular in this chapter are:

- Melde: *Zur Integration von Landeskunde und Kommunikation im Fremdsprachenunterricht* (Integrating *Landeskunde* and communication in foreign-language teaching) (1987).
- Zarate: *Enseigner une culture étrangère* (Teaching a foreign culture) (1986).
- Galisson: *De la langue à la culture par les mots* (From language to culture via words) (1991).
- Byram: *Cultural Studies in Foreign Language Education* (1989).

The USA in the 1980s

In the USA, the 1980s involved a shift in the field of learning theory from an interest in defining necessary cultural knowledge to one in the individual student's qualifications and motivation – and gradually in the actual cultural learning process as well. At the same time, there are also several signs of a more practice-oriented, dynamic conception of culture. This can be seen, among other things, from an article written in 1984 by Crawford-Lange and Lange. The authors of this article strongly stress the close interrelationship between language and culture and the necessity for language teaching to fully realise this interrelationship. At the same time, they emphasise that 'culture is in the process of becoming and should therefore be taught as a process' (Crawford-Lange & Lange, 1984: 142). They come up with proposals for how linguistic and cultural learning can be integrated, outlining a theme- and problem-oriented programme in which students singly and in groups are guided through a series of phases in connection with a cultural or societal theme, and in which they are encouraged to engage in independent critical discussions and get involved in the theme (with a reference to the pedagogical ideas of P. Freire). They also claim that a language subject that tackles cultural content in such a way will be well suited to be taught at a school that works for 'global education'. The movement for 'global education' is based on an awareness of multiculturality in the world and in the individual school class, and argues that this should strongly influence all subjects at the school, cf. for foreign languages the anthology: *A Global Approach to Foreign Language Education* (Conner, 1981).

In 1984, a new edition appeared of Seelye's book from 1974, *Teaching Culture*. It is symptomatic that, while the former edition had the subtitle *'Strategies for foreign language educators'*, the new edition was given the subtitle *'Strategies for intercultural communication'*. The new edition, however, was only quite superficially revised to fit an intercultural paradigm. It is just as goal-oriented as its predecessor – no wish is expressed, for example, that students should gain any reflexive understanding of their own cultural background.[1]

Culture pedagogy in the 1980s was also linked by a number of other authors to the area of intercultural communication. In 1987, for example, a book appeared on culture pedagogy by Louise Damen: *Culture Learning: The Fifth Dimension in the Language Classroom*. It is a fairly thorough introduction for student teachers within *inter alia* English as a foreign and a second language, within which language and culture pedagogy is described as part of the field of intercultural communication (represented by Gudykunst & Kim [1984] among others). This led to Damen's version of culture pedagogy acquiring the weakness that also characterised the field of intercultural communication in the same period and partially still today: a positivist-oriented view of communication linked to a holistic and functionalist view of culture.[2]

With the rapprochement between language and culture pedagogy and intercultural communication arose – initially in the USA – a shift of emphasis from 'the culture-specific' (which culture pedagogy had emphasised up until then) towards 'the culture-general' (which intercultural communication most emphasised). In other words, there was now more focusing on the psychological aspects of intercultural competence: ability to adapt and the development of a general awareness of cultural differences.[3] On the other hand, specific knowledge of the target language countries was toned down to a certain extent.

Neither Seelye nor Damen display any knowledge of (language and) culture pedagogy in Europe. Crawford-Lange and Lange know something about language pedagogy in Europe (references to van Ek, Wilkins and Widdowson), but not about European culture pedagogy.

Europe in the 1980s

A cultural turn, from an overall point of view, took place in European culture pedagogy in the 1980s. Whereas a social orientation had dominated the 1970s, reflected in such terms as *Landeskunde* and *civilisation* (Fr.), other terms were now under discussion, including the term 'culture', which until then had been used rather sporadically (except in the *Kulturkunde* movement). The reason for this was partly the general postmodern tendency from the USA, which brought cultural (especially ethnic) differences into the foreground, partly – linked to this – the conservative backlash of the 1980s, which led to a toning-down of social analysis and social criticism, and partly the European process of integration, which placed the question of national identities in Europe on the agenda.

Within English as a foreign language more and more people felt inspired by British Cultural Studies or American Studies, and many references were made (as already mentioned) to Geertz's interpretive anthropology, which underlined the perspective of 'the natives', their self-perception and symbolic systems. It was still predominantly the holistic concept of culture – culture used as an overall concept – that was centre stage – and almost always understood in national terms. But, just as in the USA, there was a shift away from focusing on the topic matter – knowledge of culture and society in the target language countries – to focusing on the students' learning processes. And this meant, potentially, a greater degree of individualisation.

In language pedagogy that was specifically geared to language, an awareness gained ground in the 1980s that it was also important to deal with the cultural content of language teaching. In West Germany, the national association of language teachers, *Fachverbund Moderner Fremdsprachen*, had *Landeskunde* as the main theme at its annual convention in 1982. It was the first time in Europe that a national language-teacher association (covering all foreign languages) put culture pedagogy on the agenda. The conference has been documented in Raasch, Hüllen und Zapp (1983) and discussed in Buttjes (1982).

Under the impact of the European process of integration and the growing visibility on the world stage of postcolonial societies, culture pedagogy in the 1980s widened the geographical horizon from not focusing exclusively on the most central target-language countries – the UK/ USA, France, West Germany/GDR – to also including other countries inside and outside Europe: Ireland, Belgium, Austria, Switzerland, Canada, Australia, India, English- and French-speaking Africa, etc. At the same time, international and global topics were being included to an increasing extent: colonialism and post- and neocolonialism, transnational environmental issues, the arms race (cf., for example, Risager, 1989a).

Until the 1980s, culture pedagogy was principally a debate about the objectives and content of language teaching – a programmatic, normative debate. But in the course of the 1980s, empirical research and the development of theories got under way. It is worth noting that it is particularly in Europe that there have been major empirical projects on the cultural dimension of language teaching, student attitudes, and the cultural and social content of textbooks. Even though the content of school textbooks has also been discussed in the USA, the more large-scale analyses of textbooks have been a European speciality, which presumably has something to do with the interest in the images that language teaching communicates, or tries to communicate, about other European countries, seen in the light of the European process of integration and the incipient interest in 'European identity'. Generally speaking, these analyses do not deal explicitly with the national but, fairly innocently, with 'the country' or 'the countries', thus supplying good examples of 'banal nationalism' (Billig, cf. Chapter 1).

The Council of Europe in the 1980s

The Dutchman van Ek, one of the most active in the Council of Europe's language projects, developed in a series of publications in the 1980s (van Ek,

1986 and 1987) a model for communicative competence that incorporated a sociocultural component. In van Ek (1987), he describes it as one of a total of six components (subcompetences): linguistic competence, sociolinguistic competence, discourse competence, strategic competence, sociocultural competence and social competence. They are summarised as follows:

> *Linguistic competence*: the ability to produce and interpret meaningful utterances which are formed in accordance with the rules of the language concerned and bear their conventional meaning.
>
> *Sociolinguistic competence*: awareness of ways in which the choice of language-forms – the manner of expression – is determined by such conditions as setting, relationship between communication partners, communicative intention, etc., etc. ('features of the communication situation').
>
> *Discourse competence*: the ability to use appropriate strategies in the construction and interpretation of texts, particularly those formed by stringing sentences together.
>
> *Strategic competence*: the ability to use 'verbal and non-verbal communication strategies to compensate for gaps in the language user's knowledge of the code or for breakdown of communication for other reasons'.[4]
>
> *Sociocultural competence*: awareness of the sociocultural context in which the language concerned is used by native speakers and of ways in which this context affects the choice and the communicative effect of particular language forms.
>
> *Social competence*: the ability to use social strategies appropriate to the achievement of one's communicative goals. (van Ek, 1987: 8)

It should be noted that van Ek describes sociocultural competence as awareness, i.e. knowledge and consciousness, not as ability. We are not dealing with a behaviouristic understanding of the cultural side of language teaching. He also writes about sociocultural competence that:

> the use of a particular language implies the use of a reference frame which is at least partly determined by the sociocultural context in which that language is used by native speakers. Competent use of that language, then, presupposes a certain degree of familiarity with that sociocultural context. For want of a more adequate term the German word *Landeskunde*[5] is often used for this. (van Ek, 1986: 35, italics in the original)

This 'familiarity' van Ek develops in an attitude-oriented and student-oriented direction typical of the approach of the Council of Europe since the 1970s:

In order to serve its purpose, teaching and learning for sociocultural competence should go beyond the cognitive domain and address the learner's attitudes, opinions, value-systems and emotions as well. This can only be done if the learning-content is clearly related to the learner's own experience and interests and if the learning-activities engage the learner not only as a learner but as a human being. (van Ek, 1986: 60)

Van Ek does not develop further what sociocultural competence can or must contain, so on this point the Council of Europe did not have much to say in the 1980s. But in 1991, a new version of _Threshold Level_ (van Ek & Trim, 1991) appeared, and it contains a little more in the sense that a simple list is provided of (1) subject areas that the student must know something about: everyday life, life conditions, interpersonal relations, important values and attitudes, and (2) social conventions and rituals that the student must be familiar with: body language, situations in connection with paying visits, eating and drinking rituals. There is also a lengthy section on conventions of politeness.

West Germany in the 1980s

Reaction against the _Landeskunde_ concept

During the 1980s in West Germany there was growing criticism of the concept of _Landeskunde_. It was seen as being too unscientific (_Kunde_ being an everyday term) and as being exclusively cognitively oriented, i.e. knowledge-dominated.

Some people chose to shift the focus away to everyday knowledge (_Alltagswissen_), e.g. Firges and Melenk (1982). This tendency was based on phenomenological sociology of knowledge and ethnomethodology and it focused on individuals' cultural experiences and notions about unfamiliar forms of culture. Advocates suggested that one should study foreign-language concepts as generalised everyday experiences and they worked with cultural shifts of perspective in language teaching, also using the heading _konfrontative Semantik_ (Elbeshausen & Wagner, 1985, Müller, 1981).

Some of those who found themselves more on the socially oriented wing chose to retain the term _Landeskunde_. This applied, for example, to Peter Doyé, who chose to keep the term because he was interested in retaining the social and political aspect of the concept of _Landeskunde_ in order to stress that language teaching must contribute to the students' _politische Bildung_ (political education). The same applies to Wilma Melde, whom I mentioned in Chapter 3, who pursued further the idea of emancipatory language teaching, publishing in 1987 the book *Zur Integration von Landeskunde und Kommunikation in der Fremdsprachenunterricht* (Integrating *Landeskunde* and communication in foreign-language teaching). This book is the only culture-pedagogical monograph that contains an analysis of culture pedagogy on the basis of one particular social theory where the general tendency has otherwise been – and is – that one adopts a more eclectic attitude to the choice of inspirational sources from cultural anthropology and social science. The social theory chosen by Melde was that of Habermas, particularly his *Theorie des kommunikativen Handelns* (theory of communicative action). I will deal with Melde's book in the next section.

Melde's colleague Baumgratz continued her studies from the 1970s on *transnationale Kommunikationsfähigkeit*, publishing them in the book *Persönlichkeitsentwicklung und Fremdsprachenerwerb* (Baumgratz-Gangl, 1990) (Personal development and learning a foreign language). Like Melde and several others, she also designed, in connection with R&D work at *Das Deutsch-Französische Institut Ludwigsburg* (The Franco-German Institute Ludwigsburg), interesting teaching materials for French teaching (Alix *et al.*, 1988, Ammon *et al.*, 1987, Schumann, 1986).

Buttjes was one of those who located himself midway in the transition between *Landeskunde* and 'the intercultural', which was to become the central concept of the 1990s. He spoke, for example, about *interkulturelle/ landeskundliche Kompetenz* (Buttjes, 1986: 67ff.).

One of those who first expressed himself consistently within the intercultural paradigm was Meinert Meyer, in connection with a major school investigation carried out in Nordrhein-Westfalen in 1976–86. It aimed at integrating general and vocational schooling at *Sekundarstufe II* (schooling for 16–19-year-olds). Meyer carried out classroom observation as well as various experiments at some of the schools involved with 'double qualifying' classes in English. In his book, which presented the results of the project, *Shakespeare oder Fremdsprachenkorrespondenz?* (Shakespeare or foreign language correspondence?) (1986), he distinguishes between four subdimensions of foreign-language communicative competence: firstly, the interlingual dimension, which exists in the tension between first-language competence and target-language competence. Secondly, the intercultural dimension, which is defined as:

> the capacity to be able to behave adequately and flexibly regarding the expectations of the communication partner from other cultures, to become aware of the differences and interferences between one's own and a foreign culture and form of life and to remain true to oneself and

one's cultural origins in the transmission between cultures. (Translated from Meyer, 1986: 265)

Thirdly, the language-analytical, argumentative dimension, i.e. the all-round educative dimension, which is developed via analytical work with literary and other texts, and, fourthly, the action- and role-oriented dimension, i.e. the dimension that prepares for a vocation, which focuses on more subject-related and functionally delimited communicative genres.

The investigation does not result in concrete organisational and didactic proposals for a reform but in a relatively loosely formulated utopia for each of the four dimensions and for integration between them. Even so, the project is epoch-making. It is one of the first and largest pieces of empirical work that illustrates various aspects of intercultural competence within the field of education. Moreover, the project demonstrates an unusual breadth, since it cuts across educational programmes that are both general and vocational.

Within the field of textbook analysis, there were two major projects in West Germany in the 1980s. J. Krauskopf carried out an investigation of the picture of France conveyed by German textbooks for French teaching and the picture of Germany conveyed by French textbooks for German teaching (Krauskopf, 1985). And within English teaching a broadly based investigation was carried out of German and English students' conceptions of England, the USA and Germany, compared with an analysis of curricula and textbooks (Friz, 1991).

Melde: *Zur Integration von Landeskunde und Kommunikation im Fremdsprachenunterricht* (1987) (Integrating *Landeskunde* and communication in foreign language teaching): Presentation

Unlike the works referred to earlier by Seelye, Erdmenger and Istel, Vereščagin and Kostomarov and, to a certain extent, Fichou, Melde's book is not addressed to teachers but to an academic audience, which means that it is less accessible to the ordinary reader, although more rewarding from a strictly theoretical point of view. Her project is to provide a cohesive theoretical justification for integrating the two sides of language teaching: communication and *Landeskunde*, and in order to do this she mainly draws on Habermas' theory of communicative action seen as a cooperative process of interpretation (Habermas, 1981). Her reason for emphasising the cohesive theoretical understanding of the (cultural and linguistic) content of language teaching is the weak theorising that otherwise exists in culture pedagogy, e.g. in Erdmenger and Istel, who operate with a large number of knowledge-elements of various kinds that come from a wide range of subjects: geography, history, political science, etc. – an additive and subjective selection without any other justification than the assumed communicative needs of the group of students involved and the orientation needs that result from them.

Melde's concrete point of departure is French teaching in West Germany, and it is the relations between West Germany and France that she focuses on. She subjects both states to a symmetrical treatment, partly in the form of a comparative overview of their economic and political structures and the historical relations between the two countries, and partly in the form of a discussion of notions and attitudes held by one country about the other. She adopts, then, a clearly intercultural point of departure, without actually formulating it as such.

Habermas distinguishes between two layers in society: the life-world and the system. The life-world is to be understood in phenomenological terms as the world as it appears to human beings and in which they communicate and try to understand each other, and where they reproduce themselves at a symbolic level. The system consists of the societal structures that have taken shape in the course of history and which have acquired ever greater importance in the development of modern societies in relation to the life-world. The system's forms of communication do not, as in the life-world, aim at intersubjective understanding but are of a more rational, goal-oriented nature. Habermas attempts, then, in his theory to combine an understanding sociology (like that of Weber) with a system-theoretical approach.

With reference to Habermas' broad concept of communication, Melde criticises the communicative approach in language pedagogy for limiting itself to the level of the individual.[6] She emphasises that only if one operates with a broader concept of communication that also includes the higher levels of society can one link the life-world to the social system. This link is crucial if one wishes to integrate the communicative (linguistic) and the societal content with each other in language teaching. As she formulates it:

> Only when the political system is defined as a communication system does the connection ensue between social players and system structures, between communicative processes and system level. (Translated from Melde, 1987: 80)

Melde (1987): The relationship between language and culture

Melde begins her book with a critical account of culture pedagogy in (West) Germany, including the *Kulturkunde* movement and its use of the traditional German concept of culture.[7] She uses the term 'identity hypothesis' to describe the movement's identification of people, language and culture, and explicitly distances herself from such a hypothesis. Because she distances herself from both the *Kulturkunde* movement and its identity hypothesis, she hardly uses the concept of culture at all. In addition, and in accordance with Habermas, she does not use the concept of language very much, preferring that of communication. Thereby she avoids addressing the question of the relationship between language and culture by reinterpreting the theoretical construction and placing it in the overall universalistic understanding that Habermas represents. One could say that in her discourse she operates at the generic level as regards her conception of language (language and communication in general), despite the fact that it is the differential (and specific, cf. Chapter 1) level that is the challenge in practice (teaching of French in particular). Her theoretical point of departure is sociological and language-philosophical, not language-pedagogical.

So one does not find any hypothesis about the inseparability of language and culture in Melde – nor, on the other hand, a hypothesis to the contrary. The pair of concepts is made irrelevant in her presentation. This, however, leads to a loss of certain dimensions in the understanding of the life-world: Melde does, for example, deal with regional identities, but not with the question of ethnic identity regarding immigrants and refugees. She does not deal with France as a multicultural society. The bilateral scheme: comparison between France and West Germany is central and, in addition, there are references to various geographical, regional identities and to the European context. Melde (1987) clearly supports a political-national paradigm, but with inner social and regional differentiation.

Melde (1987): The relationship between language teaching and culture teaching

Apart from the reference to Habermas, Melde also discusses how one can develop the cognitive, developmental side of language teaching by including aspects of critical psychology, cognitive developmental psychology (Piaget) and the theory of critical socialisation, each of which illustrates in its own way the interpretative schemes that students develop or ought to develop, but I do not intend to deal with them here.

All of these theories are extremely abstract in nature and it is not easy to concretise them for use in language teaching. Melde nevertheless attempts to do this by distinguishing between three levels or phases in language teaching and by ordering them in a systematic scheme (Melde, 1987: 262ff.). The three levels are:

- the life-world (especially the private sphere);
- the politico-cultural public world;
- the socio-scientific observer perspective.

At all three levels, there are comparisons between the two states (here France and West Germany). At the first level, it is a question of comparisons between life-worlds in the two countries, including the various forms of communication. At the second level, it is a question of comparing the two social systems and the more general forms of communication that characterise the politico-cultural public world, including the mass media. These comparisons lead to a juxtaposition of various perspectives. At the third level, an attempt is made in a good universalist spirit to step outside the two individual country perspectives – and this is important because it enables decentring, perspective coordination and social criticism to take place, both of the target country and of the students' own country. Melde gives an overview of these levels with suggestions for concrete assignments linked to interviews, role-play activities, narrative presentations, media analyses, political commentaries, information via statistics, an understanding and clarification of differences and conflicts, etc.

Melde is the first person within culture pedagogy as a whole who has attempted systematically and in an entire monograph to find a theoretically based solution to the problem of integration in language teaching. She has not been completely successful, for the differential level in the form of work with one particular language does not have any obvious place in the theory. Another weakness is that she does not deal with working with various types of literature in language teaching, except for work with narrative presentations concerning the life-worlds of various groups. But, all in all, Melde marks in her approach an innovative high point for the German social and critical approach to culture pedagogy, and in (West) Germany she represents a counterweight to Erdmenger and Istel's more pragmatic approach.

France in the 1980s

From an encyclopedic to a student-centred approach

In the course of the 1980s, considerable conflict arose between those who claimed that the teaching of culture ought to give students a coherent understanding of culture and society and those who claimed that one ought to have as one's point of departure the students' prior qualifications and allow them to explore (*découvrir*) the foreign culture. The principle of the intercultural – that what was at the centre was the relation and interaction between the various cultures – began to make headway. In the intercultural paradigm, the concept of *civilisation* does not really have any assigned place: one cannot say that civilisations interact, and there is no concept à la *intercivilisationnel*. For that reason it is possible to say that when one uses the term *civilisation*, one focuses more exclusively on the target-language country – and it is still most usual to do so at university level. The use of the concept of *civilisation* interpreted in terms of the intercultural became more widespread.

François Poirier, who works on the teaching of English at university and upper-secondary levels, is one of those who argued in favour of a scientifically (sociologically) based teaching of culture. In an article in 1983, he emphasised that all knowledge and all scientific theory is characterised by a particular philosophical or ideological point of view, but that this must not prevent one from adopting an objective stance to society. He feels that one ought to base oneself on the Marxist-inspired concept *formation sociale*, which conveys both unity and internal tensions, both process and product, and he describes a *civilisation* as a group of social formations. He proposes that one develop culture pedagogy in a sociological direction, first and foremost with reference to Bourdieu.[8]

Louis Porcher adopted a mixture of a positivist and a more socialisation-oriented position, for example in an anthology published by him in 1986, *La civilisation*. He had taken part in the Council of Europe's project on threshold levels, and this work also influenced his thoughts within the field of culture pedagogy. In his book he gives an account of his thoughts concerning the development of a culture pedagogy which, along the lines of the communicative approach of the Council of Europe, comprises a description of needs, student groups, aims, content and methods of assessment. The teaching of culture is to be based on an objectivising and classifying approach towards the foreign culture. Students must first and foremost be able to find their bearings in the cultural universe. To be able to do so, they must construct a system of reference points or bench marks (*repères*), i.e. facts within history, geography, institutions and cultural life (in the aesthetic sense) – and also be trained in learning how to seek information for themselves.

However, this fact-oriented content must, according to Porcher, be supplemented by awareness-raising activity. While taking the students' notions (*représentations*) concerning the foreign culture as the point of departure, one has to try to counteract tendencies towards ethnocentrism, sociocentrism and egocentrism by confronting stereotypes with cultural variation with regard to age groups, social groups, gender, etc. The aim here is decentring. Here, according to Porcher, there is an important parallel with the principle of language pedagogy to have the individual student as one's point of departure.

A stark contrast to Porcher's sociological and objectivising approach is to be found in the work of Geneviève Zarate, who develops in her book *Enseigner une culture étrangère* (Teaching a foreign culture) (1986) a predominantly (social-)anthropological approach to culture pedagogy which emphasises that there is a difference between acquiring one's native culture and acquiring a foreign one. Whereas the first process in particular is implicit, the other one, because of the geographical distance involved, can broadly speaking only be explicit. Therefore, the most important challenge facing the teaching of culture is to make that which is implicit for natives explicit for students. It should be noted that Zarate uses the concept of *culture* and not of *civilisation*. I will deal with her contribution in the next section.

There was also another approach represented in France – a lexicological, semantic approach, because of the work of Robert Galisson, which I will return to later in this chapter.

Zarate: *Enseigner une culture étrangère* (1986) (Teaching a foreign culture): Presentation

Geneviève Zarate is active within French as a foreign language for adults, and the book has been written for teachers. As mentioned above, within the French discussion she is located among those who advocate student centring and a reduction in the demand for overall canonical knowledge of culture and society. In this, she is the diametric opposite of Fichou and also, partially, of Porcher. She refers to various different researchers who are interested in everyday practice and the implicit rules for interaction and communication, including Goffman and Bourdieu – and she also refers to Barthes' mythological studies of the sign systems and symbolics of everyday life.

Zarate's main idea is that there is a difference between learning a foreign culture and learning one's own culture in the course of childhood and adolescence. In the latter instance, there are many relations that are implicit and never verbalised. But when one is to learn a foreign culture, it is necessary to take a longer route where the implicit is made explicit. It is necessary to contextualise and explain many kinds of institution and behaviour that natives take for granted. To learn a foreign culture is to develop from an ethnocentric to a relativist standpoint and thereby become conscious of one's own identity.

Zarate (1986): The relationship between language and culture

Zarate's point of departure is not linguistic but sociological and anthropological. She does not deal with the relationships between language and culture, but contents herself with very briefly underlining the close connection between *langue* and *civilisation*:

> Reflection on the relationship between language and civilisation has been developed over these last fifteen years, insisting on the close link between the two domains from the outset of learning. (Translated from Zarate, 1986: 135)

This makes it clear that there is a link here between the general and the pedagogic level: the first part of the sentence deals with the relationship between language and culture (*civilisation*), the second part with the learning process in teaching. Zarate also refers to Porcher, who in an article from 1982 emphasises the close relationship between *langue* and *civilisation*[9] with the following words:

> Language is totally marked by civilisation, partly because it is a sociohistorical product and partly to the extent it is always initially a social practice. Similarly, no feature of civilisation exists independently of language. (Porcher, 1982: 40, cited in Zarate, 1986: 147, translated)

Zarate thus makes herself an advocate of the hypothesis concerning the inseparability of language and culture, even though she hardly touches on language questions in her approach – and does not deal at all with language-pedagogical questions. Here the hypothesis features only as a legitimising basis for dealing at all with teaching culture – in this particular case with French culture.

Zarate (1986): The relationship between language teaching and culture teaching

The cultural aim of teaching is to develop cultural competence, which, as Zarate sees it, is almost exclusively cognitive (i.e. knowledge-oriented) in its orientation: it deals in particular with understanding written and spoken texts – and here one can refer to the French tradition of detailed textual analysis (*explication de texte*). It also deals with using various sources of information, identifying stereotypes and other representations, contextualising information, explaining one's own culture to foreigners and establishing personal contacts with foreigners and preparing trips to a target-language country (Zarate, 1986: 146). Cultural competence is for her first and foremost a matter of gaining insight into various cultures and into one's own culture. She is operating here with a concept of culture that internally is sociologically differentiated. But there is nothing in her book to indicate that she finds it important to represent France as a multi-cultural or multiethnic society. On the other hand, she includes such subjects as nationalistic discourses and the necessity of contextualising the national. So one cannot say that Zarate's discourse is characterised by banal nationalism in Billig's sense (cf. Chapter 1).

A historical understanding counts for quite a lot in Zarate's universe. Emphasis is placed on cultural understanding also having a historical dimension and on historical documents being able to help create an understanding of one's own identity – in both time and space. This aware-ness of the historical dimension is typical of the French tradition within culture pedagogy, cf. Fichou and others (it also often applies to the teach-ing of French abroad, cf. Melde above).

When it comes to the question of assessing cultural competence, and also when it comes to intercultural competence Zarate has to refer to the USA, where assessment criteria were established early. This is a result both of the long history of culture pedagogy within the USA and of its practical, more or less positivist orientation, cf. Seelye above.

Despite the fact that Zarate underlines the inseparability of language and culture, she does not make any attempt to combine language teaching and culture teaching into a whole.

Galisson: *De la langue à la culture par les mots* (1991) (From language to culture via words): Presentation

At the same time as Zarate, Porcher, Poirier and others, another Frenchman, Robert Galisson, has worked on the culture-pedagogical area, though with a completely different approach, one that is linguistic and semantic. Galisson is a lexicologist/lexicographer, and he is especially interested in the development of the monolingual (French) dictionary, not only as a reference work but also as a real pedagogical tool in teaching French as a foreign language.

Galisson wants by means of his semantic point of departure to place work on the vocabulary at the centre of language teaching, and in doing so he is harking back to language teaching prior to the audio-visual method and the communicative approach, both of which he feels marginalised vocabulary by focusing on situation-determined conversational routines and language functions and communication, without any particular inter-est in the semantic dimension.

Galisson has worked on semantic fields (*centres d'intérêt/domaines d'expérience*) in French vocabulary since the 1970s, and since the 1980s he has taken this work in a more explicitly culture-oriented direction. He has therefore come to deal with the relationship between language and culture, and he understands this question in lexicological terms: culture he describes as contained in the vocabulary of the language – and certain parts of the vocabulary have more cultural charge than others.

Galisson (1991): The relationship between language and culture

Galisson believes that language teaching must grant access to the cultural knowledge that all natives share, and he emphasises that the best way into this culture is the language. Language and culture are naturally bound up with each other and to try to separate them is artificial. We are dealing with a symbiosis:

> It is as a social practice and socio-historical product that language is permeated by culture. The game of symbiosis in which language and culture function means that they are the reciprocal and compulsory reflection of each other. Didactologists/didacticians clearly ought to take account of this commensalism, making sure they do not dissociate the study of culture – the study of language, and vice-versa. (Translated from Galisson, 1991: 119)

Galisson is one of those who use the compound word *langue-culture*, and he also talks about *langue-culture-source* and *langue-culture-cible* (Galisson, 1994: 95). But even though language is completely permeated by culture, it is the words that are centre stage:

> If language is permeated by culture, it is not in a uniform manner. As preconstructed receptacles and thus stable and economical in use compared to utterances which have to be constructed, words are the privileged places of permeation for certain cultural contents that settle there, that end up by sticking there, and thus add another dimension to the ordinary semantic dimension of signs. (Translated from Galisson, 1991: 119)

Galisson calls the 'other dimension' *charge culturelle* (cultural load) and he underlines the fact that what one should deal with in particular in language teaching and in the dictionaries that are intended for it is the words' *charge culturelle partagée*, i.e. the cultural load that is common to the entire language community. The words that can be described as having a common cultural load he calls *mots à charge culturelle partagée* (abbreviated *mots à CCP*). He also uses the term *la lexiculture partagée* (common 'lexiculture'). All words that have a common cultural load he feels should be gathered together in a new type of French-language dictionary, specially designed for foreigners. As an example of such a word that is not given sufficient treatment in traditional dictionaries he lists *inter alia* the word *carotte*, which is thought to make one friendly and give one rose-red thighs:

> So, the *Petit Robert*, for example, signals that the *carrot* is 1. 'an edible (umbelliferous) plant with a revolving root', 2. 'a conical root, rich in sugar', and there are fodder carrots as well as white, yellow or red carrots'. On the other hand, it says nothing about the commonplaces inspired by the *carrot*: the popular clichés, the absorption of this vegetable is fact supposed: 1. make more friendly 2. cause rose-red thighs! (Galisson, 1991: 122)

Galisson discusses four types of words that have a tendency to be linked with those kinds of popular notions (he does not, however, undertake this categorisation himself):

- Common words, e.g. words that describe animals (as cunning as a fox, as dirty as a pig, to have the memory of an elephant, etc.), plants (the rose as a symbol for love, etc.), things (as hard as stone), colours (as red as blood), festivals and special days and things typically associated with them: Christmas: Christmas tree, Christmas fare, etc., etc.
- Proper names, e.g. geographical names and the names of well-known people: there are, for example, mutual associational links between 'Dijon' and 'mustard', between 'Limoges' and 'porcelain', between Henri IV and peace, reconciliation and humanism, etc.
- Brand names. Galisson means here the cultural loads that (for Frenchmen) lie in such words as 'Michelin', 'Kodak', 'La vache qui rit', etc.[10]
- Hybrid words, i.e. words that are formed by joining two words together, e.g. *franglais* (a blend of *français* and *anglais*) and *crottoir* (a blend of *trottoir* and *crotte*).[11] This type of word, of which there are a great number in French, Galisson calls 'mots-valises',[12] and he feels that this type of linguistic creativity is full of CCP – and, in addition, typical of our age (Galisson, 1991: 106).

Galisson does not want to use the term 'connotation'. He distinguishes between the denotative meaning of the words (signs) and their CCP. He prefers the latter expression to the term 'connotation', which for him is too individual. It is precisely not the individual variation he is after but that which is common to the entire language community. He also points out that a CCP can clearly be common for a number of language communities at the same time. He provides as examples various ideas of the cow as a domestic animal when thinking of meat production v. the cow as a sacred animal – ideas that cut across a number of different language communities.

Galisson's method of describing the lexiculture has as its point of departure an anthropological division of the world into zones, e.g. 'the human race and space' and 'the human race and time'.[13] 'The human race and space', for example, is divided into 'the body', 'the immediate surroundings', 'social, political, cultural and religious life', 'means of communication and transportation', 'the state', etc. – an arbitrary and atheoretical division that may, however, be of certain assistance in trying to gain an overview of the semantics of the vocabulary in a more denotative sense.

Like Vereščagin and Kostomarov, Galisson does not believe that all 'culture' is exhausted by looking at the vocabulary of a language. He says, for example, that 'culture inside language and culture outside language form a whole that should be exhaustively explored and that provides complementary access routes' (Galisson, 1991: 103). But he does not deal with 'culture outside language'.

The concept of culture we have in *la culture dans la langue* (culture inside language) can be characterised as cognitive, as it deals with the associations particular words evoke in language users. In Galisson's version, it has a folkloristic, idealistic orientation, since it deals more with the notions and attitudes that are evoked than with knowledge, insight or understanding of the real world. We are not dealing with an understanding of society here (or with a societal orientation, as with Vereščagin and Kostomarov).

Regarding the national, Galisson can hardly be called explicit. He frequently refers to the first-language speaker (*le natif*), and it is only implicitly apparent that what he is thinking of here is the French national language norm in France. He recognises that the cultural load of words can differ in various groups of the population, since he talks of *une sectorisation culturelle* (a cultural sectorisation), e.g. bourgeois v. popular, literary v. scientific culture. But he is interested only in the common cultural loads – and this has presumably something to do with his pedagogical intention to give the students in initial teaching access to the common culture (*la culture partagée*). So he is not interested in sociosemantics, nor in sociolinguistics in general – including the question of the multilingual society which France clearly is.

Galisson (1991): The relationship between language teaching and culture teaching

Galisson's main aim is not pedagogical, nor does he say anything about the practical use of his (future) culture-oriented, pedagogical dictionary. He does not adopt a critical attitude at all to the possibility that teaching that focuses on words with a common cultural load can help reproduce stereotypes that are widespread among native French speakers. When he names examples such as 'mustard' that associates with 'Dijon', and vice versa, it will only be an example of commercial utilisation of all types of association. Apparently, he does not see any problem in language teaching possibly becoming the learning of brands, advertising slogans and other automated notions. There is, of course, nothing wrong with dealing with these subjects, but in that case it must take place in a critical context, as is done, for example, within (socio-)semiotic media studies. Galisson's implicit pedagogical position is thus not intercultural but monocultural in the sense that he does not deal with comparative or contrastive aspects of the vocabulary – unlike Vereščagin and Kostomarov, for example.

Galisson writes in a strange isolation in which he does not mention the many other researchers who have also worked on vocabulary and culture.[14] He possibly wishes to justify this professional isolation by the scientific programme for which he is one of the advocates, i.e. the develop-ment of an independent discipline called *didactologie des langues-cultures*. This discipline is characterised by not being 'colonised' by other sciences. It is a discipline that does not have the role of an applied discipline (like *linguistique appliquée*) but which develops its own theory on the basis of its own needs (*théorisation interne*).[15] Here, though, I completely disagree with Galisson: I believe that language and culture pedagogy – especially culture pedagogy – can develop further only via dialogue with adjacent disciplines.

Galisson (1991) represents a specially culture-oriented semantic posi-tion within culture pedagogy that is partly at odds with Vereščagin and Kostomarov's more socially oriented position. It is not uninteresting for a foreigner to know widespread connotations of words in a language, and it will not be irrelevant to work (critically) with such connotations in language teaching. The problem is that Galisson's theoretical and methodological basis is too loose, and he does not have an eye for the pedagogical danger of ending up giving very narrow, monocultural and uncritical language teaching. He stands for a reifying/essentialising view of both language and culture and his implicit conceptual framework is national.

Great Britain in the 1980s

The beginnings of empirical research within culture pedagogy

Culture pedagogy in Great Britain only really got under way from the early 1980s onwards, with the work of Michael Byram. He was, on the other hand, the first person within culture pedagogy to write a truly research-based monograph that tried to develop the entire area theoretically and thereby establish culture pedagogy as an academic discipline: *Cultural Studies in Language Education* (1989), see below. Byram had a broad grasp of European culture pedagogy – as well as a knowledge of American – and he included research from anthropology and (social) psychology. The book was partly the result of a major empirical research project in the north of England in the mid 1980s (*The Durham Project*). It dealt with teaching in French, including the students' knowledge of and notions about France (published in Byram & Esarte-Sarries, 1991 and in Byram, Esarte-Sarries & Taylor, 1991).

Byram was also involved in the late 1980s in a project with German culture pedagogues (within English) from Braunschweig (*The Braunschweig-Durham Project*), led by Byram and Doyé respectively, on the reciprocal assessment of textbooks (Doyé, 1991 and Byram, 1993). It contains partly a number of thoughts about the role of foreign-language teaching and textbooks in the development of international understanding and *politische Bildung*, and partly certain criteria for assessing textbooks used in German teaching in Great Britain[16] and English teaching in (West) Germany.[17]

During the same period Hugh Starkey was active within the teaching of human rights and *world studies* in connection with language teaching, especially French (Starkey, 1991a, which I will return to in Chapter 5).

Byram: *Cultural Studies in Foreign Language Education* (1989): Presentation

Byram deals with 'the hidden dimension of foreign language teaching': the cultural dimension and its significance for the general education of the students, which he describes as 'an emancipation from the confines of one's native habitat and culture' (Byram, 1989: vii). He wants to develop the theoretical basis of language teaching, both as regards cultural theory and cultural studies and as regards the psychological processes that take place in connection with cultural-studies learning. He wants to create an 'integrated discipline of teaching language and culture' (Byram, 1989: 23).

He carries out this enterprise on the basis of a major empirical project on culture pedagogy and of a broad knowledge of research and debate within the field. The book is the first monograph that attempts to describe the entire area, pose the relevant questions and point to potential areas of development and research tendencies. It is enquiring and debating by nature and takes many different approaches into account.

Byram does not adopt a linguistic point of departure but an anthropo-logical and psychological one. Within anthropology he refers mostly to the American tradition of culture anthropology that has been interested in studying culture as analogous to language: E.T. Hall (1959), Goodenough (1964), Geertz (1973). His main reference is to Geertz, whose definition of culture (from Geertz, 1973) he cites – and, all in all, his approach in 1989 is clearly interpretive in its orientation. He also talks a lot about various perspectives and whether one ought to learn to work within language teaching with 'the insider perspective' – although he does not provide any specific references to this more hermeneutic orientation. Within psychol-ogy he refers in particular to such concepts as intercultural psychology and to such concepts as acculturation and culture shock, including R.W. Brislin (Brislin *et al.*, 1971) and A. Furnham and S. Bochner (Furnham & Bochner, 1986).

Byram introduces cultural studies as his term for the field. It is, however, interesting that he has only a few sporadic references to the actual Cultural Studies movement in Great Britain in connection with the Centre for Contemporary Cultural Studies in Birmingham. This has perhaps to do with two things. Firstly, his aim is to question the domi-nance of literature in language teaching, which is why he defines a subject area that is fundamentally non-literary in its orientation. That is not how the Cultural Studies movement sees things (R. Williams, R. Hoggart), where the reaction was against a humanist[18] concept of culture that favoured a high-culture canon. They therefore defined culture more broadly, allowing it to include popular literature and other symbolic forms of culture. Secondly, Byram's approach is not as clearly political and ideological as Cultural Studies. On the other hand, one can find in some of Byram's statements an inspiration that comes from Cultural Studies, e.g. Byram, 1989: 15: 'by culture and civilization I refer to the whole way of life of the foreign country, including but not limited to its production in the arts, philosophy and "high culture" in general' (Byram, 1989: 15). So one can identity an inspiration from Cultural Studies at a fundamental level.

In his book Byram also includes the Norwegian anthropologist F. Barth's theory of ethnic boundaries (Barth, 1969). Barth's point is that ethnic groups are formed and maintained via the drawing of boundaries between groups, and that the concrete cultural content one associates with the identity of the groups can change, while the actual boundaries continue to exist. So ethnic identities come into being by virtue of the fact that a boundary is set up in relation to another ethnic identity. This idea is transferred by Byram to national identities, and he claims it would be a relevant method in foreign-language teaching to focus on national identities as boundary phenomena, to investigate the contrasts that result from cultural encounters. He also reacts against the tendency to perceive cultures as homogeneous entities:

> The tendency to homogenize 'British' or 'French' culture by reference to national boundary phenomena distorts the experience of cultural identity which 'British' and 'French' people really have. (Byram, 1989: 93)

Foreign-language teaching is a context in which national identities are typically thematised: 'In foreign-language teaching learners are presented with national identities and are thereby implicitly encouraged to respond in terms of their own national identity' (Byram, 1989: 93). And this leaves one with the problem that Byram refers to as 'the simplifications of high level identity', in this case national identity – a problem which, in my opinion, will always be latent in the discourse of culture pedagogy (cf. Chapters 9–10).

Byram (1989): The relationship between language and culture

Byram deals in some detail in one of the chapters in the book with the relationship between language and culture. He underlines that the relationship between language and culture is highly complex and that it can be considered at various levels. 'The relationship between language and culture, whether in general or in a particular case, is of course an extremely complex problem' (Byram, 1989: 40).[19]

There is a lengthy passage to do with this relationship which I would like to quote in full here, since perhaps – considering the importance and widespread nature of the book – it could be said to be a central passage in European culture pedagogy regarding the fundamental assumption concerning the relationship between language and culture:

> Thus language pre-eminently embodies the values and meanings of a culture, refers to cultural artefacts and signals people's cultural identity. Because of its symbolic and transparent nature language can stand alone and represent the rest of a culture's phenomena – most successfully in the literary use of language – and yet it points beyond itself and thereby constantly undermines its own independence.

Language in use by particular speakers is constantly referring beyond itself irrespective of the intentions of the speaker: language cannot be used without carrying meaning and referring beyond itself, even in the most sterile environment of the foreign-language class. The meanings of a particular language point to the culture of a particular social grouping, and the analysis of those meanings – their comprehension by learners and other speakers – involves the analysis and comprehension of that culture.

The pedagogic separation of language from culture is thus justified in the sense that language can and does stand alone. It does so most obviously in literature, and the long association of language and literature teaching is some explanation for the separation. On the other hand, the tendency to treat language quite independently of the culture to which it constantly refers, cannot be justified; it disregards the nature of language. That tendency is not necessarily an intended distortion of language and is seldom taken to its potential extreme. No doubt all language teaching contains some explicit reference to the cultural whole from which the particular language is taken. Even when a deliberate attempt to transfer its use to a different culture is made, as in those countries where English is taught from textbooks which refer only to the native culture of the learners, the absolute separation of lexical items from their original reference is extremely difficult (Byram, 1989: 41–42).

As is evident, the first paragraph deals with the relationship between language and culture and the second with the relationship between language teaching and culture teaching. I reproduce them here in context, since it is interesting to see how they are linked in the text.

Byram expresses here a concept of language that in many ways is on a par with the interest of sociolinguistics at that time in linguistic practice and the importance of language in terms of identity. It is not possible for me to comment on all the aspects of the concept of language here, so I will restrict myself to emphasising three problem areas.

Byram seems to be mixing the generic and the differential levels in his text. He bases his fundamental assumption on 'the nature of language', and with this concept he is really at the general level, which deals with 'language' as a universal human phenomenon. But the text as a whole otherwise treats language at the differential level, i.e. the relationship between a language and (in Byram's words) 'the culture to which it constantly refers'. In my opinion, Byram formulates himself somewhat ambiguously as to whether he is thinking of the generic or the differential level in the quotation. There is an example of this as early on as the first line: 'language' without an article (which could justify a generic reading) is linked to 'a culture' (which calls for a differential reading).

In addition, Byram uses in this passage (and the rest of the book) the term 'reference' in an unclear way. It is apparently used both for what the semanticist J. Lyons calls reference and for what he calls denotation (Lyons, 1995). When Byram talks about 'the culture to which the language constantly refers', he is clearly referring *at the same time* to the meanings of language (denotation) independently of the specific context and to the cultural reference that the language user undertakes in a specific speech situation. But language as a system cannot (in Lyons' conceptual apparatus) refer to anything. Reference is an act, so it is individuals or other social agents who can refer. Denotation is the relationship between a linguistic expression and its conceptual content ('denotatum'), e.g. the relationship between the word (expression) 'breakfast' and its conceptual content. This content has been developed and accumulated in close connection with the sociocultural context within which the English language (spoken and written) has developed. But to call this context 'a culture' is a problematic abstraction – something I will return to in Chapter 7. It should, however, be pointed out that there are many other people who use the term 'reference' for what I (or Lyons) call 'denotation'. One ought nevertheless to distinguish between the two concepts in some manner or other.

Byram's conception of the relationship between language, literature and culture in the quotation is interesting. He apparently distinguishes between literary use of language, which he sees as being more or less independent of culture (here 'language stands alone'), and all other use of language, which is dependent on culture. Here, though, I disagree with him. Literary texts are always produced and received in some cultural (micro- or macro-) context or other, but one can say that a written literary text presupposes a particular communication situation by virtue of what one has referred to as the literary contract. Byram's main concern is to react against a teaching of literature that treats literary texts as linguistic works of art without any particular connection to the cultural and social context – and perhaps one can say on the basis of this pedagogical criticism that he is drawing conclusions 'in reverse' and claiming that literature in general is not connected to the cultural context – which is obviously untenable.

Byram also implies in another passage that language can actually be separated from culture. Here he uses a metaphor that emphasises that language and culture are interwoven without being identical: 'Although the warp of language can be teased out from the weft of culture, the learner needs to see the web of the whole' (Byram, 1989: 42).[20] Here the general level and the pedagogical level are closely linked but as opposites: *even though* language and culture can be separated, Byram feels that the student needs to see the whole of language and culture. Here, then, we have the pedagogical programme advanced on the basis of an understanding of the relationship between language and culture which claims that they are both separable and inseparable – an assertion that I will also argue in favour of, although in a completely different way (Chapter 7).

Byram (1989): The relationship between language teaching and culture teaching

As mentioned, Byram stresses throughout the book the necessity of integrating language and culture teaching during the entire language-teaching programme, and at the end of the book he presents a model for foreign-language teaching. It is, as one can see from Figure 4.1, divided into four fields, with language learning only being assigned one of these fields.

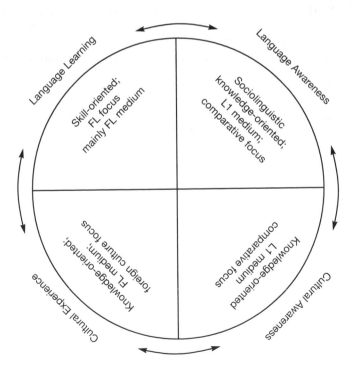

Figure 4.1 Byram: Model of foreign-language education

The model stresses the necessity of developing both language awareness, cultural awareness and cultural experience. The last-named Byram believes is best gained by the students having a stay in the target-language country, where they can experience interrelationships between language and culture in practice. But they can also gain it at school if they are taught in other subjects, e.g. geography or domestic science, in the foreign language concerned, e.g. French, and at the same time taught in a way that would be characteristic for education in the target language country, e.g. France.

The idea of cultural experience is also found elsewhere, cf. the German expression *erlebte Landeskunde* (experienced *Landeskunde*) in connection with student exchanges and trips abroad in general, but it has a special basis in the English system for educating language teachers, where it is obligatory for all future language teachers to spend a year in the target-language country. So future teachers of French normally live for a year in France, typically as language assistants who teach French students English. The idea of cultural experience is also an expression of Byram's ethnographical orientation, one which he has subsequently done much to develop further and implement in relation to foreign-language teaching, cf. Byram, 1997b; Byram & Fleming, 1998; Roberts *et al.*, 2001 (concerning the last-mentioned, see Chapter 6).

Along with Seelye and, to a certain extent, Fichou, Byram is one of the few culture pedagogues who has also taken an interest in sociolinguistics, in the sense that he deals with language variation and links between language and identity. He is also well aware of the fact that students already have a first language which can be made use of in foreign-language teaching, especially in developing language awareness and cultural awareness (cf. the fields with 'L1 medium' in the model). In doing so, he is also helping to break with the tradition that comes from the emergence of the direct method towards the end of the 19th century (in connection with the reform movement) and which requires one to use the target language only in language teaching.

Byram suggests that all four components of the model are always present in teaching, but that one should alter the relative amounts of time spent on the various components, e.g. that in the initial phase the most emphasis should be on language learning, but in the final phase on cultural experience.

Byram (1989) is a key text in culture pedagogy, because it is relatively explicit about the content of the assumption concerning the relationship between language and culture. But Byram has since modified his position, especially in a publication from 1997 (Byram, 1997a), which I will return to in Chapter 5.

Language and Culture in Language Teaching: The Marriage Metaphor

I would like to comment on a metaphor that has particularly become widespread since the 1980s in the USA, though also in Europe: the relationship between language and culture is described as a marriage. In the above-mentioned text of Crawford-Lange and Lange there is a statement that 'although culture and language are in reality "married", language curricula respond to them as if they were still only "engaged"', and, a little further on: 'this inclusion of cultural content continues to be seen as an issue separate from that of language. The groom is still waiting at the altar' (Crawford-Lange & Lange, 1984: 140–41).

Galisson uses a similar image. He emphasises that language and culture must not be treated separately in language teaching; to integrate culture teaching in language teaching is to 'consommer un mariage jusqu'alors un peu trop blanc' (consummating a marriage a little too unconsummated up to that point) (Galisson, 1991: 151). It is quite normal in culture-pedagogical discourse to find places where one insists on 'the intimate relationship between language and culture'; 'language and culture may not be divorced'; 'the interdependence of language and culture'; 'the interpenetration of language and culture' (see also the analysis in Murphy, 1988) and 'the inseparability of language and culture'. Lastly, there is also the expression where the pair of concepts are organised as one and the same lexeme: 'language-and-culture', *langue-culture*.

It is obvious that the marriage metaphor gives rise not only to an objectivisation but also to a personification and animation of the two concepts – a transformation that goes against the post-structuralist, anti-essentialist tendency that has otherwise characterised treatment of the concept of culture in particular, but also to a certain extent the concept of language, since the 1980s. The marriage metaphor is a good expression of the tension that exists between the conviction that the two concepts are inseparable in some sense or other, and the great difficulties involved in 'integrating language and culture' that can constantly be ascertained in language teaching. When the metaphor is expressed narratively, with the bridegroom waiting at the altar, or the unconsummated marriage, it links together the two levels I was talking about earlier: the general level (where language and culture are seen as being inseparable) and the pedagogical level (where people feel that language and culture ought to be integrated, but where they all too often are not).

It should be noted in the above quotation from Crawford-Lange and Lange that it is the man who is waiting at the altar, for it is the man who is language and the woman who is culture. This gender metaphor cannot but help to conjure up associations with a logos-eros polarisation when, for example, one looks at this passage about language and culture from the American culture pedagogue Wendy Allen. She comments on language teachers' tendency to prefer to teach grammar because it is ordered as opposed to culture, which is felt to be diffuse:

> Grammar offers several advantages over culture: it is the concept around which most textbooks and materials are organized; it is finite and can be ordered in either a linear, sequential plan of study or else in a cyclical one; mastery of it can be easily tested and evaluated; and, finally, it is a subject matter the classroom teacher can teach himself or herself, if necessary, using an advanced grammar text, and which, once mastered, is unlikely to change. Culture, by contrast, is diffuse; difficult to grasp, translate into instructional goals, test, evaluate, and order; prodigious in quantity; and ever-evolving. (Allen, 1985: 145)

The task of the language teacher is to unite these opposites as does the minister in the church. Language and culture are seen as being equally important in language teaching, and not until they are united – by virtue of the holy sacrament – can language teaching be made whole.[21]

There can be no doubt that, for some language teachers and for language pedagogy researchers who are relatively empirically minded, we are talking about a boundary that has to be gone beyond. One can often notice a great fascination with the cultural among language teachers and language pedagogues, but often also a hesitation about entering that area, as in the following statement from a researcher on language pedagogy in connection with a conversation about Bakhtin: 'Yes, it's very exciting. But it cannot of course be operationalised.'

Conclusion

In the 1980s, the discourse on language and culture becomes generalised and normalised in culture pedagogy at the pedagogical level, while the basic assumption of the inseparability of language and culture typically adopts the form of an extremely brief assertion somewhere at the beginning of the pedagogical argumentation.

The 'anthropological concept of culture' becomes a common reference, and with it comes the idea of the intercultural task of language teaching. It is interesting to note that the concept of culture is now introduced into West Germany, but with a semantic content that focuses on everyday life: the reaction against *Kulturkunde* has been implemented. The concept of culture is still dominated by the holistic mode of thought that stems from American cultural anthropology in the period from the 1930s to the 1950s, but is beginning to shift towards an interpretive approach represented by Geertz among others. But the concept of culture in Europe also encounters competition from the more differentiated and critical concept of culture from the Cultural Studies and American Studies traditions, particularly because English as a subject in Germany and France gains inspiration from them.

The concept of culture, however, does not reign supreme. The concepts of civilisation/*civilisation* (Fr.) and *Landeskunde* are still used by those who stress insight into social structures. Regarding the national paradigm, there are a few (e.g. Zarate and Byram) who take up issues to do with nationalism and national identity and thus problematise the national paradigm. The four examples of culture-pedagogical positions consist of one that has a linguistic point of departure, and three that have a cultural or social point of departure:

Point of departure in linguistics:
• Galisson: a semantic, culturally oriented approach.

Point of departure in the humanities and the social sciences:
• Melde: a social-sciences, politically oriented approach.
• Zarate: a sociological, anthropological approach.
• Byram: an anthropological, psychological approach.

Melde occupies a special position by explicitly distancing herself from the idea of the inseparability of language and culture and by distancing herself from the problem area, as she operates with the concepts of communication and society instead. But these two concepts are otherwise kept together with the aid of a sustained binational paradigm: France v. West Germany. In addition, there is – with the slight exception of Byram – a general under-lining of the relationship between language and culture, which is expressed in such new coinages as 'language-and-culture' and *langue-culture*.

It is still the predominant attitude that culture pedagogy has to do with the thematic content of language teaching. First and foremost, we are dealing with a *content-oriented culture pedagogy*. But with the shift towards the students' own qualifications and experiences, content-oriented culture pedagogy begins to become interested in the students' knowledge of their own country, their perception of themselves, their national identity. Byram is at the forefront of this development, and the appearance of his book in 1989 marks a great step forward for culture pedagogy in the estab-lishing of an academic discipline based on empirical studies.

There is in Byram's presentation – apart from the content-oriented culture pedagogy – a certain emphasis on a *context-oriented culture pedagogy* because of his interest in a sociolinguistic *language awareness*, i.e. an interest in the relationship between language use and the cultural/social context. On the other hand, interest in a culture pedagogy that includes *the poetic dimension of language* (Chapter 1) is strictly limited among the culture pedagogues of the 1980s (as in the 1970s). Such an interest belongs to the 1990s.

Both Zarate and Byram are among those who have developed a more student-oriented and process-oriented culture pedagogy, with the focus being on cultural learning. Because of the emergence of this new emphasis, one is able in the subsequent culture pedagogy to distinguish between a learning-oriented culture pedagogy, which adopts a student perspective and is interested in the social and psychological learning processes that take place in connection with teaching, and a teaching-oriented, didactic culture pedagogy, which adopts a teacher perspective and is interested in the ends and means of teaching, ways of organising and assessing it, etc.

The 1980s were, as mentioned, the decade when culture pedagogy became generalised and normalised as an academic discipline alongside or as an extension of the more specifically linguistically oriented language pedagogy. Its legitimacy was supported by a dual overall idea: that of the indissoluble connection between language and culture, and that of the as-yet unrealised connection between language teaching and culture teaching. In this respect, the marriage between language and culture was a very useful image. But such metaphorics presupposed a distinct dichotomous separation between language and culture, and this I will attempt to argue against in Chapter 7.

The history of culture pedagogy is one of how the discourses on culture have spread from country to country and from language to language. Each time the term 'culture' has been imported into a new language, it has been incorporated into a new semantic context. I have mentioned that the (north and south) American concept of culture was introduced into French culture pedagogy in the 1970s and entered into a new semantic relationship with the already existing individual concept of culture. I have also stated that the concept of culture 'returned' to Germany in the course of the 1980s, packaged in the derivative 'intercultural', so it was able to replace the *Landeskunde* concept without being confused with the former *Kulturkunde* concept.[22] In this way, the history of culture pedagogy is an example of something I will return to in Chapter 7: the spread of discourse across languages.

Notes

1. In a newly written chapter at the end of the book Seelye declares he is a supporter of the movement for 'global education'.
2. See, for example, Risager, 2005.
3. Here Robinson (1985) ought also to be mentioned, which draws on American cultural anthropology and social psychology.
4. The passage between inverted commas is a paraphrase of M. Canale and M. Swain's article from 1980 on communicative competence.
5. Cf. Chapter 3. Byram was obliged to introduce the term 'cultural studies' here (Byram, 1989).
6. Her criticism is also of the German language educationalist E. Piepho even though he has also been inspired by Habermas' concept of communication.
7. Her criticism is also of the culture-anthropological concept of culture introduced by Rebouillet and others in France in the 1970s.
8. Poirier mentions (but does not recommend) Guy Michaud and Edmond Marc's *Vers une science des civilisations?* (Towards a science of civilsations?) (1981), which is an attempt to elaborate a unifying system for interdisciplinary social analysis, comprising a political system, an economic system, a cultural system and a biosocial system. It is not particularly designed for language teaching, but many people within language subjects in France are familiar with it. It is one of the most ambitious models for a comprehensive analysis of society (understood as a state). (cf. Nostrand's *emergent model*, which is, however, constructed quite differently because of its affiliation with the Parsonian tradition – Chapter 2).
9. Porcher describes the close relationship between language and culture as a fundamental epistemological principle for culture pedagogy. But that, I think, is misleading. The question of the relationship between language and culture is a theoretical question of an ontological nature: what is the ontological status of language and culture, and how does one construct the theoretical relationship between them? The epistemological aspect, in my opinion, has to do with the epistemological role of language in relation to knowledge, and that is not a central issue in culture pedagogy (even though it is not irrelevant, either).
10. In 1999 he published a dictionary of brand names: André and Galisson (1999). See also Galisson (1992).
11. *Trottoir* means pavement, and *crotte* means (dog) excrement.
12. 'Portmanteau word'.
13. Galisson refers here to Hallig & Wartburg, 1963 (1952), which contains a proposal for a conceptual system for French.
14. As stated, he mentions Hallig and Wartburg (1963), who build on the long-standing German tradition of studies within semantic fields. But he could, for example, also have mentioned American cognitive anthropology (ethnosemantics) or Thesaurus work within information theory or contemporary cognitive semantics – or just the French lexicological tradition, i.a. Gougenheim's articles on the cultural history of French words: *Les mots français dans l'histoire et dans la vie* (French words in history and in life) from 1966.
15. It is Galisson who invented the word *'didactologie'*, which is fairly widespread today, cf. Puren (1999).
16. *Deutsch konkret, Deutsch Heute, Los geht's, Zick Zack* and *Einfach toll*.

17. *Let's go, Learning English, English H, English G, English Live, English in Action, Contacts Basic Course and Contacts Enriched Course.*
18. In the sense in which the word is used in pedagogical philosophy, where it means an emphasis on a person's moral development through intensive work on particularly valuable cultural manifestations.
19. By 'general' and 'particular', Byram is thinking of the two levels within the differential level: the general and the specific, cf. Chapter 1 (personal communication, Nov. 2001).
20. 'Warp' and 'weft' are technical terms from weaving (cf. Geertz's metaphor: web).
21. In this quotation, Allen expresses an untenable, autonomous conception of grammar – one that I will argue against in Chapters 7 on the concept of languaculture.
22. It is possible to notice that there seems to be a transition from 'people' to 'culture' in West German culture pedagogy from the 1970s to the 1980s (Kramer, 1997: 20), especially in the form of a replacement of *Völkerverständigung* (cf. Erdmenger & Istel) by contexts which include *'interkulturell'*.

Chapter 5

Culture Pedagogy in the 1990s: Internationalisation and the Intercultural

Introduction

During the 1980s, the basis of an international professional network for culture pedagogy began to emerge – a tendency that intensified during the 1990s. It expressed itself in a growing familiarity with each other's work and a certain exchanging of views.

In the 1990s, it became increasingly common for people with a background in language pedagogy to begin to become interested in the cultural side of language teaching, often without knowing much in advance about the more culturally and socially oriented aspects of culture pedagogy. Language pedagogy (and linguistics in general) witnessed a cultural turn. This meant a breakthrough for culture pedagogy as a new part of language pedagogy, resulting among other things in AILA's world congress in Amsterdam in 1993 devoting a special section to this field, called *'The cultural component in language teaching'*.[1] Interest in the cultural side of language teaching, then, really took off in the 1990s, since when it has spread to many countries around the world.

The 1990s were very much characterised by internationalisation. There was a marked increase in study travel, especially within the Common Market/EU as a result of the major exchange programmes – and this benefited language teaching. The explosion within ICT, including the Internet, also came at this time. These developments led to far greater access to transnational personal contacts than before: some language teaching students – potentially at least – gained greater opportunities of meeting students from other countries, either physically via student exchanges and school trips (this especially in Europe), or via e-mail, etc. This meant that the teaching of culture tended to become more oriented towards experienced culture and personal cultural encounters.

Another field in which much took place in the 1990s was assessment. Comprehensive projects were undertaken in both the USA and Europe on developing criteria for the evaluation of cultural competence – a sign that this competence had now acquired such societal importance that language-teacher organisations (in the USA) and school authorities (in Europe) felt that there was a need to clarify and regulate its content.

The specially treated examples of culture-pedagogical approaches in this chapter are:

- Kramsch: *Context and Culture in Language Teaching* (1993)
- Byram: *Teaching and Assessing Intercultural Communicative Competence* (1997a)
- Starkey: *World studies and foreign language teaching* (1991a)
- Brøgger: *Culture, Language, Text* (1992)

The USA and Canada in the 1990s

Kramsch: Context and Culture in Language Teaching (1993): Presentation

In the USA, a poststructuralist shift of paradigm took place in the early 1990s with a number of publications by Claire Kramsch, especially her book from 1993, *Context and Culture in Language Teaching*. She adopts a linguistic, discourse-analytical approach and is highly critical of culture pedagogy up to that point, in particular the positivist American strain. She mainly teaches German, and is well-oriented in European culture pedagogy.[2]

Kramsch uses a linguistic starting point, her book being the first monograph within culture pedagogy that unites a linguistic main perspective that is theoretically well founded with a non-essentialist treatment of the cultural dimension. Even so, I have some reservations that I wish to examine below.

Kramsch is first and foremost a linguistic discourse theorist. She does not refer to 'critical discourse analysis' but draws on a number of various other approaches to the study of linguistic practice (discourse) seen in relation to its context (Halliday, Hymes, Gumperz, Tannen, Friedrich, Saville-Troike, Ochs, Goffman *et al.*). She has been particularly inspired by Bakhtin and therefore argues in favour of experimenting with dialogic language teaching, where the emphasis is on the differences or struggle between the many voices in the texts, and in classroom discourse. Moreover, she has more generally been inspired by the German text-hermeneutical tradition. On the other hand, she does not subscribe to the American Cultural Studies tradition – apart from sporadic references to the educationalist Giroux and the media researchers Fiske and Hartley.

She severely criticises the positivist, pragmatic tendencies in mainstream language teaching. In fact, she is referring to language teaching in the USA, although she does not limit her statements to this:

> By refusing to be ideological, this approach (foreign-language education up to now) has in fact espoused a middle-ground conservative ideology, recognizable by its positivistic, pragmatic bent, intent on assimilating conflicts by minimizing them. However, as in other sectors of education, questions are being raised about a purely pragmatic type of foreign language education. (Kramsch, 1993: 12)

It is in particular the universalist tendency in pragmatic language and culture teaching that Kramsch objects to: the idea that everyone can understand each other, if only they use the same code. Such language teaching values consensus and negotiation of understanding. She calls it 'the teaching of forms to express universal meanings' (Kramsch, 1993: 2). Against this she places a particularist programme, taking as her point of departure a conflict-perspective on meaning: there is always variability in meanings and contexts, and the classroom in language teaching is full of cultural faultlines that ought to be made visible.

If Kramsch's critical standpoint is compared with that of Byram, there is a great difference in what each of them is opposing: whereas Kramsch is against the positivist, pragmatic orientation of American culture pedagogy, arguing that there should be a move in a social-constructivist and dialogic direction, Byram is against the literary tradition in (British) foreign-language teaching and wishes to introduce a more realistic kind of teaching that deals with 'the real world': everyday life, values and institutions in the target-language countries – a criticism that has a long prehistory dating back to the European reform movement in the late 19th century. Byram stresses the necessity of reflecting on cultural differences and boundaries – and it is here that his position is also that of Kramsch.

Kramsch (1993): The relationship between language and culture

Kramsch examines the relationship between language and culture at many points in her book, but there is no real systematic treatment of the subject.[3] In a passage dealing with both the general and the pedagogical level simultaneously, she emphasises that language in itself is culture. This is the principal thought underlying her position:

> The dichotomy of language and culture is an entrenched feature of language teaching around the world. It is part of the linguistic heritage of the profession. Whether it is called (Fr.) *civilisation*, (G.)

Landeskunde, or (Eng.) *culture,* culture is often seen as mere information conveyed by the language, not as a feature of language itself; cultural awareness becomes an educational objective in itself, separate from language. If, however, language is seen as social practice, culture becomes the very core of language teaching. (Kramsch, 1993: 8)

Culture is 'a feature of language itself': even though the passage is talking in general about the differential level (since it deals with language teaching), I feel that Kramsch is making a statement here about language at the generic level: 'language' as such is always culture, or: language practice seen as a social practice is always culture at the same time. When she talks about the differential level (different languages), she links language and culture according to the formula: one language – many cultures that vary according to different parameters:

> Even if learners share a common native language, the fact that they partake of a multiplicity of 'cultures' (e.g. socio-economic status, gender, sexual orientation, visible and invisible disabilities) is rarely acknowledged. (Kramsch, 1993: 93)

That linguistic practice in itself is cultural practice is something I agree with Kramsch about, but I see a problem in her describing the dialectic between linguistic practice (which in itself is culture) and cultural context as being so close that it is not possible to distinguish between the two:

> foreign-language study [...] takes cultural context as its core. The educational challenge is teaching language 'as context' within a dialogic pedagogy that makes context explicit, thus enabling text and context to interact dialectically in the classroom. (Kramsch, 1993: 13, quotation marks in the original)

Her point of view is that the cultural context is variable and dynamic. But is the cultural context language in itself? Kramsch uses the expression 'teaching language "as context"', and places 'as context' in quotation marks, but by this indication she is not far from claiming that text and cultural context are identical – which could be seen as a translation to the poststructuralist context of the hypothesis of the identity between language and culture.[4] Kramsch is right, in my opinion, in saying that there is always a dialectic connection between the concrete language utterance/interaction and the context within which it takes place. And this context could also be called 'cultural', but if so we are talking about culture at the generic level: one is talking about 'culture' in general, no matter what this phenomenon contains and where it comes from in the historical process.

Kramsch justifies the unity between text and cultural context by means of a fairly radical social-constructivism, since she maintains that: 'Culture should [...] be viewed not as a natural given, but as a social construct, the product of linguistic choices made by two or more individuals interacting through language' (Kramsch, 1993: 46). In my opinion, this radical form of social constructivism is untenable. When talking of the context of language use, a distinction must be made between the aspects of the context that are directly created via the linguistic interaction, e.g. the immediate social relations, and the aspects of the context that exist in advance as objective facts[5] and that constitute the historically specific setting, but which will always be coloured by the interpretation of the implied language users, for example, their deictic markers.[6]

At a single point in the book she mentions the concept 'linguaculture': 'Culture, conceived here as linguaculture, emerges dynamically from actual, concrete exchanges between individuals in the classroom' (Kramsch, 1993: 30). This concept, with which I will deal in much more detail in Chapters 7 and 8, figures here simply as a harmless interpolation; there is no reference to a source, and the word cannot be found in the index. But it has been taken from Friedrich (1989). She actually uses the term herself in an earlier article from 1989, where she concludes with these words:

> A proposal is made here to develop an intercultural approach to the teaching of linguaculture at all levels and in all aspects of the curriculum. This approach takes discourse as the integrating moment where culture is viewed, not merely as behaviors to be acquired or facts to be learned, but as a world view to be discovered in the language itself and in the interaction of interlocutors that use that language. (Kramsch, 1989: 10)

But Kramsch clearly prefers in her book of 1993 to tone down the use of this concept.

Kramsch is very interested in the poetics of language (referring, among others, to Tannen and Friedrich), and she strongly advocates not simply including literary texts in language teaching but making them the focal point. She stresses that literature and culture are inseparable – unlike Byram, who from his perspective believes (in Byram, 1989) that one-sided literature teaching has had the tendency to separate literature (= language) from culture. My own position is that literary practice is a form of linguistic practice, and therefore an analysis of the relationship between language and culture is in a certain sense no different as far as literature is concerned from how it is for all other forms of linguistic practice.

As regards the national paradigm in language teaching, Kramsch clearly distances herself from it, which is a natural result of her poststructuralist basis. She talks about cultural variability and about international cultures: 'Once we recognize that language use is indissociable from the creation and transmission of culture, we have to deal with a variety of cultures, some more international than others, some more conventionalized than others' (Kramsch, 1993: 9). And she also points out that: 'too many textbook publishers believe that there is a universally "German" link between the German language and any German speech community, and that any speaker of German is automatically representative of any given German society' (Kramsch, 1993: 181).

Kramsch (1993): The relationship between language teaching and culture teaching

Since Kramsch basically believes that culture is a characteristic of language itself, and since there is a smooth transition between linguistic practice and cultural context, there is in principle no integration problem in teaching: all work on linguistic material provides cultural insight. Kramsch also believes the converse: culture pedagogy should deal with cultural reality only to the extent it is expressed through language, i.e. in linguistic discourse (a language-inherent approach that has certain similarities with what Erdmenger and Istel represent – Chapter 3). But her programme of focusing on cultural faultlines means that discourses (texts) have to be selected that can give rise to a struggle between voices in the foreign-language classroom. And here she proposes giving literary texts preference since she underlines that 'cultural imagination' is no 'less real' than cultural reality' (Kramsch, 1993: 207). Regarding selection, she prefers selection based on aesthetics rather than one based on themes:

> Rather than selecting a text exclusively in the basis of thematic interest and linguistic simplicity, the teacher may wish to consider other criteria:
>
> * Does the text lend itself more to an efferent or an aesthetic kind of reading?
> * Is the narrative structure predictable or unpredictable?
> * Are the cultural allusions clear or unclear to foreign readers?
> * Are the silences in the text understandable to foreign readers? (Kramsch, 1993: 138)

On the basis of such texts, one can be fortunate enough to experience a 'dialogic breakthrough', Kramsch says, referring to Friedrich, among others. Classwork is seen as a kind of interdisciplinary fieldwork in itself, where everyone is both informant and ethnographer. Here, there are two types of dialogue: a teaching dialogue where the cultural status quo of the school is confirmed and validated, and a dialogue where ideas and emotions are exchanged via language, which offers the possibility of questioning the status quo and thereby gaining new awareness, i.e. experiencing a dialogic breakthrough. By means of this, students get the chance to develop a cross-cultural personality, and Kramsch calls the special semantic constellations that arise in the class 'third places', new awarenesses that are created on the basis of a synthesis between meanings of various origins.

Kramsch represents an exciting and promising culture pedagogy, seen from a linguistic discourse point of view. It is interesting to note that she underlines the poetic dimension of language, which has otherwise been very underexposed or even completely neglected in the culture-pedagogy discussion up to that point (which has been separate from the literature-pedagogy discussion). My reservations have to do with two aspects of Kramsch's position.

Firstly, she does not approach sufficiently analytically the discussion of the relationship between linguistic practice (as cultural practice) and cultural context: what, actually, is 'cultural context', and what aspects of the cultural context are most connected to the specific linguistic practice, and vice versa?

Secondly, Kramsch has a too negative attitude to being updated as regards the outside world and to understanding some of its mechanisms. In other words, I miss a social angle that, among other things, would valorise knowledge, including factual knowledge. If teaching is built up round literary texts, it can well end up consisting of various exchanges of opinion and understandings of the texts, without any overall educational aim: should dialogues have to do only with anything the teacher and the students come up with? As already stated, I feel there ought to be an overall aim that includes gaining a greater knowledge of the world.

The concept of culture at its most language-bound: An example

In 1999, an anthology appeared in the USA called *Culture in Second Language Teaching and Learning*, edited by Eli Hinkel. It can be contrasted with Kramsch, as it is an example of a publication that, from a language-pedagogical point of view as regards language acquisition, contains exciting things, including sociocultural approaches, but which operates with a conception of culture that, unlike that of Kramsch, is chronologically earlier and is not supported by any reflections on the nature of culture.

We are dealing with one of the first publications that attempts to draw together certain strands from the language-pedagogy and culture-pedagogy traditions, seen from a main perspective that is basically that of language pedagogy. References are made to American second-language teaching (English), to foreign-language teaching, including Kramsch, and – more sporadically – to European foreign-language teaching, including Byram, Morgan, Zarate and Meyer. In the introduction, the editor writes that the aim of the book is to investigate '…the relationship between culture, language teaching, and learning by showing how cultural factors influence many different aspects of second language learning and use' (Hinkel, 1999: ix).

On reading through the book, it becomes clear that the dominant view of language and culture is that there is a 'culture' for every 'language'. There are many expressions like: 'a second language and a second culture' (p. 73), 'the target language culture' (p. 110), 'second culture acquisition… (henceforth SCA)' (p. 28), 'the learning of a second culture' (p. 9), and it is emphasised that 'Culture and language are inseparable and constitute "a single universe or domain of experience"' (p. 6, where there is a quotation from Kramsch, 1991: 217). And it is emphasised that 'the teaching of the second or foreign language cannot be separated from teaching the culture of its speakers' (p. 132).

There are references almost everywhere to an undifferentiated concept of 'culture', without any attempt being made to define more closely the theoretical content of this term. One of the articles in the anthology (Lantolf, 1999: 30), however, does refer to a particular theoretical conception of culture, namely that of Geertz: 'a historically transmitted semiotic network constructed by humans and which allows them to develop, communicate and perpetuate their knowledge, beliefs and attitudes about the world.' It is commendable that Lantolf defines the concept of culture he intends to work with, although he quotes it quite incorrectly.[7] But by resorting to Geertz (1973), he ends up basing himself on an antiquated, system-oriented concept of culture that does not, at any rate, invite any problematisation of the idea that one culture corresponds to one language.[8] Lantolf, and implicitly the other contributors, are operating here on the basis of a theoretically underexposed, language-linked concept of culture – one the theoretical content of which was not worth troubling about and which therefore acquires an *a priori* status.[9]

In the USA, the document *Standards for Foreign Language Learning: Preparing for the 21st Century* appeared in 1996. It had been drawn up by a number of language-teacher organisations, and it contained objectives for the so-called five Cs of foreign-language teaching: *Communication,*

Cultures, Connections, Comparisons and *Communities.* There are many such expressions as: 'assumptions of language and culture' (p. 7), 'language and culture learners' (p. 7), 'language and culture education' (p. 7), but there are also examples of the awareness that certain languages can be used in various cultural contexts: 'the cultures that use that language' (p. 27), 'the cultures of a given language' (p. 30).[10] The document has an essentialist view of language and culture, but not in the form of the simple identification of one language and one culture that characterises the above anthology by Hinkel.[11]

Canada

In Canada no monographs have been published to do with culture pedagogy,[12] although references are often made to H.H. Stern's (posthumously published) book from 1992, *Issues and Options in Language Teaching,* which contains a multidimensional model for the organisation of language teaching, including a 'cultural syllabus'. The book is a continuation of his comprehensive book on language teaching from 1983, and it deals with a number of different syllabuses for language teaching: 'the language syllabus' (pronunciation, grammar, functional analysis), 'the cultural syllabus', 'the communicative activities syllabus', and 'the general language education syllabus'. From a culture-pedagogy point of view, however, it does not contain anything new, as it mostly attempts to provide an overview of American culture pedagogy (USA), referring mainly to Seelye. Its concept of culture is the traditional holistic one, with teaching in the culture of the target-language society being the almost exclusive aim, without there being any developed intercultural perspective. It thus represents an extension of the cultural anthropological tradition in culture pedagogy.

Europe in the 1990s

European cooperation

The 1990s saw many transnational cooperation projects within culture pedagogy in Europe, most of them the result of initiatives by Michael Byram. He was the one to organise the first European conference on culture pedagogy (in Durham in 1986), which resulted in the anthology *Mediating Languages and Cultures* (Buttjes & Byram, 1991). Some of the most important cooperation projects will be dealt with in connection with the individual countries. But, first, an account of the Council of Europe language project and of certain EU initiatives within the area.

The Council of Europe and the EU

In the 1990s, the Council of Europe took the initiative of setting up transnational workshops in connection with its project *Language Learning for European Citizenship*, which was implemented in the period 1989–96 (cf., for example, the collection of articles in Byram, 1996). This also led to work on defining the concepts of sociocultural and intercultural competence and on suggesting ways of evaluating them. Byram and Zarate were central figures in this connection, as was Gerhard Neuner, who has a background in German as a foreign and a second language (Neuner, 1994).

In their work report *Definitions, Objectives and Assessment of Sociocultural Competence* (1994), Byram and Zarate develop the concept of the 'intercultural speaker'. They use the concept of sociocultural competence as their starting point because that is the concept used in work done by the Council of Europe on communicative competence (cf. Chapter 4 on the sociocultural component in van Ek's model). But Byram and Zarate develop the concept in an intercultural direction, as they underline that the aim of language learning and teaching is to develop into an intercultural speaker (French: *intermédaire culturel*), i.e. a language speaker who does not strive to attain the hopeless ideal of approaching native-speaker competence linguistically and culturally, but who develops his or her ability to mediate between a number of cultural perspectives and between the target language and the first language. They distinguish between four aspects of sociocultural/intercultural competence:

- *Savoir-être* (attitudes and values): An effective capacity to relinquish attitudes towards and perceptions of otherness and a cognitive ability to establish and maintain a relationship between native cultures and foreign cultures.
- *Savoir-apprendre* (the ability to learn): An ability to produce and operate an interpretative system to gain insight into hitherto unknown cultural meanings, beliefs and practices, either in a familiar or in a new language and culture.
- *Savoirs* (knowledge): A system of cultural references that structures the implicit and explicit knowledge acquired in the course of linguistic and cultural learning, and which takes into account the specific needs of the learner in his/her interaction with speakers of the foreign language. The notion of intercultural speaker … presupposes that this system of references incorporates native-speaker perspectives … and an awareness of the relationship with foreign-speaker perspectives on the issues in question.

- *Savoir-faire* (knowing-how): A capacity to integrate *savoir-être, savoir-apprendre* and *savoirs* in specific situations of bicultural contact, i.e. between the culture(s) of the learner and of the target language.[13] (Condensed from Byram & Zarate, 1994).

The publication in question does not contain any indication of what the relationship is like between the four *savoirs* and communicative competence. I will return to this presentation later in the chapter when discussing Byram: *Teaching and Assessing Intercultural Communicative Competence* (1997a).

The Council of Europe project was published in the document *Modern Languages: Learning, Teaching, Assessment. A Common European Framework of Reference* (1996). It does not contain all that much about sociocultural/ intercultural competence, and parts of Byram and Zarate's proposal have not been included. The *Framework* and the accompanying document, *European Language Portfolio*, are consensus documents for all the member states of the Council of Europe, the aim of which is to improve mobility and transnational cooperation in Europe. It is therefore not surprising, perhaps, that *Framework* is characterised by a Eurocentrism that favours the majority languages in Europe and the European majority cultures – and that it ignores the entire rest of the world outside Europe, where of course the major European languages also happen to be widespread. Consider, for example, the following passage at the beginning of the section on 'sociocultural knowledge': 'The features distinctively characteristic of a particular European society and its culture may relate, for example, to: ...' (followed by the classification of "features", such as everyday life, life conditions, interpersonal relations, values, etc.) (*Framework*, 1996: 40–41).[14]

Germany in the 1990s

Culture pedagogy in Germany, reunified in 1991, experienced a veritable intercultural boom, but the intercultural was associated with another concept of culture than the one found in the former idealistic concept of *Kulturkunde*. It was a concept of culture that was especially psychologically oriented and cognitive, taken originally from American cultural anthropology (Keesing *et al.*), but mediated by the field of intercultural communication.[15]

In the 1990s, the concept of intercultural communication gained a pivotal role in German foreign-language pedagogy, and with it came intercultural learning, intercultural didactics, intercultural competence and the intercultural speaker. This development must be seen in conjunction with the growing importance of German as a second language both for immigrants/ refugees and for re-emigrants (*Aussiedler*) who wished to resettle in Germany after the collapse of the Eastern Bloc. Intercultural learning in language teaching was often thought of as a part of a more general cross-disciplinary intercultural education/upbringing. The stronger emphasis on intercultural competence meant, among other things, an upgrading of affective goals, such as understanding foreigners, tolerance and a critical distance towards one's own cultural experiences.

One of those most active in this development was Bernd-Dietrich Müller-Jacquier, who had already worked in the 1980s on *Konfrontative Semantik* (contrastive semantics) (see Chapter 4), and who from the late 1980s onwards built up the field of *Interkulturelle Didaktik*, the emphasis being on methods of developing awareness of linguistic and cultural aspects of intercultural contact, especially including semantics ('the reconstruction of foreign meaning') (Müller-Jacquier, 2000).

At the same time, a rapprochement took place between culture pedagogy and literature pedagogy, under the aegis of *Didaktik des Fremdverstehens* (didactics related to the understanding of the foreign). One of the main representatives here is Lothar Bredella, who has been extremely active in the research environment set up in 1990 connected to *Fremdverstehen* in Giessen. This environment, which has been behind several large anthologies, including Bredella and Delanoy (1999), has facilitated broad discussions of the role of literature in language teaching, being not least interested in reading comprehension from a hermeneutic perspective, including such psychological-cognitive skills as empathy, perspective awareness, perspective differentiation, perspective takeover and perspective coordination in connection with the pedagogical work on fictional texts in a foreign language (see also Burwitz-Melzer in Chapter 6). Some of the representatives place their research within the interdisciplinary field of *Xenologie* – the study of constructions and experiences of the foreign in a multicultural society.

The intercultural paradigm was also criticised, however, from three angles: *firstly*, some people felt that focusing on the intercultural meant a culturalisation of culture pedagogy that got in the way of a critical and political awareness of society. These included the aforementioned Jürgen Kramer, who speaks of 'cultural and social studies' (Kramer, 1992 and 1997), and Peter Doyé and Meinert Meyer and Arnim Mennecke, who retain the concept of *politische Bildung* (education for citizenship) as being central. Mennecke, for example, is of the opinion that cultural content must contain the following dimensions, of which intercultural learning is only one (under Cultural Studies):

Landeskunde mediates background and orientation knowledge for future encounters by learners with speakers of the foreign language or manifestations of the foreign culture and economy.

Cultural Studies emphasise, apart from the pure mediation of knowledge about *Landeskunde* in the stricter sense, the aspects of intercultural learning that have to do with the acquisition of the foreign language.

Politische Bildung sees promoting international understanding as making a contribution that enables foreign-language teaching to become an interdisciplinary politically educative school activity.

World Studies[16] mediates knowledge and attitudes that are indispensable for finding one's bearings in a world that is becoming increasingly enmeshed, interdependent and multicultural. (Translated from Mennecke, 1992: 184)

I also agree that it is important to maintain this breadth in the content dimension of culture pedagogy, even though I do not structure it in that way.

Secondly, Willis Edmondson and Juliane House criticise the concepts of intercultural communication and intercultural learning from a linguistic and language-pedagogy point of view. They feel that these concepts are too imprecise and that the concept of intercultural learning is meaningless as a process concept and therefore should be dispensed with. For there are no specifically intercultural learning processes or learning strategies. For Edmondson and House, language itself is cultural: 'Languages (are) cultural occurrences and carriers of culture' (Edmondson & House, 1998: 185), and therefore the above concepts are in fact superfluous: all foreign-language teaching is intercultural (cf. Kramsch's position: culture is a feature of language itself). Even so, they acknowledge that the concept of intercultural communication can be used when the cultural aspects of foreign-language learning are to be emphasised. They prefer, however, the term 'cultural sensitising'.

Thirdly, social-constructivist objections can be pointed to, as advanced by Adelheid Hu (1999), who, in criticising Edmondson and House, favours a reorientation of foreign-language teaching via the development of narrative-constructivist concepts for culture, communication and intercultural learning.

Eike Thürmann is one of the few who deal systematically with the question of the national in language teaching.[17] He criticises the binational paradigm in language teaching and the equal status of target language and target culture. He does so on the basis of experiences gleaned from a pedagogical development programme, *Lernen für Europa* (learning for Europe), which included a project in which Dutch, German and Danish students stayed together in a Danish summer cottage and – with the aid of English as a language of communication – worked on learning each other's languages. He writes:

> What are the features that '*Landeskunde*'-like or intercultural learning can use to orientate itself in foreign-language teaching: the social and cultural extent of the 'major' languages and their function for the internationalisation of life-worlds, or the culture-historical status of European national states? (Translated from Thürmann, 1994: 321)

He does not believe that one should turn away from the classic target-language countries and their cultural plurality, but would like to find transnational cooperation where students use the target language as a lingua franca (see also Byram & Risager, 1999). Furthermore, a number of the authors in the above-mentioned Bredella and Delanoy (1999) question a national understanding of the cultural, including Adelheid Hu, who writes about identity issues in migration societies and what this can entail for foreign-language teaching (Hu, 1999).

A major historical study of textbooks, etc. has also appeared in Germany in the 1990s, this time by Anke Wegner (1999), which deals with the last century of the teaching of German as a foreign language in France and England, with particular interest in the linguistic and cultural content of the textbooks as well as their methods.[18]

France in the 1990s

The intercultural paradigm has also been strong in France. Geneviève Zarate in particular has been active in this area and has focused on cultural representations, otherness (*altérité*) and the shaping of identity from a Bourdieu-inspired and anthropological perspective (e.g. Zarate, 1993, and Cain & Zarate, 1996). She has been involved in the work of the Council of Europe on the concepts of sociocultural and intercultural competence, but she has not dealt specifically with the relationships between language and culture.

Albane Cain and Claudine Briane led a major empirical project around 1990 on the representations and stereotypes of French school pupils concerning a large number of countries. The survey covers teaching in eight languages (German, English, Arabic, Chinese, Spanish, Hebrew, Portuguese and Russian) and 45 countries around the world where these languages are spoken. It covers lower- and upper-secondary schools throughout France, with pupils ranging from 11 to 18 (*collège* and *lycée*). The results show, among other things, that the pupils' representations of other countries are very stable throughout the entire period of teaching. This project does not deal with the relationship between language and culture as such, but there is a considerable amount of material that has to do with the culture-specific connotations of words (Cain & Briane, 1994).

On several occasions, the heavy emphasis on the unity of language and culture (represented by, for example, Galisson) is questioned, although this discussion is not the main focal point. Benadava writes that the concept of *langue-culture* has meaning in only two contexts: when speaking of how various languages divide up reality (*classent la réalité*), and when speaking of language communication in relation to the natural context (*communication en milieu naturel*) (Benadava, 1990: 79). This distinction between language system and linguistic practice is important for the discussion, and I will return to it in more detail in Chapter 7.

Porcher, for his part, focuses on the thematic content side of language teaching, stating that it is possible to speak about a culture in any language whatsoever (a position that is far too simple, however, in relation to my own:

> As a result of preaching the indissolubility of language and culture (which is nothing else than a truism), experts in didactics lose sight of the fact that it is possible to speak about a foreign culture in any language whatsoever and learn it in the same way. (Translated from Porcher, 1994: 196)

Puren has reservations, too, and says: 'The forms of the language-culture relation are diverse and tend to diversify. [...] The indissolubility of language and culture ought therefore to be considered from a perspective of the plural and dynamic relations between the two terms' (from Puren, 1998: 45).

Great Britain in the 1990s

A European synthesis

In Great Britain, there has not been any real *discussion* of culture-pedagogy-related subjects; no clearly differing positions have been disputed. On the other hand, Byram has been extremely active in research and development work, both in Great Britain itself (along with others such as Carol Morgan and Celia Roberts) and in the Council of Europe (along with, for example, G. Zarate). He has also been the initiator of or participant in a whole range of projects in collaboration with others in various parts of Europe, including such East European countries as Bulgaria, and in East Asia. It was also Byram who took the initiative for an international language-teacher project, along with myself (Byram & Risager, 1999). Byram's orientation towards and impact in Europe must be seen against the background of the lesser impact he has had in Great Britain. The approval and implementation of the National Curriculum in England and Wales in the 1990s may have meant that teachers and educational planners in language subjects have focused a great deal on the testing of communicative competence and had correspondingly little time and energy left to get involved in intercultural competence – which is of course less suitable for being assessed by quantitative methods.[19]

In the 1990s, Byram dealt with a wide range of subjects within culture pedagogy: the development of ethnographic methods in connection with study trips and longer stays abroad, e.g. as a 'language assistant' (Byram, 1997b) (cf. also Roberts *et al.*, 2001, dealt with in Chapter 6), the development of the concept of citizenship in a European context (Byram, 1996), the investigation of language teachers' perception of themselves as mediators of culture in a European cultural and political context (Byram & Risager, 1999), and the development of the concept of 'intercultural speaker' along with Zarate, which led to the book *Teaching and Assessing Intercultural Communicative Competence* (1997a), dealt with in more detail below.

Byram's professional and academic position is the expression of a kind of European synthesis. His approach combines a British pragmatic approach with a German (moderate) approach that is critical of society and aware of the political aspects of language teaching. The approach contains a clear anthropological interest with inspiration from both the USA (Geertz), Great Britain and France.

At the same time as Byram, Hugh Starkey has continued to be active in the teaching of human rights and foreign languages. He stands for a particular position within language teaching, one that stresses its possibilities in relation to the students' moral development and their knowledge of the world ('world studies'). This I will return to after a discussion of Byram (1997a).

Byram: *Teaching and Assessing Intercultural Communicative Competence* (1997a): Presentation

This book derives from Byram's cooperation with Geneviève Zarate in the Council of Europe project on intercultural competence. But while this cooperation took place within a European framework, Byram's book is of a more general and universal nature. He underlines the diversity of the contexts in which language teaching takes place around the world and proposes a general model for the teaching and assessment of intercultural communicative competence that can be fleshed out locally, taking local conditions into account. In his book he concretises the concept of the 'intercultural speaker', created by Zarate and himself (Byram & Zarate, 1994). Because the book deals with intercultural competence, it adopts an individual- and target-oriented perspective: what does the individual's intercultural competence consist of, how can one distinguish between various levels of intercultural competence and how can one assess this competence? I intend to concentrate mainly on the first question: what does the individual's intercultural competence consist of?

Byram (1997a): The relationship between language and culture

The book marks a partial break with the concept of culture Byram has previously represented (Byram [1989], but also, for example, Byram, Morgan and colleagues, 1994). His discourse represents in 1997 a view of culture that is less system-oriented. There are no longer any references to Geertz. Byram talks about 'cultural beliefs, behaviours and meanings' (Byram, 1997a: 12), but otherwise refrains from discussing or defining the concept of culture further. At the same time, he presents a view of culture that is more practice-oriented. This change has, among other things, been inspired by a number of articles by the anthropologist John Gulløv Christensen (especially Christensen, 1994). Byram now writes: 'We have to be aware of the dangers of presenting "a culture" as if it were unchanging over time or as if there were only one set of beliefs, meanings and behaviours in any given country' (Byram, 1997a: 39) and 'we should not think in terms of encounters between different language and culture systems, but rather of encounters between individuals with their own meanings...' (Byram, 1997a: 40). This understanding characterises the whole book, although there are still traces of the earlier understanding at various points, as the expression 'language and culture' is still to be found (pp. 3, 42, 46) (although now without a hyphen). So there are certain discrepancies in Byram's text between earlier and more recent understandings of language and culture.

Generally speaking, it can be said that Byram (1997a) keeps a low profile with regard to the relationship between language and culture. There is no hypothesis of the inseparability of the two, nor any analysis of what the relationship between them might be. Language and culture are treated as two separate entities – and here Byram's approach is completely different from that of Kramsch, as Kramsch underlines that linguistic practice is cultural in itself.

The relationship between language and culture must be seen as both a societal/historical and a psychological/learning question. Admittedly, Byram's book does deal indirectly with linguistic and cultural learning. But these processes are expressed in competence terms and mainly conceived in connection with formal teaching.[20] So the focus is on the desired competence development, i.e. a normative point of departure is taken. For this reason, I intend to discuss Byram's theory of intercultural communicative competence under the heading 'The relationship between the teaching of language and culture'.

Byram (1997a): The relationship between the language teaching and culture teaching

Byram presents the following model for intercultural competence[21] (Byram, 1997a: 34) (Figure 5.1).

As can be seen, the model includes components that have to do with knowledge, attitudes and skills. And when the development of intercultural competence takes place in a teaching context, Byram also believes that cultural learning should have a more educative role: education, which he specifies with the aid of the words 'political education' and 'critical cultural awareness'. 'Political education' is a translation of the German expression *politische Bildung*, and Byram refers here to Doyé, who has worked a great deal on this concept in relation to language teaching.

	Skills interpret and relate (savoir comprendre)	
Knowledge of self and other; of interaction: individual and societal (savoirs)	**Education** political education critical cultural awareness (savoir s'engager)	**Attitudes** relativising self valuing other (savoir être)
	Skills discover and/or interact (savoir apprendre/faire)	

Figure 5.1   Byram: Intercultural competence

Byram writes about *politische Bildung*, which is meant as an educational goal relevant for all subjects, including language subjects, that it can be analysed in three orientations, on a par with intercultural competence: knowledge, attitudes and skills:[22]

- cognitive orientation: the acquisition of concepts, knowledge and modes of analysis for the understanding of political phenomena;
- evaluative orientation: the explanation and mediation of values and the ability to make political judgements on the basis of these values;
- action orientation: development of the ability and the readiness for political engagement. (Byram, 1997a: 43)

Byram also refers to Melde, who has designed a model for integrated teaching in communication and *Landeskunde* – a model that places considerable emphasis on political socialisation (Chapter 4). Finally, he refers to Starkey's work on such concepts as world citizenship and global education in connection with foreign-language teaching (cf. later in this chapter). But Byram adopts a quite neutral attitude to these approaches and does not engage in an explicit discussion of them. Regarding critical cultural awareness, Byram advances the view that if educational authorities and teachers do not want to introduce political education as such into their teaching, they must under all circumstances support the development of a critical awareness of values and meanings in cultural practice in the target-language culture and – if this is politically possible – in the students' own culture. He suggests gaining inspiration from the Cultural Studies tradition in Western Europe and North America. He also mentions Alastair Pennycook's discussion of the possibilities of basing oneself on a critical pedagogy in English teaching in postcolonial contexts (Pennycook, 1994). In my opinion, a transnational language and culture pedagogy must strengthen political and critical cultural awareness.

Unlike Kramsch, Byram represents a position that sees it as important that language teaching does not seek only to equip students with methodological skills in accessing and analysing cultural practice in general but also seeks to help them acquire (construct) knowledge. What, then, does Byram mean by knowledge (cf. the knowledge component in the model in Figure 4.1)? If we look at his proposal for concretisation, it is clear that the knowledge he is thinking of is generally speaking couched in national terms. He lists knowledge about:

(a) historical and contemporary relationships between one's own and one's interlocutor's countries ...

(b) the means of achieving contact with interlocutors from another country (at a distance or in proximity), of travel to and from, and the institutions which facilitate contact or help resolve problems ...

(c) the types of cause and process of misunderstanding between interlocutors of different cultural origins ...

(d) the national memory of one's own country and how its events are related to and seen from the perspective of other countries ...

(e) the national memory of one's interlocutor's country and the perspective on them (*sic*) from one's own country ...

(f) the national definitions of geographical space in one's own country, and how these are perceived from the perspective of other countries ...

(g) the national definitions of geographical space in one's interlocutor's country and the perspective on them from one's own ...

(h) the processes and institutions of socialisation in one's own and one's interlocutor's country ...

(i) social distinctions and their principal markers, in one's own country and one's interlocutor's ...

(j) institutions, and perceptions of them, which impinge on daily life within one's own and one's interlocutor's country and which conduct and influence relationships between them ...

(k) the processes of social interaction in one's interlocutor's country. (Byram, 1997a: 59ff.)

This focusing on the national is a conscious strategy on Byram's part, as is expressed in his explicit use of the word 'national'. So we are not dealing here with a more or less unconscious banal nationalism, and he is well aware of the dominance relationships that are implied in the unified conception of national culture, as he writes elsewhere:

> It has been the tradition of FLT to analyse in terms of national divisions and national identity, tacitly accepting the fact that this is also above all the analysis of the culture of a dominant elite. Is this tradition justified? (Byram, 1997a: 19).

On the other hand, Byram does not justify the strong national focusing on the above-mentioned categories (a)–(k), apart from raising the issue of the existence of national education systems at another point in the book:

> It is evident that other geo-political entities may be more relevant in some situations. I do not wish to imply ... that countries and nation-states are the inevitable entities of linguistic and cultural allegiance, but they are currently dominant and are the basis on which education systems are usually organised. (Byram, 1997a: 54f)

It is probably correct that most people have been socialised in a national school system and have acquired national school knowledge there. But, in my opinion, this does not justify foreign-language teaching underpinning this state of affairs. It is of course relevant to know of the national self-understanding that characterises the national education system in the country the interlocutor comes from. But it is precisely foreign-language teaching that has the potential to support a transnational approach – one that questions this national binding and its side effect: the belief in the inseparability of the national language and the national culture. What is needed is a more dynamic understanding of how linguistic and cultural flows characterise the world today.

Byram distinguishes between intercultural competence and intercultural communicative competence. The former is a competence that the native speaker has or can develop, and which enables this person, among other things, to interact with people talking their language as a foreign language (second language). The latter is a competence that enables a person to interact with others whilst talking a foreign language (second language). This latter competence, then, is more complex and specific than the former. Against this background, it is strange that Byram presents a model for intercultural communicative competence – as if the former were a supplement to the latter (see Figure 5.2). And it is so only from a theoretical-historical point of view in van Ek's model (van Ek, 1986), which Byram bases himself on and reformulates.

In most of his book, Byram deals with how the intercultural speaker can develop his/her competence to interact with people who speak the language in question as their first language. At times, however, he touches on the use of the target language as a lingua franca, which is a new angle for him – and for culture pedagogy in general:

> FLT has a central aim of enabling learners to use that language to interact with people for whom it is their preferred and 'natural' medium of experience, those we call 'native speakers', as well as in lingua franca situations where it is an estranging and sometimes disturbing means of coping with the world for all concerned. (Byram, 1997a: 3)

He does not, however, deal all that much with the issue of lingua franca, focusing on it only in a brief concluding chapter. There, however, it proves that he is in actual fact only thinking of English (using the abbreviation Elf) (Byram, 1997a: 112ff.), despite the fact that in principle any language can of course be used as a lingua franca, for example the use of German in

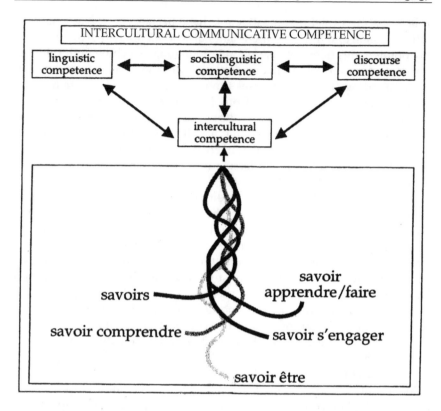

Figure 5.2   Byram: Intercultural communicative competence

international school networks where German classes in various countries communicate with each other. Byram does not raise the discussion of what the relationship between language and culture looks like when the language is used as a lingua franca.[23]

If the approaches of Byram and Kramsch are compared, the differences are considerable. As mentioned earlier, Byram keeps the categories of language and culture apart, yet claims at the same time that there is a complex relationship between them – typically within a (political) national context. Kramsch claims there is an identity between language and culture in a practice-oriented framework, i.e. linguistic practice is seen as cultural practice in itself, and a national understanding of the relationship is rejected. Furthermore, Kramsch favours the use of literature in teaching, whereas Byram mainly ignores such material. Lastly, Byram believes that language teaching – via such activities as fieldwork – is to give students a critical insight into the world, with the emphasis on the implied national cultures (and fieldwork is supported by the relatively short travelling distances in Europe), whereas Kramsch rejects the idea that it is the teacher's responsibility to deal with anything else than the themes and self-understandings that can be derived from the discourse of, and on, the chosen texts. As Kramsch says: 'The responsibility of the language teacher is to teach culture *as it is mediated through language*, not as it is studied by social scientists and anthropologists' (Kramsch, 1998a: 31, italics in the original).

Starkey: *World studies and foreign language teaching* (1991a): Presentation

This is an article by the Englishman Hugh Starkey, who has written and edited a number of books and articles about world studies and related issues, with the particular aim of developing foreign-language teaching in the direction of political science.[24] The article has the subtitle *'Converging approaches in textbook writing'*, as it also deals with pictures of society in textbooks. Starkey has been active in the Council of Europe in developing human-rights teaching in schools, has developed intercultural programmes for French students (Starkey, 1996) and has been co-author of a textbook in French that reacts against national stereotypes and adopts a critical and global perspective (*Orientations*, Aplin *et al.*, 1985). He has also been involved in developing language-teaching materials for adults at the Open University.

'World studies' is the term that has been used in Great Britain to denote 'studies which promote the knowledge, attitudes and skills that are relevant to living responsibly in a multicultural and interdependent world' (Starkey, 1991a: 210). Some people prefer the American terms 'global education' and 'peace education' – a pedagogical trend that wishes to promote a globally oriented and committed teaching in all subjects, including language subjects.[25] It focuses on political education and seeks to further 'the development of democracy and active citizenship' (Starkey, 1999: 156).

Starkey (1991a): The relationship between language and culture

Starkey's view of the relationship between language and culture does not emerge clearly from Starkey (1991a), but in Starkey (1996) there are explicit references to Byram, Morgan and colleagues (1994) and thereby to the fusion expression 'language-and-culture'. He says 'learning a language is also learning another culture on its own terms' (Starkey, 1996: 103). In Starkey 1999: 155 he says for example: 'A language is an expression of a culture', and quotes favourably a passage from Doyé that I have already quoted in an earlier form (from 1966, Chapter 3), and that Doyé writes with a direct reference to the longer quotation I have mentioned above from Byram (1989) (Chapter 4):

> If language is considered as a system of signs, and signs are character-ized by the fact that they are units of form and meaning, it is impossi-ble to learn a language by simply acquiring the forms without the content. And as the content of language is always culture-bound, any reasonable foreign-language teaching cannot but include the study of a culture from which the language stems. (Doyé, 1996: 105, quoted in Starkey, 1999: 159)

The decisive factors for me here are firstly that I believe language not to have a fixed content (it is always up for negotiation), and secondly that this relatively fluid content has admittedly been developed in particular cultural contexts over time, but to say that it is bound to 'a culture' in an abstract sense is a discursive construction that is highly problematic (cf. Chapter 7). Starkey, however, adopts the position here – as does Doyé – that to every language there belongs a culture, yet states at the same time that he supports global teaching.[26] This must mean that he perceives the world as consisting of language communities each of which has its own culture. So my criticism of the identification of language and culture must also apply to his position.

Starkey (1991a): The relationship between language teaching and culture teaching

Starkey distinguishes between two dimensions in world studies or global teaching, no matter what the subject: the teaching methods and the content. With regard to the methods, he places special emphasis on teach-ing that creates both a sense of security and a challenge. Much work is done with activities that strengthen cooperation skills, self-confidence and tolerance, and on outgoing activities such as making collections, writing letters to authorities, organising exhibitions, etc. Starkey points out in this connection that the development of the communicative approach to language teaching (the use of language in pair-work interaction and in larger groups, task-based activities, etc.) is a good basis for integrating it into global teaching. With regard to the content, the emphasis is on teach-ing being able to demonstrate that there are various views of the world and that it can promote the students' receptiveness to other perspectives than their own. Here, Starkey stresses that language teaching ought to be considered as a central subject as 'there is no more direct route to the heart of a culture than through its language' (Starkey, 1991a: 217). He gives the following comment on the textbook system *Orientations*:

'The authors of *Orientations* selected authentic French texts which would promote a world view, which would challenge racist and sexist stereotypes and which would show concern for the environment. The unit on fashion, for instance, contains an interview and a map illustrating the links between French fashion and India where the garments are actually made. The section on "La nature" includes a description of a Greenpeace protest on nuclear testing in Nevada. The unit on food contains illustrated material on the links between colonisation in Senegal and present-day food shortages. The accompanying exploitation of this material asks students to prepare a television debate on world hunger. Another exercise involves students in a role-play on how they might react to a racist incident on the Paris Metro. The photo illustrating a text on the women of Tchad shows three women cradling Kalashnikoffs.' (Starkey, 1991a: 219)

The pedagogical principle of emphasising transnational connections is an obvious selection, in my opinion, as part of globally oriented language teaching.

This approach emphasises knowledge of the world, insight into social interconnections, experience in thinking in systems and structures that have meaning for the global situation. In relation to Byram, it could be said that this approach places the model of the intercultural speaker in an explicitly global context. World studies or global teaching represent an interesting and necessary approach to language teaching as well, an approach that encourages both cooperation and meaningful work outside school or between schools in a network. But Starkey does not examine the relationship between language and culture, so here his position has to be developed further.

Other European Countries in the 1990s

Denmark, Norway, Greece and Finland

In *Denmark*, I was working in the 1990s on how language-teaching topics were in the process of transcending national frameworks (see, for example, Risager (1989a) on international and global topics in language subjects), and on the necessity for language teaching to take an interest in code-switching and code-mixing (Risager, 1993), on how the perspectives for textbook criticism can be expanded (Risager, 1991b and 1999a), and on the development of teaching materials (Risager & Aktor, 1999; Aktor & Risager, 2001). At the same time, the international research project on (English and) Danish schoolteachers in English, German and French was implemented with a project group (Byram & Risager, 1999). One of those taking part in the group, John Gulløv Christensen, wrote an article in that connection in which he criticised the reified concepts of culture in culture pedagogy, using Bourdieu's practice and field concepts as his starting point (Christensen, 1994).

In *Norway*, Fredrik Christian Brøgger published his book *Culture, Language, Text* (1992), which I will deal with in more detail below. In *Greece*, Bessie Dendrinos took an interest in how critical discourse analysis (as developed by Fairclough) could be applied to language teaching, especially English as a foreign language in Greece. She dealt in particular with the ideological content of textbooks and with pedagogical and political discourse in relation to the subject of English (without making use of the concept of culture) (Dendrinos, 1992).

In *Finland*, Pauli Kaikkonen and others worked on intercultural learning in connection with foreign-language teaching (Kaikkonen, 1991 and 2001). He refers most to the field of intercultural communication, speaking in favour of a cultural determinism that is characteristic for mainstream thinking within this area. He writes, for example, that 'Human beings are products of their own cultures, and can by nature understand the people of other cultures to a limited extent' (Kaikkonen, 2001: 100). He also talks about 'the shell of the native language and culture' and says that 'the most important goal of foreign language education is to help learners grow out of the shell of their mother tongue and their own culture' (Kaikkonen, 2001: 64).

Brøgger: *Culture, Language, Text* (1992): Presentation

Fredrik Christian Brøgger teaches American Studies at the University of Tromsø, and his book, with the subtitle *'Culture Studies within the Study of English as a Foreign Language'*, is an analysis of how a subject such as English can be described and developed at university level. Brøgger presents a picture of the tripartite university study plan in languages, comprising language, literature and culture. His aim is both to analyse the part that deals with cultural studies and to describe this part as an integral part of the overall study of language. He would like language subjects (at university level) to develop into new philologies, i.e. subjects characterised by the study of texts from a linguistic, a literary and a culture-theoretical point of view – both in teaching and in research. He speaks in favour of interdisciplinarity (not multidisciplinarity) in language subjects, so that teachers / researchers have a primary competence in one discipline and a secondary competence in one of the two others. He does not believe that people should be employed from other subjects (history, social sciences, etc.) in language subjects – these should be taken care of by people who have specialised in the study of language and literature or culture.[27]

Brøgger distinguishes between 'culture studies' on the one hand, which take place within the framework of language subjects focusing on the language in question as a foreign language, and 'cultural studies' on the other hand, which relate to a language area where the language is the first language,[28] like American Studies or British Studies as carried out in the USA and Great Britain respectively. The concept of 'cultural studies' is more inclusive, while 'culture studies' in foreign-language subjects must have a more precise focus on language and on the relationship between language and culture (and on the teaching of language and culture).

Brøgger's book is important in a culture pedagogy context because it is the only one to think of outlining a subject-related structure for language subjects as wholes (both language, literature and culture; teaching and research) and which also includes a chapter with a systematic discussion of the relationship between language and culture. A distinction is made in the book between:

- culture studies as a laissez-faire discipline;
- culture studies as an American Studies discipline;
- culture studies as an anthropological discipline;
- culture studies as a linguistic discipline;
- culture studies as a literary-oriented discipline;
- culture studies as a historical discipline;
- culture studies as a philological discipline;
- culture studies as a didactic discipline;
- culture studies as a research discipline.

In this connection I will deal mainly with the chapter on *culture studies as a linguistic discipline*.

Brøgger's concept of culture in this book is semiological and interpretive in its orientation, taken mainly from American cultural anthropology – especially Geertz (1973 and earlier). But he also refers to Gramsci's concept of hegemony and to Bakhtin and thus to a more practice-oriented and dialogic, heteroglossic approach. There are, on the other hand, no direct references to the Cultural Studies movement (Williams, Hall, Grossberg, etc.). Brøgger defines 'culture studies' as:

> the study of mutually confirmative and conflicting patterns of domi-
> nant assumptions and values signified, explicitly or implicitly, by the
> behavior of members of a social group and by the organization of their
> institutions. (Brøgger, 1992: 38)

The 'behavior' Brøgger is mainly thinking of here is production and understanding of non-literary (written) texts seen in relation to their social and cultural context ('cultural texts'). Via textual analysis he wishes to analyse the ideological implications of what takes place in society. When in his definition he talks about a 'social group', he means all forms of group, ranging from 'the nation as a whole' to 'a particular group of people within the nation' (Brøgger, 1992: 38f). So the frame of reference is basically the national paradigm.

Brøgger (1992): The relationship between language and culture

As far as Brøgger is concerned, language and culture are closely inter-woven. He says, for example, in a concluding passage in one of the chap-ters: 'Culture, it repeatedly turns out, is language, and language is culture' (Brøgger, 1992: 135). He also says that 'culture and language are inextrica-bly interrelated and interdependent' (Brøgger, 1992: 27).

Brøgger notes that recent developments within linguistics – functional linguistics, sociolinguistics, pragmatics and discourse analysis – have enabled a rapprochement between the studies of language and culture to take place, especially in the form of studies of the interdependence between language and cultural context and the interplay between language and ideology (Brøgger, 1992: 47). He also refers to critical linguistics (Kress, Hodge), but not to the various forms of critical discourse analysis that were becoming more widespread just before the publication of *Culture, Language, Text* – Fairclough's approach, for example. He prefers a purely linguistic conception of discourse: 'discourse analysis will be limited to […] the use of sentences in combination' (Brøgger, 1992: 48).

There is a need for a cultural linguistics, says Brøgger: a development of a cultural syntax and morphology, a cultural pragmatics and semantics, a cultural discourse analysis. But he does not believe that all aspects of language use necessarily have cultural significance:

> We may say that neither sociolinguistic, functionalist, pragmatic, nor
> discourse-oriented aspects of language use are necessarily culturally

significant. It is only when they can be shown to have a specific ideological signification and function that they become objects of study of the field that I would term cultural linguistics. Such cultural linguistics may be defined as the study of the ways in which patterns of dominant assumptions and values are the product of certain language uses, and vice versa. (Brøgger, 1992: 49)

In my opinion, though, all aspects of linguistic practice have ideological potential in some way or another. Furthermore, it seems strange that Brøgger believes the horizon of cultural linguistics ought to be restricted to dominant conceptions and values. I agree with him that there is a need for a more highly developed cultural linguistics, but it must be linked to a view of society that reflects the struggle for meanings at all levels of society, and which is just as interested in non-dominant as in dominant forms of culture.

Brøgger discusses a number of examples of where a cultural-linguistic analysis can be introduced, examples that will also be typical for most approaches within critical discourse analyses in the 1990s: the difference between saying 'Feminists clash with right-to-lifers' and 'Right-to-lifers clash with feminists' (in Halliday's terms a matter of transitivity). Or the difference between saying 'a black female doctor' and 'a female black doctor'. Or the conservative ideological construction that consists in equating 'individuals, business and local communities' in this sentence: 'The government will ensure self-determination and independence for individuals, business, and local communities'. By means of such examples – and others that focus on cultural exploitation of linguistic means at the level of discourse – Brøgger wishes to demonstrate to students that 'grammar and culture are inextricably related' (Brøgger, 1992: 55). As something quite central he wishes to develop a cultural semantics, inspired by, among others, Bakhtin (1981): 'Each word tastes of the context and contexts in which it has lived its socially charged life...' (Brøgger, 1992: 87).

The relationship between language and culture (and literature, which I have not dealt with specifically) is described in Brøgger by the model shown as Figure 5.3 (Brøgger, 1992: 108).

As can be seen, the model indicates that certain aspects of culture are non-linguistic. These include gestures, clothing, rituals and objects (artefacts) that, in Brøgger's opinion, ought to be included in the teaching of culture even if the main purpose of this is to develop communicative, i.e. linguistic competence (Brøgger, 1992: 98). At the same time, the model implies that certain aspects of language (and literature) are non-cultural,

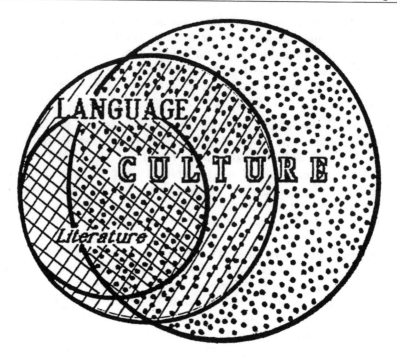

Figure 5.3   Brøgger: Culture, Language, Literature

and Brøgger justifies this by linguistic and literary practice being able to display purely individual, idiosyncratic features – and such features cannot be called 'cultural' insofar as they are not shared by others.

Brøgger (1992): The relationship between language teaching and culture teaching

Brøgger suggests a procedure in teaching culture that consists of three stages: first, social analysis, then cultural analysis and finally textual analysis (Brøgger, 1992: 113), possibly followed by a linking-back to cultural and social analysis once more. Textual analysis includes an analysis of the cultural, ideological implications of the linguistic choices that have been made. This indicates an integration of the teaching of language and culture: The texts used in English teaching are in English and deal with/come from American culture (or British culture, etc.). The teaching focuses on mainstream culture, seen as an essence that exists in a sociocultural dominance structure:

> This book ... is based upon the supposition that there *is* something that must be characterized as mainstream culture in the United States, the study of which may illuminate the processes of sociocultural domination and subordination in American life. (Brøgger, 1992: 106, italics in the original)

This accentuation by Brøgger implies a criticism of the traditional teaching of culture, which in his opinion can be characterised by four pitfalls or syndromes: 'the institutions syndrome' (one-sided emphasis on institutional teaching), 'the excess information syndrome' (one-sided emphasis on statistical information about populations, etc.), 'the social engineering syndrome' (one-sided emphasis on social problems and their resolution), and 'the minority syndrome' (one-sided emphasis on various minorities to such an extent that the mainstream culture of the majority becomes invisible).

Brøgger's conception of culture studies is unambiguously directed at the target-language country: the USA (or Great Britain). He does not deal with cultural relations in Norway or with Norwegian students' own cultural experiences in Norway. In other words, there is no comparative or intercultural aim in Brøgger's approach in this book. The pedagogical approach is clearly influenced by a focusing on the teaching process, not the learning process or other pedagogical-psychological relations, as is the case with Byram, for example. Brøgger represents a cognitive, didactic orientation that is probably characteristic of the culture pedagogy that exists at university level. Brøgger's approach is similar to that of Poirier (the teaching of British *civilisation* at French universities, cf. Chapter 4). Furthermore, Brøgger's approach is heavily text-oriented and without the ethnographic elements that Byram, for example, works with in connection with stays abroad by students and pupils.

The national paradigm is prominent in Brøgger, even though he also mentions in passing that 'many "American" patterns of belief are cross-cultural ones, shared by many Western cultures' (Brøgger, 1992: 111). We seem to be looking at a more or less enclosed space: the USA as revealed via social analysis, cultural analysis and textual analysis. In addition, I would describe this as an object area that is characterised by linguistic and cultural flows and which is seen as part of a global dynamics, cf. Chapter 7.

Brøgger cannot be completely identified with the tradition of culture pedagogy. He does not refer to anyone in international culture pedagogy, not even American or British writers. He is mainly part of a specifically English-subject discourse.

When compared to Kramsch, there are certain similarities: the post-structuralist inspiration is something they both share, although it is more pronounced in Kramsch. Both of them react against more positivist understandings of culture teaching as the mediation of factual knowledge, focusing on the understanding and interpretation of texts in a cultural context characterised by dominance structures. Both of them have an extremely vague and all-inclusive concept of context – 'the cultural context' – which gives them an alibi for claiming that linguistic practice and cultural context are always inseparable. But where Kramsch suggests cultural texts with a preference for literary ones, Brøgger distinguishes between the literary and cultural sides of language subjects with such comments as this one:

> The generalizations in culture studies are often *supra*-textual ones, that is, constructions of collective issues that may not be fully present and developed in any one text; the generalizations of literary studies, however, have often remained purely *intra*-textual ones, i.e. constructions of the intrinsic characteristics of one specific text. (Brøgger, 1992: 88, emphasis in the original)

This difference can have something to do with the different levels of learning with which they are working. Kramsch works with beginners/continuers, where it is not so relevant to angle the texts in a distinctly literary-aesthetic or historical way, as opposed to a culture-analytical angle.

Outside Europe and the USA/Canada in the 1990s

Morocco, Mexico, Australia, Sri Lanka

K. Adaskou, D. Britten and B. Fahsi (*Morocco*) have discussed in an article from 1990 an issue that has also become topical elsewhere – at any rate in the Arabic-speaking and/or Muslim countries (cf. Byram, 1997a: 23 regarding Qatar). This issue has to do with the cultural content of English teaching, and with the contexts presented in, for example, textbooks. The authors argue in favour of English teaching not dealing with cultural and social relations in countries such as Great Britain and the USA but with those in the pupils' own country, i.e. Morocco. English teaching is to focus on how Moroccans use English in their everyday lives in Morocco itself, as when receiving guests from abroad or corresponding with people abroad. The aim is to avoid the pupils (and the teachers) becoming dissatisfied with material conditions in Morocco when these are compared to (middle- and upper-class) conditions in Great Britain and the USA. This would be at variance with the educative aims of the education system as a whole.

The authors do not, however, imagine a 'culturally neutral' English being introduced. They emphasise that there are culture-specific aspects of the pragmatics and semantics of the English language that under all circumstances ought to be dealt with.

In *Mexico*, Phyllis M. Ryan has studied Spanish English teachers' metaphors concerning the concept of culture (Ryan, 1996). Ryan has examined both unsolicited and solicited metaphors about culture during her conversations with teachers, and she discusses their content and use in language teaching: a ball of yarn, an impressionist painting, a machine with all its parts working together, overlapping circles, a mosaic, a fabric with the warp and weave, a bubble each of us has. There are also examples of metaphors to do with language and culture that visualise their inseparability, e.g. two circles inside each other that are constantly changing position in relation to each other, so that the culture ring is sometimes on the outside, sometimes on the inside. Or language and culture seen as two metal rings that interlock and can be pulled apart only with difficulty (cf. Chapter 4 concerning the marriage metaphor).

During the same period, Alastair Pennycook (*Australia*) has written about the cultural-political role of the English language and about how it is possible to work in a critical pedagogical way with English teaching from a postcolonial perspective (Pennycook, 1994 and 1998), and A. Suresh Canagarajah (*Sri Lanka*) has written about how linguistic imperialism can be resisted in English teaching, also from a postcolonial critical perspective (Canagarajah, 1999).

Conclusion

In the 1990s, the idea of intercultural learning became widely recognised. Brøgger makes no use of the concept and in this sense represents the 1980s rather than the 1990s. Apart from him, most of the theorists within culture pedagogy deal with intercultural issues and thereby with the learning processes that bridge cultural differences, whether viewed within a national framework or not.

Of the four examples of culture pedagogy positions, one adopts a linguistic point of departure, while the other three have the humanities and / or social sciences as their point of departure.

Point of departure in linguistics:
- Kramsch: a linguistic, discourse-theoretical approach.

Point of departure in the humanities and the social sciences:
- Byram: a psychological, ethnographic approach – with a more practice-oriented concept of culture than previously.

- Starkey: a social sciences, politically oriented approach (world studies).
- Brøgger: a humanities and social sciences, textually oriented approach.

It is still the case that the prevailing view of the relationship between language and culture is that they are inextricably linked. But in the course of the 1990s, this conviction has split into a structuralist and a (new) post-structuralist variant, i.e. one that focuses on language as a system (*langue*, competence) and one that focuses on language as practice (*parole*, performance): the traditional structuralist variant is found in many theorists, including Starkey and Brøgger (and Hinkel). The poststructuralist variant is most consistently expressed by Kramsch, and partly by Byram, who is, however, ambivalent on this point. The poststructuralist variant claims an inseparability between concrete linguistic practice (the linguistic event) and the 'cultural context'.

If we look at the three dimensions of the cultural side of language teaching, the content, context and poetics dimensions, we can in the 1990s observe growth in the last two and a certain weakening of the first. A swing has taken place towards a pragmatic and contextual orientation, represented by Kramsch and, in part, Byram. The content dimension is still championed by Byram, Starkey and Brøgger: language teaching is, among other things, to give the students the opportunity to develop a knowledge that is as cohesive as possible about the target-language countries and perhaps also the larger global context. Kramsch, on the other hand, does not feel that attempts should be made to create a cohesive knowledge of the world: the aim of language teaching is first and foremost to interpret texts, not least literary texts, and thereby develop an intercultural personality – no matter the thematic content of the selected texts. My position here will be to argue for the importance of the content dimension, whilst also arguing in favour of a non-structuralist understanding of language and culture.

The national appears explicitly in Byram in connection with the knowledge component of intercultural competence: knowledge of the national self-understanding of the target-language country. But there is no theoretical problematising of the national as a cultural construction in Byram. Kramsch criticises the idea of, for example, a general link between the 'German language' and any 'German language community', but she too does not discuss the national as such. The other theorists (Starkey, Brøgger) seem to operate unreflectingly within a national paradigm. Among the few to discuss the national question are Hu (1999) and Thürmann (1994). The criticism of the latter focuses on binational thinking in language and culture pedagogy – a criticism that has as its point of departure the actual student mobility that exists in connection with internationalisation.

Notes

1. *AILA = Association Internationale de Linguistique Appliquée*. Culture educationalist Claire Kramsch was a keynote speaker at the congress.
2. Kramsch has a European background, as she was born and grew up in France and has been married to a German and studied in West Germany.
3. There is such a treatment, though, in her book *Language and Culture* (Kramsch, 1998a), see, for example, the discussion in Risager (2006).
4. Elsewhere in the book she also talks about 'teaching the interdependence of language and culture' (Kramsch, 1993: 236).
5. Cf. Berger and Luckman (1966), whose version of social constructivism is more in agreement with mine.
6. Note that the English word 'construction' is ambiguous, since it can be formed both from 'construct' and 'construe'. This is why it is possible to distinguish between strong ('construct') and weak ('construe') uses of social constructivism. It would often be clearer to use the word 'construal', as it is obviously derived from 'construe'.
7. Lantolf reformulates the passage in his own words, although quotation marks are used. The passage in Geertz is as follows: 'an historically transmitted pattern of meanings embodied in symbols, a system of inherited conceptions expressed in symbolic forms by means of which men communicate, perpetuate, and develop their knowledge about and attitudes towards life' (Geertz, 1973: 89).
8. In a later edition, Geertz got closer to a more pluralistic conception of culture than he had previously expressed. He emphasised, for example, that the role of an ethnographer was to 'enlarge the possibility of intelligible discourse between people quite different from one another in interest, outlook, wealth, and power, and yet contained in a world where, tumbled as they are into endless connection, it is increasingly difficult to get out of each other's way' (Geertz, 1988: 147). Lantolf could also have gained inspiration from this view.
9. This layman's attitude would seem to be very widespread among language people. In my conversations with linguists of various observances about the subject the relationship between language and culture, a very common reaction is: 'It's all a matter of what language is.' But not a single one has said to me: 'It's all a matter of what culture is', or 'It's all a matter of what language and culture are'. 'Culture' would still seem to function as a kind of 'stop word' that prevents any further discussion (cf. Hermann & Gregersen, 1978: 31).
10. Here it could be asked whether it is a given language that has cultures, or cultures that have a language?
11. An approach reminiscent of that of *Standards*, can be seen in Oxford (1994).
12. John H. Schumann's acculturation theory (e.g. Schumann, 1978) and R.C. Gardner's work of motivation (e.g. Gardner, 1985) are related to culture pedagogy.
13. This shortened form of expression might give rise to the question: who is it that has 'culture', the people or the language?
14. This is a highly deliberate linguistic and cultural move on the part of the Council of Europe. Michael Byram has informed me that those involved in *Framework* were expected to refer to countries in Europe and not attend to the potential for its use outside, although this has now become common in East

Asia (with a translation into Japanese, for example) and North America (February 2006).

15. This field had already been developed in Western Germany by such a person as J. Rehbein, e.g. Rehbein (1985).

16. Called *Weltkunde* (knowledge of the world) by some people (which has the same unfortunate positivist connotations as *Landeskunde*).

17. Also worthy of mention is Claus Altmayer, who criticises the concept of culture used in intercultural Germanistics and re-interprets it as a social habitus (Altmayer, 1997). There is also comprehensive German research into national stereotypes (Löschmann & Stroinska, 1998).

18. M. Erdmenger, one of the authors of Erdmenger and Istel (1973), which I dealt with in Chapter 3, published in 1996 the book *Landeskunde im Fremdsprachenunterricht*, which, with a few exceptions, restates his position from 1973.

19. However, it was at a symposium in Manchester in the early 1990s that the then staff director 'discovered' the intercultural and ensured that it became part of the curruculum (but not of the assessment) – so the phrase 'cultural awareness' was a direct but necessarily unacknowledged consequence of that weekend (Michael Byram, personal communication, April 2006).

20. Byram does emphasise, however, that intercultural competence can also be developed outside a teaching context.

21. Also referred to as 'the model of the five *savoirs*'. The term *savoir* originates from Byram's collaboration with Zarate.

22. These three components Byram has from Doyé (1993), who in turn has them from the German researcher in education Gagel (Gagel, 1983).

23. Subsequently, Byram has written an article about English as a lingua franca (Byram, 2000b) in which he argues that a language cannot be culturally neutral but where, in my opinion, he lacks the concept of languaculture to make the issue more clear (Chapter 7).

24. Including Starkey (1988, 1989, 1991b, 1996 and 1999).

25. Cf. also Risager (1989a), which is an example of this.

26. Also like Doyé.

27. I think this is an unnecessary restriction of the profile of language subjects. Cf. Sevaldsen and Thorsen (1994) as an example of a societal approach to language subjects.

28. The predominant first language, it should be added, but Brøgger does not mention this proviso.

Chapter 6

Culture Pedagogy Today – Questioning of the National Paradigm

Introduction

In this chapter I wish to discuss certain important contributions to culture pedagogy in the years after 2000, and then attempt to take stock of the present-day culture pedagogy situation. I do so on the broadest basis possible, but naturally it is impossible to include everything. For culture pedagogy has spread to most parts of the world since the 1990s, not least in connection with the expansion of English as a foreign and second language. There are many PhD students working in the field, and many international cooperations, conferences and networks. There is at present a growing interest in the field in Australia and East Asia.

Europe still accounts for the most publications in the area (monographs and anthologies). At the same time, the many publications are an expression of a great diversity when it comes to approaches. Quite a few of them are the result of transnational cooperations, including Eastern Europe. Without doubt, it is the need for intercultural communication in multilingual and multicultural Europe that is the basis for the continuing interest in the theory and practice of culture pedagogy there.

The specially treated examples of culture pedagogy approaches in this chapter are:

- Roberts *et al.*: *Language Learners as Ethnographers* (2001).
- Burwitz-Melzer: *Allmähliche Annäherungen* (Gradual Approaches) (2003).
- Guilherme: *Critical Citizens for an Intercultural World* (2002).
- Risager: *Det nationale dilemma i sprog- og kulturpædagogikken* (The National Dilemma in Language and Culture Pedagogy) (2003).
- Crozet and Liddicoat: *Teaching Culture as an Integrated Part of Language* (2000).

The USA in the Years after 2000

Claire Kramsch, whose book of 1993 has had a great influence on language and culture pedagogy, has in the years around 2000 not devoted most of her efforts to the theory of language and culture teaching, but instead worked more specifically with the relationship between language and culture from an ecological perspective, looking particularly at linguistic socialisation and the multilingual subject, cf. Kramsch (2002), (2004), (2006), (forthcoming). In addition, I would mention an interesting article by Aneta Pavlenko (2003). Pavlenko, who comes from Russia, is a specialist in cognitive studies of bilingualism, but in this article (which has the title 'Language of the enemy: Foreign language education and national identity') she discusses how the foreign-language teaching and foreign-language policy of a country are deeply affected by the conceptions prevailing at any given time of the country's national identity and geopolitical situation. She compares the situations in the USA after the First World War (when German changed from being the largest foreign language to being almost completely eradicated, dragging other foreign languages down in its wake, so that the very fact of knowing a foreign language became suspect), the USSR after the Second World War (when great efforts were invested in foreign-language teaching as the opportunity was seen here for spreading communist propaganda)[1] and Eastern Europe after the fall of the Wall (when the dominance of the Russian language was replaced by an enormous interest in, particularly, English). It is an article that reveals how the national paradigm does not necessarily have to do only with content (French teaching focused on France and Frenchmen, etc., cf. Chapter 1) but also that the status and specific content of foreign languages is strongly influenced by the contemporary national identity politics.[2]

As a clear illustration of this one could mention the recent initiative launched by President Bush, The National Security Language Initiative, described on the website of ACTFL (American Council on the Teaching of Foreign Languages) in the following way:

> President Bush today launched the National Security Language Initiative (NSLI), a plan to further national security and prosperity in the 21st century through education, especially in developing foreign language skills. The NSLI will dramatically increase the number of Americans learning critical need foreign languages such as Arabic, Chinese, Russian, Hindi, Farsi, and others through new and expanded programs from kindergarten through university and into the workforce. The President will request $114 million in FY07 to fund this effort.
>
> An essential component of U.S. national security in the post-9/11 world is the ability to engage foreign governments and peoples,

especially in critical regions, to encourage reform, promote understanding, convey respect for other cultures and provide an opportunity to learn more about our country and its citizens. To do this, we must be able to communicate in other languages, a challenge for which we are unprepared.[3]

Europe in the Years after 2000

The Council of Europe publication *Common European Framework of Reference for Languages* (CEF) (2001), which I have already mentioned in Chapter 5, has at present a major influence as a guideline document for language teaching and language assessment around Europe. CEF is based on a view of language that is integrative and pragmatic in orientation, but its conception of the relationship between language and culture, and that between language teaching and culture teaching, is unclear and without theoretical foundation. The same can be said for the supplementary project, The European Language Portfolio. CEF is part of work done by the Council of Europe on the concept of *European citizenship* – a concept which the council has disassociated itself from in favour of the expression *democratic citizenship in Europe* so as not to have its work directly associated with the political conflicts in connection with EU citizenship. In connection with the council's work, Michael Byram is developing the concept of 'intercultural citizenship'.

Much cooperation is taking place between people in Great Britain and France – English is of course the first foreign language in France, and French the first foreign language in Great Britain – among which I would like to emphasise a project carried out by Carol Morgan and Albane Cain (2000).

Practically speaking, the project had to do with a cooperation between a school class in France and one in England. The pupils learned English and French respectively as foreign languages and were around 13–14 years old. The actual teaching project lasted six weeks, and the common topic for the two classes was 'Law and Order'. Each class was to produce some material about the subject in their first language (possibly supplemented by representations in other media) and send it to the partner class. At the same time, they were to send a help sheet in the target language that gave certain cultural and linguistic explanations. The material for this help sheet arose as a result of a number of interviews with the pupils (in their first language) done by the researchers. Theoretically speaking, the authors base themselves on a dialogic and sociocultural view, referring here to Bakhtin and Vygotsky. They investigate the entire cooperation process, especially the many dialogic relations and processes in the classes, between the classes, between the pupils, teachers and researchers, etc. Furthermore, they look at interactions between the various media (writing, photos, drawings, etc.) and refer here to the critical semioticians Kress and Hodge. This approach is quite reminiscent of Kramsch's. As regards the national, the project must clearly be said to be an extension of the national paradigm, since we are dealing with a binational design where two different linguistic/cultural worlds interact.

Michael Byram has been highly active as an editor since the 1990s, working partly on the *Routledge Encyclopedia of Language Teaching and Learning*, which appeared in 2000, and in which the cultural dimension is well represented, and partly on a number of anthologies about various aspects of culture pedagogy: Byram, Nichols and Stevens (2001); Byram and Grundy (2003); Alred, Byram and Fleming (2003).[4] All these publications contain articles by authors from different countries and continents – but from Europe in particular. Another major cooperation in which Byram also has participated will now be looked at in more detail here.

Roberts *et al.*: *Language Learners as Ethnographers* (2001): Presentation

This book has been written by an interdisciplinary team of sociolinguists, culture educationalists and anthropologists (Celia Roberts, Michael Byram, Ana Barro, Shirley Jordan and Brian Street) and is the first major monograph that describes the ethnographical method in language subjects. It is based on a development project for university students (the Ealing Project) and contains both a theoretical introduction and a detailed description of the project, including the education of language teachers in ethnographic fieldwork, the development of a course in anthropology and ethnography for the language students, examples of the students' own fieldwork (at home and abroad) and project writing, etc. These are examples of a culture-pedagogy approach that has a linguistic point of departure (with reference to Gumperz and Roberts' own work), linking this to an anthropological-ethnographic one (with reference to, among others, Agar and Street himself).

Roberts *et al.* (2001): The relationship between language and culture

The authors explicitly disassociate themselves from the national paradigm, stressing the importance of Michael Billig's concept of 'banal nationalism'. They place great emphasis on local knowledge, both geographical and social, and by combining interactional sociolinguistics, linguistic anthropology and cultural and social anthropology their theoretical structure shows great similarities with mine in Risager (2003), (see below). They emphasise the practice dimension of both language and culture: languages must be studied as linguistic practice in particular situations and contexts, and linguistic practice must be seen as cultural practice, where the individual is not a 'culture bearer' but is actively creating culture – a social-constructivist point of view (they refer to such writers as Gumperz and Kramsch). By entering into linguistic interaction we help give meaning to the world; at the same time we are in the middle of a linguistic socialisation process (here they refer to Ochs) in which we are developing ourselves as social beings. This also occurs when we acquire a foreign language. With the aid of our linguistic (cultural) resources we create discourses and representations of the world, e.g. about our own and others' changing national and ethnic identities (where they refer to Gilroy and other representatives of the Cultural Studies movement).

The writers' aim is not, however, to discuss the structure of the connection between language and culture in a critical way. Their research and development programme is to clarify the connection between language and culture, to plead for language and culture as a unity, so as to thereby neutralise the traditional dichotomy between 'language' on the one hand and 'culture' on the other. They argue that language is never culturally neutral (Roberts *et al.*, 2001: 7); they say, for example, that 'language and culture are inextricably connected' (Roberts *et al.*, 83), they say 'cultural learning *is* language learning, and vice versa' (Roberts *et al.*, 5), and they use the expressions 'language-and-culture learning' (Roberts *et al.*, 6) and 'language-and-cultural practices' (Roberts *et al.*, 55). My attitude here, as mentioned earlier, is that language must be seen from an integrative perspective, and that linguistic and (other) cultural practices are always inseparable at the *generic* level (cf. Chapter 1). But the authors do not distinguish clearly between language at the generic and at the differential level: at the differential level it would here be, for example, the French language. What is 'the French language' (or linguistic practice in French, inseparable from? In my opinion, this is an empirical question, one I will return to in Chapter 7. The writers come to represent a point of view that language and culture constitute one single universe, and thus also for the already-mentioned first-language bias (native-language bias) (cf. Chapter 1).

This clashes with their concept of 'the intercultural speaker', which implies knowledge of two different languages, one of which will normally be the first language and the other a foreign or second language. In my opinion, by introducing the concept of languaculture and using it in a particular way it is, however, possible to get out of such difficulties, see Chapter 7.

Roberts *et al.* (2001): The relationship between language teaching and culture teaching

The most important aim of 'the Ealing Project' has been to help university foreign-language students develop that part of their intercultural competence that has to do with accessing information for themselves and with creating their own insight into life in the countries where their target language is the first language (discover and/or interact, cf. Byram in Chapter 5). They wanted to educate them to be a kind of ethnographer (not professional anthropologist) who had the most necessary tools for carrying out fairly short-term ethnographic fieldwork, make (participant) observations, do interviews, etc., as well as gather all this together and write a cohesive, focused and reflective report on the target language when they came back to the university. So the students (and their teachers) were to be prepared for this via courses in basic anthropological concepts and in ethnographic fieldwork, completing the course by carrying out a home ethnography (where they do a small-scale piece of fieldwork in their own country). All of this is to prepare the students for acquiring some integrated linguistic and cultural experiences during their stay abroad: they use the language and at the same time develop their cultural practice and cultural insight.

This is a very promising programme for language studies in an age of exchanges, not least in Europe. The programme also avoids the national paradigm, as the ethnographic studies must by nature have a local focus that can counterbalance any eventual national stereotypes. The approach is therefore clearly postnational, oriented towards a concept of culture (and one of language) that examines practice and its dynamic. However, the approach is less transnationally oriented than mine is, as we see below.

In *Germany* and *Austria* there is much activity particularly within the above-mentioned field of *Didaktik des Fremdverstehens* (didactics related to an understanding of the foreign), with comprehensive discussions of the role of literature in foreign- and second-language teaching. I would like to draw attention to Bredella und Burwitz-Melzer's major literature-pedagogical work (2004) and to Delanoy (2005), and below I will pay particular attention to the approach in Burwitz-Melzer (2003).[5]

Burwitz-Melzer: *Allmähliche Annäherungen: Fiktionale Texte im interkulturellen Fremdsprachenunterricht der Sekundarstufe 1* (Gradual approaches: Fictional texts in intercultural foreign language teaching at secondary level) (2003): Presentation

Eva Burwitz-Melzer works within English and has carried out a large-scale empirical project on the use of fictional texts with children in various types of school in Germany at *Sekundarstufe 1* level, i.e. students aged between 10 and 17. This is the first major empirically based investigation of the foreign-language area to focus on literature pedagogy as culture pedagogy, and the investigation is also special in that it looks at relatively young pupils whose foreign-language skills are typically not all that developed.[6]

The overall aim of the project is to study what is needed for the students to undergo an intercultural learning process, i.e. first and foremost that they are able to carry out shifts of perspective and relate the various perspectives to their own experiential world. The centre of focus in the teaching is a fictional text (short story, poem, youth novel, comic strip) that the class works with in various ways (role-play activities, letters to the main characters, poems, etc.) and talk to each other about afterwards.

In the project, Burwitz-Melzer has examined 14 different teaching sequences at various class levels. In each case, she has chosen the text and prepared the teaching along with the teacher and has observed and videoed the actual teaching. In addition, she has given the teacher a questionnaire. She has subsequently done retrospective interviews with the teacher and with a selected group of students. All the data has been ordered according to a comprehensive categorisation table that gives a good picture of the many facets of intercultural learning.

Burwitz-Melzer (2003): The relationship between language and culture

Burwitz-Melzer does not adopt a linguistic point of departure but a literary-critical one and is thus one of the culture educationalists that take the humanities and/or social sciences as their point of departure. The understanding process in relation to 'the foreign-cultural text' is centre stage.

Burwitz-Melzer's view of the relationship between language and culture is contradictory: on the one hand, there are a number of examples showing that she wishes to emphasise a view of culture that is complex. She refers to, among others, Kramsch (1998b) and Risager (1998), both of which stress in their separate ways the importance of paying attention to cultural complexity and of avoiding the essentialisation of culture,[7] and she writes:

In present-day multicultural societies, which clearly show us every day just how far we have come from being homogenous cultures, a multicultural dialogue will reveal overlaps, complexity and blurred boundaries that make it more difficult to speak of an absolute foreigner. (Translated from Burwitz-Melzer, 2003: 45)

Her choice of texts in the survey also makes it clear that she wishes to promote intercultural learning via texts that thematise such subjects as racism, migration and cultural identities, and that a central aim of the teaching is to avoid prejudices and stereotypes. She also reflects on the fact that in many of the classes there are students who speak German as a first language and others who speak it as a second language.

On the other hand, there are many points in the book where the common pattern of thought that for 'the foreign language' there is a corresponding 'foreign culture' finds its way into the discourse, e.g. in the concept 'the foreign-language and foreign-culture reader' (Burwitz-Melzer, 2003: 6), and 'foreign-language teaching that presents its students with three levels of foreignness: the foreign language, the foreign culture and meeting foreign people...' (Burwitz-Melzer, 2003: 42).

It would seem that, when talking about *culture*, it is possible to conceptualise diversity and complexity, but when talking about *language*, this is not the case. This is perhaps because foreign-language teaching is dominated by an essentialising and homogenising view of language. When there is a need to talk about *both language and culture*, the common essentialising of language rubs off on the view of culture, and 'language' and 'culture' are made to coincide. This identification is eventually modified in such a way that for one language there are a number of (national) cultures, as, for example, when the English language is seen as linked to British culture, American culture, Australian culture, etc. Both understandings can be said to be an expression of banal nationalism.

Another example of this is when Burwitz-Melzer uses two terms for the texts she works with: foreign-language texts and foreign-culture texts. But she does not discuss the distinction between the two terms, and the question is whether she believes that the foreign-language texts simply are foreign-culture texts. This is a problematic identification. I, for example, who have Danish as my first language, can point to many Danish-language texts that are foreign-culture texts to me, and to many English-language texts that are not the least foreign-culture texts to me. In Burwitz-Melzer's context I believe it would be more precise to talk about English-language texts and then define which of these could be the most foreign-cultural for the students involved – and in practice that is probably what she has done.

Burwitz-Melzer (2003): The relationship between language teaching and culture teaching

The project is very valuable as a broadly-based investigation of intercultural learning processes in the classroom and has resulted in a task typology of literature pedagogy that has five phases: *1. The student and the foreign cultures*: Preparation, warm-up, with the aid of such activities as talking about objects, visual stimuli, book covers, etc.; *2. The student and the original text*: Reading, conversations and tasks such as text puzzles, characterisations, etc. (preparing shifts of perspective); *3. The student and the student text*: The students produce various types of play, parody, poem, etc. on the basis of the original text (perspective-taking); *4. The student, student texts and the other students*: Class conversations about various possible perspectives, e.g. from inside and outside (shifts of perspective and coordination of perspectives, e.g. comparison of perspectives); *5. Reflection*: Class conversation about the teaching content and about intercultural learning – meta-discussion of stereotypes and the significance of attempts to change perspectives. The title of the book, *Allmähliche Annäherungen* (Gradual Approaches), should mainly be understood as a reference to the potential of foreign-language teaching to get students to bring their originally outside perspective into the proximity of an inside perspective induced by experiencing the text.

In the teaching sequences there was relatively close integration between language teaching and culture teaching in the sense that it is constantly noted how one can see in the students' use of language what perspective they are speaking from: the use of personal pronouns, stylistic level, etc. – and these things are also discussed in class. Burwitz-Melzer also feels it is acceptable for students to use their first language (or for minority students to use their second language) if they need to, in order to clarify their experiences and understandings.

If this is compared with Roberts *et al.* (2001), it can be seen at once that the overall aims are the same: it is a question of coming into contact with other ways of living, other ways of thinking. But where Roberts *et al.* emphasise independent experience and interaction in the local contexts where the target language is used, Burwitz-Melzer emphasises the experience of foreignness via fictional texts in the classroom. This also has something to do with the very different teaching levels involved here: university students in the first instance, young school pupils in the other.

In *Belgium*, Lies Sercu has been active within the development of teacher-education courses and has also carried out a project on intercultural learning, looking in particular at Flemish students' relation to Germany and Germans and at the potential of German textbooks with regard to the students' development of intercultural communicative competence (Sercu, 2000). Furthermore, she has spearheaded an international empirical research project which, via a coordinated questionnaire survey (in 2001), seeks to define an average profile of the foreign-language teacher with regard to the conception of the cultural dimension of foreign-language teaching and of the concept of intercultural competence. The survey involved teachers in Belgium, Bulgaria, Poland, Greece, Spain and Sweden, and also Mexico. The project is reported on in Sercu *et al.* (2005). In respect of the national, this project clearly belongs to the national paradigm, insofar as it deals with national comparison.

In *Sweden*, there have been a number research projects on intercultural understanding in school English teaching and on internationalisation: Lundgren (2001), Gagnestam (2003), Tornberg (2000) and Brodow (2005). In *Portugal*, Manuela Guilherme has dealt with critical cultural awareness and the development of the critical citizen, which I intend to look at in more detail next.

Guilherme: *Critical Citizens for an Intercultural World* (2002): Presentation

Manuela Guilherme works within the subject of English in Portugal and has carried out a major empirical investigation of Portuguese language teachers' understanding of the concept of critical cultural awareness (the central component in Byram's model of intercultural communicative competence, see Chapter 5). In connection with this project, she has carried out a thorough and interesting discussion of the concept of citizenship from a social scientific and pedagogical point of view. What does it mean to develop a critical citizenship in an intercultural world? Guilherme represents, then, the most socially-oriented wing of culture pedagogy, as she takes as her starting point the humanities and social sciences, with considerable emphasis on political and moral education, as do Melde and Starkey.

Guilherme (2002): The relationship between language and culture

The book does not have a linguistic background – and language is in fact not present at all in the argumentation. The point of departure for the whole project is of course foreign-language teaching, specifically English, but the actual language is out of sight and (therefore) insufficiently dealt with from a theoretical point of view. At the same time, the view of culture is well-theorised and presented, and it is clear that Guilherme represents a postnational and transnational understanding of language and culture. She wishes, along with the American critical educationalist Henry Giroux, to 'explore the potential for the improvement of our societies and for the development of a new ethics that suits the fabric of our multicultural and transnational communities' (Guilherme, 2002: 34). Elsewhere she says:

> Postmodern concepts of identity [...] attempt to respond to postnational, multicultural societies, racial and ethnic hybridity, improved longevity, and social movements that enhance the legitimacy of beliefs of each possibility. (Guilherme, 2002: 44)

When language is mentioned, it is practically always in collocation with culture, i.e. as part of the expression 'language/culture'. She talks about 'foreign languages/cultures', 'foreign language/culture learning', 'foreign language/culture education' and 'foreign language/culture educators'. In other words, for each language there is a corresponding culture. It would seem as if we are dealing here with a traditional structuralist concept of language and, at the same time, an identification of language and culture.

It is also striking that Guilherme does not mention that societies apart from being multicultural can also be multilingual, and that apart from thinking about critical cultural awareness it is possible to think of critical language awareness (as, for example, in Fairclough, 1989 and 1992b or Schieffelin *et al.*, 1998).

While Guilherme, then, would thus appear on the one hand to stand for a structuralist concept of language and a reductionist, language-derived understanding of culture, she formulates on the other hand a postmodern (language-independent) conception of culture that focuses on the relationship between knowledge and power and on processes that create antagonisms, differences, diversity, hybridity and border-crossing. In this respect, her view of the relationship between language and culture can be compared with that of Burwitz-Melzer (and Zarate in many of her recent writings).

Guilherme (2002): The relationship between language teaching and culture teaching

As Guilherme is not interested in language as such, she does not come up with any proposals either as to language pedagogy measures, or reflect on the relationship between language and culture learning or teaching. There are, however, some exciting (though also highly ambitious) proposals as to how it is possible to develop an interdisciplinary approach to promoting critical citizenship. Such teaching must constantly seek to provide students with resources for reflection, wondering, criticism and hope, and awaken their commitment to transformative action and border crossing. The teacher is invited to gain on-going inspiration from Human Rights Education and Education for Democratic Citizenship (here Guilherme refers to Hugh Starkey, see Chapter 5), and to draw in particular on three broad subject-areas: Cultural Studies, critical pedagogy and intercultural communication (in the sense intercultural training or sensitising).

Guilherme's discussion of critical social philosophy (the Frankfurt School, Habermas) and critical pedagogy (Giroux, Freire) from a historical point of view is new in culture pedagogy and highly conducive to an understanding of the component that Byram calls 'critical cultural aware-ness and political education' (Byram, 1997a) and that has not been devel-oped all that much there.[8] She does not discuss what types of text could be used in language teaching and therefore it is impossible to know to what extent and in what way she would include fictional texts, as Burwitz-Melzer does.

In *Denmark*, a network has been set up for foreign-language subjects at higher-education level (Network for Language and Culture, 2002–2005). The aim of the network was to redefine modern language studies in the light of globalisation and the network's activities have resulted in a number of anthologies, including Hansen (2002), Hansen (2004), and Andersen, Lund and Risager (2006). During the same period, I have been active in establishing a new study and research environment for an MA on the subject of Cultural Encounters (Roskilde University), and have written Risager (2003). I will now give an account of this book on the same scale as the others (although I will refer to myself in the first person), after which in the following chapters I will go into slightly greater depth about my model for the relationship between language and culture (Chapter 7) and what it means for language and culture pedagogy (Chapters 8–9).

Risager: *Det nationale dilemma i sprog- og kulturpædagogikken. Et studie i forholdet mellem sprog og kultur* (The National Dilemma in Language and Culture Pedagogy. A Study of the Relationship between Language and Culture) (2003): Presentation

This book[9] came about as a reaction to two things: firstly, the far too low level of problematisation of what I refer to as the national paradigm – or what Billig has chosen to call banal nationalism (cf. Chapter 1) – in language and culture pedagogy, not only in the wording of official syllabuses and the discourse of ordinary teachers on culture but also to a great extent in the theoretical culture pedagogy discourse; and secondly, the prevailing identification of language and culture in language and culture pedagogy and in most of linguistics in general (as well as in the popular debate in society). This is an identification that implies that there is no 'culture' that is not 'language' – an absurd idea which is synonymous with denying the value of much of the research work that is taking place within the humanities and social sciences, e.g. in relation to Cultural Studies.

The basis for work on the book was partly my own experiences in developing syllabuses for foreign languages in curricula for the Danish Folkeskole (this was in the period 1993–95), and partly my experiences from an international project on language teachers, which I carried out together with Michael Byram and a number of other colleagues in 1992–97 (Byram & Risager, 1999). It all began with the rather banal experience that when, for example, a Danish teacher of French takes part in a study trip to Spain with his/her French class, the teacher has to function as a 'culture teacher' in respect of Spanish relations and not French ones – even though the French language has been used before, during and after the stay.

This led me to consider what internationalisation implies and can imply if one abandons the national paradigm (which identifies the national language with the national culture) and focuses instead on all sorts of transnational movements, processes and structures. I am not the only person who thinks that the relationship between language and culture is complex. But no one has tried to investigate *the structure of this complexity* to the extent that I have in this book, and also considered what this means for the identity of modern language studies.

Risager (2003): The relationship between language and culture

The underlying idea concerning the relationship between language and culture is that languages spread across cultures and cultures spread across languages (with reference to Hannerz's theory of cultural flows, see Chapter 1). At the same time, I attempt to neutralise the language/culture dualism by introducing certain concepts in the interface between language and culture: partly the concept of languaculture (with reference to Agar), partly the concept of discourse (with reference to Fairclough). This results in four types of practice that are enacted or 'flow' in relation to each other:

- language;
- languaculture;
- discourse;
- other forms of culture (which are complex, but not analysed by me).

Very briefly, it can be said that in my view linguistic practice in a particular language spreads via social networks of major or minor proportions throughout the world via various forms of migration, and that linguistic practice is accompanied by languaculture. When I travel about the world, I take my Danish language (my Danish idiolect) with me, including my Danish languaculture, i.e. my personal way of using the Danish language – pragmatically and semantically. I travel around in many different cultural contexts (different countries) and my Danish languaculture (as, for example, it finds expression in my use of English) spreads to other contexts than the Danish one. I come into contact with many different discourses and subjects that have diverse origins and that circulate around the world from one language community to the next (or from one linguistic network to the next) via translations and other transformations. Take a single example: discourses about terrorism spread from one language community to the next. I can talk about terrorism everywhere, using the languages that happen to be possible in the context. But linguistic practice is never culturally neutral: there are always *languacultures* involved – various ways of using language, pragmatically and semantically. My use of English, for example, displays a blend of Danish and English languaculture. My connotations for such a word as 'empire' will differ from that of most English people.

I place emphasis on describing languages in the world as practices that are spread via major or minor networks, local, national, continental and global. Even a 'small' language like Danish[10] is spoken by people spread all over the world (as a first language, second language, foreign language, community/heritage language), and something similar applies to a large number of the world's other languages because of the diverse flows of migration. To learn a language such as, for example, Danish is synonymous with gaining access to a more or less global network.

Risager (2003): The relationship between language teaching and culture teaching

On this basis, the traditional conception that attention must be directed towards how native speakers use the language in the native context in one of the countries where the language is spoken begins to crumble, as does the idea that texts and other media must be focused on present cultural and social conditions in these countries. Many other contexts, discourses and topics can be involved.

The question of the choice of cultural contexts (where in the world?) and cultural content (about which topics?) thus becomes a *pedagogical-political question*, not one that depends on the 'nature of the language'. We gain much greater freedom to organise language teaching, including now the concrete experiences and interests of the participants in relation to different parts of the world and different topics. At the centre is work on the language and its varying languaculture, and it must not be forgotten, of course, that the languaculture comes from a historical accumulation in, primarily, *first-language contexts*. These must be given their place in teaching, but they do not have to reign supreme.

Outside Europe and the USA in the Years after 2000

Among the many activities taking place around the world,[11] I would like to mention the new interest in the field in *Australia*: Lo Bianco, Liddicoat and Crozet (1999); Papademetre with Scarino (2000); Liddicoat and Crozet (2000); Lo Bianco and Crozet (2003), and Lo Bianco (2004). There are as yet no monographs to consider, but I would like here to discuss an article by two of the representatives, namely Crozet and Liddicoat (2000).

Crozet and Liddicoat: *Teaching culture as an integrated part of language* (2000): Presentation

Chantal Crozet and Anthony J. Liddicoat are Australian language educationists who, since the mid-1990s, have been involved in developing language teaching in a cultural direction. The article I mention here has as its subtitle '*Implications for the aims, approaches and pedagogies of language teaching*', and it is the introductory article in an anthology with the title *Teaching Languages, Teaching Cultures* (Liddicoat & Crozet, 2000). This anthology claims to describe 'an emerging new approach to language teaching', i.e. Intercultural Language Teaching (ILT) (Crozet & Liddicoat, 2000: 1).

The writers adopt a linguistic point of departure, referring to the various linguistic trends over the past 10–15 years that have dealt with 'how communication works across cultures': intercultural pragmatics, discourse-analysis approaches to intercultural communication, culture-oriented ethno-methodological conversation analysis, and cultural semantics (names such as Blum-Kulka, House, Kasper, J. Thomas, Brown, Levinson, Scollon and Scollon, Moermann, Wierzbicka etc.). Their goal is to 'see culture as integrated at all levels of language' (Crozet & Liddicoat, 2000: 15), cf. Brøgger's programme described from a different position, Chapter 5.

Crozet and Liddicoat represent an intercultural pragmalinguistic approach, but gain inspiration as well from Kramsch's post-structuralist and social constructivist approach. There are also references to Byram and Zarate, without this however playing any particular role in their concrete conceptions about culture teaching. For Crozet and Liddicoat (2000) has a weakly-based conception of culture.

Crozet and Liddicoat (2000): The relationship between language and culture

The concept of culture in Crozet and Liddicoat is heterogeneous and conflicting. They define culture in this way:

> Culture is a concept referring to ways of acting, believing, valuing and thinking which are shared by members of a community (social group) and which are transmitted to the next generation. A culture is dynamic and open to change as a result of a change in living conditions or through contact with other cultures. (Crozet & Liddicoat, 2000: 22)

The first part of the definition contains a traditional and holistic conception of culture, one that can be found in most of earlier American cultural anthropology (Kroeber & Kluckhohn, 1952, among others). The second part draws on a more recent discourse about a dynamic and contextual concept of culture – one that nevertheless is still understood from an essentialist point of view (a culture, other cultures). The first conception of culture is used at many points in the text by the writers, e.g. '…both learners' first and target cultures … put under scrutiny in the language class so as to make visible the differences which can potentially prevent the two cultures from relating successfully' (Crozet & Liddicoat, 2000: 3). On the other hand, they also stress that: 'culture is not a static, monolithic construct. It is dynamic and both creates and is created by every attempt to communicate' (Crozet & Liddicoat, 2000: 5).

Crozet and Liddicoat are much less specific when it comes to the relationship between language and culture. They say that there is an 'inextricable link between language and culture' (Crozet & Liddicoat, 2000: 13). As their title indicates, they believe that culture (among other things?) can be described as making up part of language, and they also use the expression 'culture-in-language'.[12] At the same time, they say that the conception of 'the language/culture nexus' has changed, so that people are now aware that all language use is cultural action – here they refer to Kramsch. In doing so, they have at this point introduced a conflicting image: how can 'culture' be part of 'language' at the same time as linguistic practice *is* always cultural practice?

In passing, the authors also introduce the concepts of globalisation and lingua franca, but without explaining their possible relevance for an understanding of the relationship between language and culture.

Crozet and Liddicoat (2000): The relationship between language teaching and culture teaching

The authors see their approach as an extension of the communicative approach. They claim that: 'culture must be taught in conjunction with language, not as an adjunct' (Crozet & Liddicoat, 2000: 14), and since they believe that linguistic practice always contains (or is?) cultural practice, they feel that language teaching must be related to culture from the very first lessons. As they mainly refer to intercultural pragmatics, the emphasis is on oral language use, and they are more production-oriented and less reception-oriented than, for example, Kramsch and Brøgger.

The aim of teaching is what they call intercultural communicative competence. But it is important to note that this concept has for them a completely different content from the one it has for Byram and Zarate. Whereas the latter work with a comprehensive concept that, apart from communicative linguistic competence, contains both knowledge about culture and society, attitudes to culture and society, and non-linguistic skills as well as political awareness and a critical cultural awareness, Crozet and Liddicoat's concept is reduced to a pragmalinguistic understanding. Intercultural communicative competence for them is the ability to communicate using language with other people and to be able to do so in a culture-sensitive way, taking as much account as possible of the cultural differences that can be predicted in the situation. So intercultural communicative competence is the ability to use language 'in culturally appropriate ways' (Crozet & Liddicoat, 2000: 3).

That emphasis is placed on the ability to use language in a culture-sensitive way is, of course, positive from my point of view – assuming that an essentialist understanding of culture is not being used. But the actual idea of an intercultural pragmatic approach is not new in language pedagogy. It has been formulated by many other writers, not least by Müller-Jacquier since the late 1980s (*Interkulturelle Didaktik*, cf. Chapter 5).

What is new is Crozet and Liddicoat's ambition to call this approach *the* new paradigm in language and culture pedagogy. This, however, I find unfortunate, for Crozet and Liddicoat have a much narrower focus in relation to most previous culture pedagogy. They know of some of this, for they refer to Byram and Zarate, and to Kramsch. While they have partially been inspired by Kramsch, they make practically no use of Byram and Zarate, and this reveals that they are not at all interested in the content dimension at text level. They are taken up with cultural differences in the use of language but not with the cultural representations that are created in connection with language teaching. This means that they actually represent a reductionist understanding of the cultural side of teaching. There is a wide gap between their pragmatic approach and (particularly) European approaches that emphasise critical insight into cultural and social conditions, such as those of Melde, Baumgratz, Byram, Zarate, Starkey, Burwitz-Melzer, Guilherme and myself.

Conclusion

An upgrading of interdisciplinary discourse has taken place in culture pedagogy in recent years. It could be said that a transition has taken place from an eclectic interdisciplinarity, as in Erdmenger/Istel and Fichou, to a focused, theoretically aware interdisciplinarity where the theoretical basis comes mainly from one or a few theorists. Examples of this are: Morgan/Cain (Bakhtin, Kress and Hodge); Roberts *et al.* (Gumperz, Agar); Guilherme (Giroux); and Risager (Hannerz, Le Page/Tabouret-Keller, Agar). An early representative is Melde (1987) (Habermas).

Among the five representatives discussed above there are three that adopt a linguistic point of departure and two that have the humanities as their point of departure:

Point of departure in linguistics:
- Roberts *et al.*: a sociolinguistic, ethnographic approach.
- Risager: a sociolinguistic, anthropological approach (world studies).
- Crozet and Liddicoat: a communicative, pragmatic, interculturally oriented approach.

Point of departure in the humanities and/or the social sciences:
- Burwitz-Melzer: a literary, interculturally oriented approach.
- Guilherme: a pedagogical, politically oriented approach.

Guilherme focuses in particular on the *content dimension*: what issues should be addressed in teaching in order to attain intercultural competence as a critical world citizen? I also focus to a certain extent on the content dimension in connection with a similar pedagogical interest in developing students as critical world citizens. Burwitz-Melzer also stresses the importance of the content dimension and textual thematic, but her main focus is on the potential of the texts to bring about a change of perspective in the students.

I am also interested in the *context dimension*, as I emphasise that the target language must be seen as a language that can potentially be used throughout the world and in all cultural contexts. I am speaking here of macro-contexts. Roberts *et al.* focus on the context dimension, as they are interested in helping students learn to use the language well and effectively in various situations in which they function as 'ethnographers'. But they also include the content dimension, since it is important for them what images of local life the students construct on the basis of the surveys they carry out. Crozet and Liddicoat are interested only in the context dimension (at the micro-level), not in the thematic content and the reflections this might produce.

Burwitz-Melzer focuses on the *poetic dimension* of language insofar as she deals with fictional texts and their semantic universes with regard to content, genre and style. I also find room for the poetic dimension in my theory, but do not develop it all that much. I do feel, however, that it is important to incorporate work on fiction into language teaching.

The predominant view in culture pedagogy of the relationship between language and culture is still that they are inextricably linked and can be lumped together in a synthetic expression à la language/culture. This is probably a result of resistance to the idea of language being an autonomous, culturally neutral entity – a view found in certain more formally oriented sections of linguistics as well as in the public debate, e.g. concerned with internationalisation and the automatic introduction of English, which is seen as a general, culturally neutral tool. But by retaining the rigid expressions 'language-and-culture', 'language/culture' and 'culture-in-language', no examination is carried out of what actually 'hangs together', and how.

Real changes are taking place with regard to the national paradigm. Both Roberts *et al.* and Guilherme (and myself) clearly disassociate themselves from banal nationalism, but in slightly different ways. Roberts *et al.* stress the localisation that lies in ethnographical work; Guilherme refers somewhat indistinctly to the postnational and the transnational as characteristic features of postmodern society. Burwitz-Melzer stresses the dangers of national stereotype-casting, while I directly thematise the transition between the national and the transnational in my work. Crozet and Liddicoat, who belong to a linguistic, pragmatic tradition, do not criticise the national paradigm or tendencies to reify language in certain ethnic communities.

The Diversity of Culture Pedagogy

In Chapters 2–6, I have attempted to provide an overview of culture-pedagogy discourse via an analysis of the international history of theoretical culture pedagogy. This overview has been structured in relation to 17 main positions in culture pedagogy, which are summarised in Figure 6.1.

That there should be precisely 17 positions is, of course, the result of an estimate. A few more positions or fewer could have been chosen. The most important thing for me has been to identify a number of clearly diverging conceptualisations of the relationship between language and culture and thereby also of the relationship between language teaching and culture teaching.

As can be seen from Figure 6.1, the main positions are placed partly in relation to the chronological sequence and partly in relation to the scientific point of departure. At the linguistic end (left) we have positions that have a linguistic foundation and look across towards the (other) humanities and social sciences. Under the humanities and social sciences (middle and right) we have positions that – still based on the language subjects – have a theory of culture or society as their point of departure, or a combination of theories, and on this theoretical basis consider and develop the language subjects. Byram, Roberts *et al.* and Kramsch, and to a certain extent Brøgger, are among those who have best been able to integrate points of view from *both* linguistics and the humanities/social sciences.

As mentioned, culture pedagogy started as a discipline that was interested in the *content* of language teaching: at text level and/or at word level, lexically and semantically. This applies to all the main positions in the 1970s and 1980s. But in the 1990s and up to the present day an interest has emerged in the context dimension and the poetic dimension. This has resulted in culture pedagogy acquiring a very large range – and it has become increasingly clear that a struggle is taking place over which academic approach is to characterise culture pedagogy: should it be anthropological, sociological, psychological, politological, pedagogical, linguistic, literary-historical, or Cultural Studies?

In this diversity, I believe it is possible to identify a basic conflict between those who support the idea that culture pedagogy is basically a linguistic discipline – an extension of language pedagogy (such as Galisson, Crozet and Liddicoat, and to a certain extent Kramsch) – and those who support the idea that culture pedagogy is an interdisciplinary field in which approaches from linguistics/language pedagogy are integrated with approaches that come from (the rest of) cultural and social sciences.

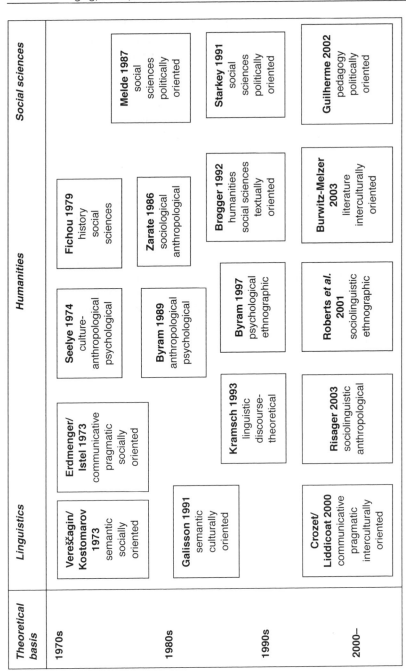

Figure 6.1 Culture pedagogy: 17 characteristic positions since the 1970s

The first group tend to believe that language teaching has *one goal*: work on the language, which in itself is cultural. The other group tend to believe that language teaching has at any rate *two integrated goals*: work on the language and something else, which can be defined as insight into cultural and social conditions, or critical cultural awareness, or understanding the other – a view of language teaching which also, by the way, makes it easier to link language teaching with other subjects in interdisciplinary cooperation. As must be obvious by now, I belong to the second group.

Since the positions stretch back to the 1970s, not all of them are still topical. But it is important to retain a knowledge of the underlying history, one that has never been fully described before. One of the reasons why it is important to know about the history of culture pedagogy is that there are signs indicating that English-language research literature in the area is beginning to become the only source of reference, the only thing that even specialists around the world know of, because of the dominant position English now has as an academic language. The German-language tradition – and partly also the French-language tradition – are in danger of being forgotten or neglected. This would be a setback for the field, for these traditions contain elements – especially social and critical ones – that are not necessarily reflected in the British, American and Australian culture pedagogy. I would even go so far as to say that, if one wants to stay updated on the discussion about culture pedagogy today, one must be able to read not only English but German as well. Even today, the culture-pedagogy debate in Germany is more substantial than in any other country.

Language, culture and nation in the history of culture pedagogy

Throughout the entire history of culture pedagogy since the 1960s, there has been the message that the idea of the autonomy of language ought to be combated. This message has underlined the link between language and society/culture and demanded that teaching language and teaching society/culture should be integrated with each other in language teaching. This emphasis has functioned as a necessary legitimisation of the actual development of culture pedagogy as an academic discipline. But the message – particularly in the 1980s – has been based on an essentialist language-culture duality, as can clearly be seen, for example, in the marriage metaphor for language and culture (Chapter 4). The duality can also be seen in the still-used coordinating links that join together language and culture to form one word: language-and-culture, *langue-culture*, etc. Kramsch resists this duality (dichotomy), but in my opinion does not put anything else in its place that is fully satisfying. Byram also takes it to task in various passages, but does not put anything in its place either. A few other warning voices can be heard: Porcher, Benadava (Chapter 5) and Widdowson (1988). But, apart from that, the hypothesis – or rather the axiom – of the language-culture duality seems to live an unnoticed, uncontested life as a common-sense idea. Because of this, sections of theoretical culture pedagogy continue to supply the scientific justification for reproducing this language-culture duality in syllabuses and practical teaching in the classroom.

The hypothesis of the close connection between language and culture has a radical and a moderate form. The radical form directly claims there is an identity between language and culture, e.g. in the form of the slogan 'culture is language, and language is culture' (and taken out of context this statement can be understood at both the differential and the generic level).[13] The radical hypothesis is not one we need today. We no longer need a firm legitimisation of the idea that language teaching must have a cultural dimension, for it is generally accepted that it must (however differently this is understood). The moderate hypothesis must content itself with claiming that there is a close connection, an interdependence, a complex relationship between language and culture (at the differential level). This hypothesis, despite its lack of clarity, is difficult to refute: there *are* of course connections between language and culture at the differential level, and very few people would deny that the relationship between language and culture is complex. In other words, there is always an alibi in the moderate hypothesis. If necessary, it also contains a possibility of carrying out a tactical retreat to the generic level, where 'language in general' and 'culture in general' will always be inseparable. In order to move on, culture pedagogy must try to create greater clarity about what it means to say that there is a complex relationship between language and culture.

Culture pedagogy between modernism and postmodernism

The history of culture pedagogy can be interpreted as a struggle between modernism and postmodernism.[14] What I will call the modernist identity was predominant until some time in the 1980s and has to do with an emphasis on the content dimension. Typical of it is that it stresses the knowledge-related result of culture teaching: as cohesive a knowledge as possible of cultural and social conditions in the target-language country or countries. The objective overview is given high priority, the realistic and all-round picture of culture and society. This understanding of culture pedagogy has gradually found expression in the cultural representations to be found in textbooks for beginners and continuers: they were modelled more or less systematically as a 'panorama' of society, as a reproduction of 'society in a nutshell' (for a discussion of this, see Risager, 1999a).

From the 1980s onwards, a postmodernist tendency was added that gradually came to dominate culture pedagogy, though without completely ousting the older view. The postmodernist tendency typically emphasises learning processes and learning strategies. It focuses on diversity in the individual students' qualifications and experiences, their attitudes and emotions, their ability to understand and deal with 'the other'. It stresses the affective dimension rather than the cognitive. The various intercultural approaches that gained ground and became predominant in the 1990s are exponents of the postmodernist tendency. The interest in the poetic dimension and narrativity are also part of this development: playing with language, working with cultural imagination, as Kramsch says. But there are still modernist features in culture-pedagogy discourse, in textbooks and official syllabuses, for example.

The postmodernist shift of perspective in culture pedagogy was/is naturally only part of a broader change in learning theory within education and in society in general. It has been necessary in order for people to understand what learning processes were required for students to develop their ability to deal with cultural differences (their 'intercultural competence'). But I believe it is important – within the framework of the postmodernist focusing on learning processes – to maintain and develop the knowledge dimension, the content dimension. It is important for cultural learning in language teaching to have a content-oriented side, a motivated educational focus. So I feel there is a need for a new educative ideal in language subjects – one that can accommodate a transnational understanding of language and culture and which aims to help cultivate world citizens. This could be formulated as a revitalisation of modernism within postmodernism in culture pedagogy.

Notes

1. See also Chapter 3 of this book.
2. Cf. Byram and Risager (1999), which deals with similar issues in the European context in the 1990s.
3. ACTFL: www.actfl.org/i4a/pages/Index.cfm?pageID=4249.
4. John Corbett ought also to be named. He has developed Byram's cultural studies approach and his model for intercultural communicative competence in English teaching, including teaching outside the public sector (Corbett, 2003).
5. Burwitz-Melzer's book has been chosen because it explicitly positions itself in relation to the culture-pedagogical tradition (Byram, Kramsch, the Council of

Europe's language projects, etc. This Bredella und Burwitz-Melzer (2004) does not – it refers to a more unambiguous literary theoretical and literary pedagogical tradition.

6. A presentation in English is to be found in Burwitz-Melzer (2001).

7. In Risager (1998), I distinguish between four approaches in culture pedagogy: the foreign-cultural, the intercultural, the multicultural, and the transcultural approach. The foreign-cultural approach focuses solely on the target-language country; the intercultural approach focuses on both the target-language country and the students' own country; the multicultural approach deals with both countries as multicultural and is interested in questions of majority and minority; and the transcultural approach focuses on cross-border processes such as transnational migration and transnational media.

8. She has also, together with Alison Phipps, edited an anthology that has critical pedagogy and language education as its theme (Phipps & Guilherme, 2004).

9. The section of the book that deals with the relationship between language and culture has been published in English: Risager (2006). The section of the book that deals with culture pedagogy and transnational language and culture pedagogy has been edited as the present book.

10. In fact, Danish is among the large languages. With its approx. five million speakers it ranks no. 68 among the world's approx. 6000 languages.

11. I would also like to mention the work of Hideo Hosokawa (Waseda University) on an individually oriented concept of culture in Japanese language education (Hosokawa n.d.)

12. In the same anthology, Papademetre uses both the expressions 'culture-in-language' and 'language-in-culture', 'culture-and-language' and 'language-and-culture', but without explaining whether there are any differences in meaning intended by the use of the different expressions (Papademetre, 2000).

13. It depends, however, on which language is used here. In English and German, both the differential and the generic interpretation are possible in 'language and culture' / *'Sprache und Kultur'*. In French, on the other hand, a distinction can be drawn between the differential: *langue et culture* and the generic: *langage et culture*.

14. It is normal to distinguish between three different dimensions of the discussion about the modern and the postmodern (cf., for example, Best & Kellner, 1991): 1. A social-scientific discussion concerning 'modernity' and 'postmodernity' (modernity theory), which is a discussion of what basically characterises the present historical epoch. 2. An aesthetical discussion concerning 'modernism' and 'postmodernism', which is a discussion of developments in – and across – various art forms. 3. A philosophical discussion concerning 'modern and postmodern epistemology', which is a discussion of issues in relation to knowledge, rationality and subjectivity. In my text, however, I do not use 'modernism' and 'postmodernism' as aesthetical but as pedagogical concepts.

Chapter 7

Language and Culture:
The Structure of the Complexity

Introduction

In this chapter I will give an overview of the most important concepts in my theoretical model of the relationship between language and culture. It will indicate – as the title of the chapter says – *the structure of the complexity*, a proposal of how the relationship between language and culture can be analysed in an internationalised and globalised world where it is becoming increasingly obvious that the national framework of reference is unsatisfactory and confining.

Conceptions of the relationship between language and culture can be positioned between two extremes: on the one hand, it is possible to see a language as being closely linked to its culture; on the other hand, it can be seen as a communication tool that does not have anything to do with culture. English when taught as an international language or lingua franca is often thought of in this latter way.

But neither of these conceptions is satisfactory. The former is all too easily associated with the idea of a closed universe of language, people, culture and history – a view inherited from the strong national-romantic current in Europe and elsewhere since the late 18th century. This idea cannot be reconciled with today's world, characterised as it is by many kinds of transnational process at many levels. The latter conception is not far removed from the classic structuralist idea of language as an autonomous structure or system. This idea is not satisfactory either, as it denies the culture-bearing and culture-creating potential of human languages.

But how can a model of the relationship between language and culture be constructed that does not lock language into a national-romantic universe, or claim that language is culturally neutral?[1]

Linguistic Flows in Social Networks

The analysis of the relationship between language and culture must start with defining the view of language. What is language, and what is linguistic practice? Here I will begin by drawing on a sociolinguistic understanding of linguistic practice, mainly with reference to qualitative sociolinguistics such as Le Page and Tabouret-Keller (1985), Gumperz (1992) and Rampton (1995), who are interested in how linguistic interaction works within a social and cultural context and helps create and shape the identities of participants in an ongoing way. Language must initially be viewed as *linguistic practice in context*. This can be the spoken language, or it can be production and reception of the written language (or a combination of both). Linguistic practice unfolds in a range of communicative events. Examples could be linguistic practice in a teaching lesson that can be analysed as one or several communicative events, according to how cohesive the lesson is, whether anyone comes in and interrupts, etc.

But I want to look at linguistic practice in a larger context. That is why I draw on studies of *intertextuality*, as represented by such writers as Bakhtin (1981) and Fairclough (1992a). Fairclough, in connection with discourse analysis, recommends also looking at how texts (oral or written) are produced in an *intertextual chain*: consider, for example, an organisation where firstly a particular subject is talked about that is to be released to the public, then a draft of the text is made in a working group, then one person makes a cohesive text that is then corrected by some other people, then it is checked by management, and then sent to the press as a press release which is referred to in various sections of the press, followed by the reactions, after which it is passed on to an international news agency, etc., etc. There are numerous instances of intertextual chains in our daily lives.

The idea of intertextual chains can be linked to research in *social networks*. In the social sciences there is considerable research into social networks, e.g. that done by the aforementioned social anthropologist Ulf Hannerz (cf. Chapter 1) (Hannerz, 1992a and 1992b). Social network theory deals with how forms of social interaction, norms and values spread in a society along lines where one person knows or has contact with other people, who in turn know others, etc., in an infinite chain. Social network theory deals with both interpersonal interaction and interaction between organisations and institutions at the macro-level.

Linguistic practice also spreads in social networks (cf. Milroy, 1980). A language such as French spreads not only in people's everyday lives but also in larger networks that potentially can cover most of the world. Apart from in the Francophone countries, French is used in practically every country and region of the world, by tourists, students, business people, diplomats, doctors, engineers, journalists, researchers, etc. The French language, i.e. people who use French, spreads across all possible cultural contexts and discourse communities. Seen from such a point of view, French is a 'world language', not only because of the number of its users but precisely because of its extent. French speakers over the whole world can communicate with each other via cell phones, e-mail, etc.

The same can be said about many other languages in the world, so that a picture emerges of a world where languages are intermixed and where innumerable language-contact situations arise. All societies are more or less multilingual – it is probable that over 100 languages are spoken in Denmark, for example.

When I talk about language users, I mean all those who speak the language, whether this is as a first language, second language or foreign language. To learn a new language is to contribute to the spreading of the language to new users – so all language teaching is an activity that is part of the continuous formation and reformation of the global network of the target language.

Since languages are not bound by territory, the concept of 'language area', e.g. the French-speaking language area, the Russian-speaking language area, etc. is problematic. Naturally, the Polish-speaking network, for example, is particularly close-meshed within the territory of the Polish state, but the Polish language, like many other languages, extends throughout the world. States have borders, but languages do not.

Linguistic practice, linguistic resources and the linguistic system

Until now, I have been focusing on linguistic practice. But this is only one of the existential loci (or ontologies) of language. One has to distinguish between three loci of language (Figure 7.1).

Linguistic practice is, as mentioned, oral and written interaction in situations knit together in ever-changing social networks, including the production and reception of literature. Linguistic practice also includes paralanguage and kinesics (or non-verbal communication accompanying verbal practice). We are dealing with processes that take place between people in real time. This is a *sociological* perspective on language; we are talking about language in society. It is important to emphasise the

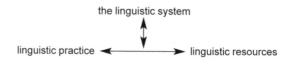

Figure 7.1   The three loci of language

transnational linguistic flows in the world that derive from the migration of language users and the communication potential that exists in transnational media.

Linguistic resources are carried by the individual subjects. They are the socially constituted knowledge of language, developed as part of the biography of the subject. In this connection, I would first and foremost refer to the sociocultural tradition represented by Vygotsky, who focuses on how the development of a person as a social and cultural being takes place via the acquisition of language as a tool for thinking and acting. That is why I would also include private and inner speech in the concept of language. This is a *psychological* perspective on language. With Hannerz (1992a) it is possible to distinguish between an external locus for language, which is linguistic practice, and an internal locus for language, which are the linguistic resources. These linguistic resources can also be considered in *transnational* terms if transnational biographies are focused on.

These two loci of language presuppose each other: linguistic practice cannot be produced and received without linguistic resources carried by individual people, and the linguistic resources of the individual cannot be developed without the experience of linguistic practice. It is necessary to have this double – sociological and psychological – perspective on language in order to understand the dialectic between the sociogenetic history of language (the history of its spread and change in society) and the ontogenetic history of language (the process of linguistic development in the individual subject as part of his or her sociocultural biography).

Whereas these two loci of language are both natural and necessary, the idea of 'the linguistic system' is not. We have to deconstruct the idea that there is a language 'out there' that we can use and study as a natural object. 'The linguistic system' is a construct or, in other words, a family of historically and discursively constructed notions ('English', 'French' etc.). At the same time it is important to note that this construct has consequences for linguistic practice and linguistic resources. The idea of the linguistic system interacts with both linguistic practice and linguistic resources, being a kind of – more or less conscious – normative factor (Cameron, 1995).

To understand the complex relationship between language and culture it is important to distinguish between *three perspectives*: a sociological and a psychological perspective, as just described, and a system-oriented perspective that focuses on 'language' as a discursive construction. The relationship between language and culture looks very different according to whether the first, second or third perspective is adopted.

Languaculture

In the above presentation of the loci of language I have had language as social practice in time and space as my point of departure. I have described a *social* view of language. Now I intend to describe a *cultural* view of language (cf. Risager, 2004). I understand culture here as *meaning*, as does Hannerz (1992a). So I will look at language as *cultural* practice, as a carrier of various types of meaning, and the intention is to argue that language is never languaculturally neutral. Linguistic practice carries and creates meaning, no matter where in the world it is used and by whom. This means, for example, that linguistic practice in French is cultural, no matter whether it takes place in France or in Sweden, and no matter whether the speaker uses French as a first language, second language or foreign language.

In order to theorise the cultural dimensions of language, I have found it fruitful to build further on the concept of languaculture, developed by the American linguistic anthropologist Michael Agar in his book from 1994.[2] In this book, languaculture is a concept that covers *language plus culture*, and Agar is especially interested in the variability of languaculture in verbal interaction, both among different native users of the same language, and among people who use the language as a first or a foreign language. Agar focuses on the semantic and pragmatic variability of linguistic practice, and invites the reader to explore 'rich points' in inter-cultural communication, i.e. examine points where communication has gone wrong.

Agar uses the concept of languaculture in order to theorise the single universe of language and culture. But that is, I think, just a continuation of the traditional romantic idea of language and culture mentioned earlier. To me it seems obvious that there are lots of cultural phenomena that are not bound to any specific language, such as foods, musical traditions or architectural styles. There may of course be lots of historical links between such cultural phenomena and the language in question, but the point is that the phenomena don't necessarily follow the same routes as the language does when language users migrate across the world. I would prefer to say that language users spread in social networks *across* cultural contexts and discourse communities, but they carry languaculture with them.[3]

Three dimensions of languaculture

The study of languaculture is the study of the various kinds of meaning carried and produced by language. I suggest that we distinguish between three dimensions of languaculture, corresponding to three well-known cultural perspectives on language:

- the semantic and pragmatic dimension;
- the poetic dimension;
- the identity dimension.

The semantic and pragmatic dimension is the dimension explored by Agar, and by many others interested in intercultural pragmatics and contrastive semantics. It has also been a long-standing focus of interest for linguistic anthropology, since Boas, Sapir and Whorf (and before them W. von Humboldt). This dimension is about constancy and variability in the semantics and pragmatics of specific languages. For example, the distinction between 'tu' and 'vous' is obligatory because of the structure of the French language, but in many cases the language user has a certain freedom to define the situation and thus choose strategically between 'tu' and 'vous'. Other instances where there will be a certain freedom to choose on a more personal basis could be the choice between 'red' and 'orange', or between 'hello' and 'how are you', etc. The boundary between which semantic-pragmatic distinctions are compulsory and which depend on social conditions and personal interpretations is not fixed but more or less open to negotiation.

The poetic dimension is especially related to the kinds of meaning created in the exploitation of the phonological and syllabic structure of the language in question, its rhymes, its relationships between speech and writing, genres etc. – areas that have for a long time interested literary theorists focusing on literary poetics, style, literariness and the like (cf. Jakobson, 1960).

The identity dimension is also called social meaning by some sociolinguists (for example Hymes). It is related to the social variation of the language in question: in using the language in a specific way, with a specific accent, for instance, you identify yourself and make it possible for others to identify you according to their background knowledge and attitudes. Linguistic practice is a continuing series of 'acts of identity' (Le Page & Tabouret-Keller, 1985) by which people project their own understanding of the world onto the interlocutors and consciously or unconsciously invite them to react. This dimension has been explored by those scholars within sociolinguistics and language and culture pedagogy who are interested in the relationship between language and identity (cf. Armour, 2000; Börsch, 1987; and Norton, 2000).[4]

As I have stressed above, languaculture is both structurally constrained and socially and personally variable. It is thus a bridge between the structure of the language and the socially constituted personal idiolect. The most interesting aspects of the concept may lie in the study of the personal side with a focus on individual semantic connotations and on the subject's language learning as a very personal process (though also structured) which is integrated in his/her life history as a speaker-hearer, a reader and a writer.

Languaculture in linguistic practice

When an utterance or a text is produced, languacultural intentions are laid down in it, intentions concerning how this utterance or text is going to function semantically and pragmatically in the communication situation. What speech acts are intended, what references are given to the context, what representations of the world are to be conjured up? These languacultural intentions are restricted or expanded during the conversation or the reception of the text. The addressees/the readers perceive and interpret the utterance or text according to their personal languacultures and their knowledge of the world. A dialogic process, a negotiation of meaning, is going on.

In situations where the language is used as a foreign language, there are many opportunities of adding even more variability than is the case with native-language use, since participants with other languages as their first languages tend to rely on languaculture (semantic connotations, etc.) stemming from their first languages or other languages they know well.

Languaculture in linguistic resources

The personal languaculture of the subject cannot be separated from his/her personal life history, socialisation and identity formation. The language-acquisition process is in any case socially differentiated, and all human beings develop their personal linguistic and cultural repertoires with which they express themselves and interpret the world. Therefore, language and culture are always different from individual to individual, characterised by a specific emotional and cognitive constitution, a specific perspective and a specific horizon of understanding. It is not possible to distinguish denotative and connotative dimensions of the personal languaculture. For example, the meaning of such notions as 'work' and 'leisure' may be quite different even within the same professional group or the same family.

What is the character of the relationship between language and culture when the language is a foreign language? A Chinese who is learning German, for instance, especially in the first stages of learning, must draw on his/her cultural and social experience related to the first language (most often a Chinese language). There are some semantic and pragmatic distinctions that are obligatory in using German, such as an appropriate distribution of 'du' and 'Sie'. But otherwise it will be natural to use the languaculture developed in relation to the first language (or other languages learnt). Personal connotations of words and phrases will be transferred, and a kind of language mixture will result, in which the foreign language is supplied with languacultural matter from another language (in this case Chinese, and possibly other languages learnt). From the learner's perspective, the alleged intimate association between German language and culture is a *normative* one, not a descriptive one. It is his/her task to establish an association, and this task has to be accomplished on the basis of a growing understanding of some of the associations and perspectives common among native speakers. But even when the learner reaches a high level of competence, his/her languaculture will always be the result of an accumulation of experiences during his/her specific life history.

Languaculture in the linguistic system

Since the linguistic system is a discursive construction, the description of languaculture in the linguistic system is a discursive construction too.[5] The description of languaculture in the linguistic system may be placed on a continuum ranging from a minimalist description of the semantic and pragmatic potential of relative constancy – the denotative core of the language – to a maximalist description in the form of a gigantic encyclopedia supplemented by a gigantic handbook of patterns of linguistic practice in specific situations. There are examples of descriptions of languaculture in the linguistic system, e.g. Summers (1992): *Longman Dictionary of English Language and Culture*, and André and Galisson (1999): *Dictionnaire des noms de marques courants: essai de lexiculture ordinaire* (Dictionary of Current Brand Names: An Essay on Ordinary Lexiculture) (cf. Chapter 4).

Discourse

Languaculture is related to one or more specific languages. But the cultural view of language should also embrace the concept of discourse.

The concept of discourse may be used as an intermediary concept between the concepts of language/languaculture and the more general concept of culture. I refer to the thinking on discourse as (for example) represented by Fairclough (1992a) and other proponents of critical discourse analysis (Wodak, Jäger, van Dijk). Discourse, and discourses, are primarily defined relative to their content: a discourse deals with a certain subject matter from a certain perspective. It is primarily verbally formed, but may be accompanied by (for instance) visual material.

Discourses may spread across languages. For example, a discourse on Christianity is not bound to any one language, although some languages are more specialised than others as to the verbalisation of topics related to Christianity. Discourses move from language community to language community (or from one linguistic network to another) by processes of translation and other kinds of transformation, and discourses are incorporated into the local language over longer or shorter periods of time. Some discourses are formed as various kinds of literature, and so literary topics, genres and styles spread from language to language.

Thus specific languages and specific discourses do not necessarily spread along the same lines. But they may exhibit parallel developments in an area or in a specific linguistic network. Pennycook is among the few people who have analysed relations between language and discourse in this way, with special reference to the question of whether colonial discourses adhere to the English language (Pennycook, 1998).

The cultural view of language, then, may be said to comprise two levels: *the level of languaculture*, bound to specific languages, and *the level of discourse*, not necessarily bound to any one language (but a discourse has to be expressed in some language at any point of time). This gives us a view on intertextuality that is double: every communicative event may be seen as a confluence of two flows: a linguistic flow in a specific language, and a discursive flow within a specific topic area. For example: a conversation in Barcelona, in Danish among Danish immigrants, about the war in Iraq, can be seen as a mixing of the transnational linguistic flow of Danish language with the transnational flow of discourses on the war in Iraq, made possible by innumerable instances of translation and other kinds of transformation from language to language.

If the above conversation in Barcelona is seen as an isolated communicative event, it is not easy to say which content elements come from Danish languaculture and which ones come from discourses about the war in Iraq – what is contained in the Danish word *krig* (war), for instance, and what connotations do those conversing have in connection with this word? But, seen in terms of spread, the conversation is a result of a confluence of flows, and it is possible to attempt to trace the flows, e.g. by carrying out sociosemantic surveys of the Danish word *krig*, and by investigating how discourses about the war in Iraq are part of intertextual chains that also include translations from one language to another, e.g. from Arabic to English to Danish.

Cultural Contexts

The communicative event (consisting of language, languaculture and discourse) always takes place in a concrete historical, social context that can be described at a number of different levels, from the lowest micro-level (the situational context) to the highest macro-level (the world-historical context).

When I use the concept of *cultural* context, it is to emphasise that every context conveys meaning. All life in society can be viewed as both social life and cultural life, and while the analysis of social life will typically be interested in the relational aspects of activities and institutions, that of cultural life will typically be interested in the aspects that convey and create meaning. These two sides cannot be separated from each other. All social life conveys and creates meaning, and all exchange of meaning is relational, embedded for example in power relations. The cultural context also includes language. Since most societies are multilingual, the context normally includes linguistic practice in several languages.

It is necessary to distinguish between objective and subjective dimensions of the context, which constantly interact: the *objective* dimension has to do with the concrete and material anchoring in time and space, and with the actual social organisation, the material interests and power relations. The *subjective* dimension has to do with the conception of the situation, with the ascribing of meaning, with how people and groups categorise and interpret the world.

First-language context, foreign-language context and second-language concept

Linguistic practice can unfold in a first-language context, a foreign-language context or a second-language context – or a mixture of these.[6]

Obviously, a language's languaculture is characterised first and foremost by the historical embedding in *first-language contexts*. But the contexts must not be understood in purely national-territorial terms. It is not 'France' that is the first-language context for 'the French language', for 'France' is a multilingual country, and French is also spoken outside France/the Francophone countries – also as a first language. When, for example, a person talks French as a foreign language in London, he/she is functioning perhaps in a foreign-language context. But if he/she visits a French-speaking family in London, we are dealing with a first-language context embedded in a foreign-language context. If he/she travels to Lyon and speaks French there, this can be a first-language context. But it can also be a second-language context if he/she is with Portuguese who speak

French as a second language. This second-language context is embedded in a larger first-language context (the French-speaking areas of Western Europe, etc.).

Life context

The concept of cultural context can also be used in relation to the individual subject's life history: a life history can be regarded as a particular type of context, i.e. a *life context,* which can also be analysed in an objective dimension, the actual sequence in real time, and a subjective dimension, the self-experienced life history that is constantly retold and reinterpreted to a greater or lesser extent. The life context has to do with the individual's social and personal development from a sociocultural perspective.

The individual's linguistic development has taken place in this life context, so a blend has taken place of the individual's linguistic experiences with the rest of the life history. The personal linguistic/languacultural resources – in one or more languages – and the discursive resources are interwoven with this life context.

Certain people in France have, for example, life experiences in which English plays an important role – perhaps they grew up as children in bilingual families where English was spoken. Others can have life experiences with very little exposure to English. They can, for example, be refugees from a country where there is little or no access to acquiring a knowledge of English. For some people English plays an important role in their life project, for others a less important role.

It must be emphasised that, while linguistic/languacultural and discursive *practice* can be separated from its cultural context and via migration be brought to another, a human being's linguistic/languacultural and discursive resources cannot be separated from his or her life context. We are dealing with an additive and integrative process. The connection between linguistic development and the life context can of course constantly be reconstructed and reinterpreted. There can be a life-historical break or a more or less split and fragmented self. But, all in all, it is nevertheless possible to say that in the individual subject the linguistic/languacultural and discursive resources cannot be separated from the life context as a whole. People do not migrate away from themselves.

The relationship between language and culture when 'culture' is cultural context

If *the sociological point of view* is taken as the point of departure and linguistic/ languacultural/discursive practice is looked at in relation to the cultural macro-context, the conclusion must be that it is quite common for language/languaculture/discourse to be separated from the first-language context and, via migration for example, to be transferred to a foreign- or second-language context, and there undergo a process of incorporation and change. From the sociological angle, language and culture can be separated.

If *the psychological point of view* is taken as the point of departure and linguistic/languacultural/discursive resources are looked at, the conclusion must be that these resources in the subject are inseparable from his or her life context. In the subject, language and culture are, then, inseparable, although their mutual relations can change in the life history and be restructured and reinterpreted in the self-narrative. From the psychological angle, language and culture cannot be separated.

If *the system-oriented point of view* is taken as the point of departure and 'language' looked at as a system, it must be said that we are dealing with a construction of constructions, where the construction of the imagined linguistic community is linked to the construction of an analogously imagined cultural community that forms the context for the linguistic. This linked community is mainly conceived within a national framework of reference, not least in Europe, although there are also examples of understandings that avoid the national framework of reference and talk instead of 'area' or 'community'. The connection between language and culture, then, is an ideological construction that can be used for various political aims. This aim could be more or less hot nationalist (Billig, 1995), but it can also be quite legitimate, e.g. linked to the struggle to preserve threatened languages, where an important element can be to state 'the inseparability of language and culture' (Fishman, 1982).

Cultural Contents

The communicative event typically has some thematic content or other (most clearly in written texts, often more fragmentary and fluid in oral communication). This thematic content of linguistic/languacultural/discursive practice can deal with all possible kinds of subject and perspective, but in this context I wish in particular to focus on those that deal with cultural and societal conditions in various places in the world (without this having to be understood in national terms). When it comes to an analysis of the relationship between language and culture, it is of particular interest to look at references to and representations of first-language contexts: in what sense is there, for example, a closer relationship between German and discourses on cultural and social conditions in Germany than between German and discourses on cultural and social conditions in France?

To clarify this, I suggest distinguishing between *internal* and *external* cultural references and representations. The internal ones relate to first-language contexts, the external ones to foreign- and second-language contexts. When talking in Japanese about (first-language contexts in) Japan, internal references are being used. When talking in Danish about (first-language contexts in) Japan, external references are being used. In language teaching it is in particular *the target-language internal references and representations* that are traditionally centre stage, i.e. the pedagogical work on the target-language countries in the target language.

Cultural references

Cultural references are a concept that is normally used about textual references to relations that are specific for a particular area – a country or a language area, for example. It is an important concept within translation theory, where it is a question of how to translate 'unmatched elements of culture' (Mailhac, 1996: 132). But when discussing cultural reference, it is important to distinguish between 'reference' and 'denotation' (cf. Lyons, 1995, mentioned in Chapter 4).

Reference is an act in which the language user refers with the aid of language to or 'points' at something in the outside world (the real world or a construed world). It could, for example, be a reference to 'New York'. The reference act is thus part of linguistic practice. Unlike this, 'denotation' is the same as meaning, e.g. the meaning of the Danish word *julenisse* (a kind of Christmas pixie), and this denotation can be used to make a specific reference to a particular *julenisse* in the outside world. So denotation is meaning potential that *can* be utilised for reference but does not have to be so. Meaning potentials are part of individual subjects' languacultural resources, accumulated via linguistic practice in lived first-language communities and spread via various networks, including such a cultural apparatus as the national school.

It is important to emphasise that, for example, French denotations do not have to be used for references to France, and that it is possible to refer to relations in France with the aid of other languages and their denotations. The French word *bûche de Noël* (a kind of Christmas cake) can be used during a journey to India to say: *Ah, ça ressemble à une bûche de Noël!* (Ah! That looks like a *bûche de Noël!*) when referring to a cake in an Indian shop. In this instance, the reference is not to relations in France. It is of course also possible to make references to relations in France in other languages than French, possibly supplemented by the necessary explanations.

Cultural words

Even though cultural reference can in principle be expressed or explained in any language whatsoever, there is a difference nevertheless in how 'easily' this can be done, depending on which language and which references are involved. This mainly has to do with the lexical loans and lexicalisations of various languages. In connection with the process of change of linguistic practice in linguistic networks, language users loan words from other languages or form new lexicalisations for the concepts needed. New words are mainly created by the formation of new compounds or by semantic differentiation.

Words like *julenisse, bûche de Noël*, etc. are sometimes referred to as cultural words (*mots de civilisation, Kulturwörter*, etc.). Within the discipline of translation, cultural words are an important concept (see for example Newmark, 1988). The prototype of a cultural word is one that can be used to refer to relations that are more or less specific to the language area involved. Such cultural words can contain translation difficulties, but Newmark also stresses that it can be even more difficult to translate certain words with an apparently more general meaning. He mentions words for morals and feelings (Newmark, 1988: 95).

In fact, the concept of 'cultural word' is problematic, for the question is whether or not all lexical units can be linked to culture-specific connotations. Even so, it can be useful to operate with a continuum ranging from relatively local denotations such as *sønderjysk kaffebord* (ritual involving coffee and many kinds of small cake, typical of Southern Jutland) to less location-bound denotations such as 'primary number'.

Internal cultural references: Are language and culture inseparable?

Are language and culture inseparable if internal cultural references and cultural words are focused on? First-language users have for centuries developed lexicalisations that have enabled precise references to be made to elements in the contexts where the language was used. These lexicalisations are part of the normal languacultural resources that have been developed in various communities. Linguistic practice can therefore not be separated from its social and cultural history. The development that linguistic practice has actually undergone in its first-language contexts and in other contexts around the world can partially be empirically reconstructed on the basis of written texts, e.g. the lexical-semantic history of the English language.

But the resources that language users carry with them are accumulated *potentials*. The word *Berufsverbot* exists in German, but this does not necessarily mean that the phenomenon *Berufsverbot* exists in the real world. The word *paradis* (paradise) exists in Danish, but the phenomenon does not need to be actualised.

If one looks backwards in time, it will be possible then to document parallel developments of linguistic/languacultural practice and other forms of cultural practice (e.g. food traditions), especially in lived first-language contexts. If one looks forward in time, this picture will of course develop, and it is important to underline that there is not any *determination* between linguistic practice in a particular language and its potential to refer to specific cultural and social conditions. Linguistic flows can go anywhere and link up with any form of context and discursive content (e.g. food traditions in other parts of the world). The languacultural potential will mix with the languacultures of other languages and change in the process, *inter alia* by developing the meaning of existing words and by new lexicalisations.

Cultural representations

Cultural representations belong to the textual macro-level, and cultural references can be part of them. Cultural representations are built up in discourses, and they convey images of or narratives of culture and society in particular contexts. One example could be a textbook section on Paris.

Two different ways of understanding the concept of cultural representation must be distinguished: it can be either a representation *of* 'culture' in a particular context, or a representation that adopts a particular cultural point of departure or *perspective*. One could refer to two kinds of look: a look at culture, and a look out from culture.

The former way of looking is the one culture pedagogy in particular has been interested in. It has been in the form of practical and theoretical issues concerning the choice of themes and texts that communicate important images of the target-language countries (e.g. Byram, 1997a). It has also been in the form of more critical approaches that make use of analyses of textbooks in terms of discourse and ideology (Dendrinos, 1992), or that discuss how production and reception of textbooks in language subjects can be linked to anthropological difficulties in ethnographical representation (Risager, 1999a).

The latter way of understanding cultural representation is often seen in the materials that base themselves on the choice of literary texts. Here the selection has traditionally concentrated on authors that speak (write) the target language involved as a first language, and the rationale for such a selection can be dual: this author has been included because (s)he is a first-language speaker, e.g. Danish, and is (therefore) assumed to represent a particularly Danish perspective on the world. The literary text does not need to base itself on material about life in Denmark; it can, for example, deal with travel and thereby convey a Danish view of the world outside Denmark – e.g. a travel account by Hans Christian Andersen.

It is important to emphasise that I am not of the opinion that it 'doesn't matter' in what language the representation is expressed. The semantic-pragmatic, the poetic and the identity-related dimensions of languaculture will probably all influence the understanding of the representation concerned in the specific reception context. If one reads, for example, about old Copenhagen in French, one's experiences with and attitude to the French language will colour the overall reception of the text.

Internal cultural representations: Are language and culture inseparable?

Are language and culture inseparable if internal cultural representations are focused on? Since any language (more or less easily) can link up with any discourse, i.e. with any subject, at this macro-level language and culture are separable. When many representatives of culture pedagogy express themselves as if they believe that language and culture are inseparable here, this can be owing to unwittingly adopting the psychological point of view.

If as a first-language user one reads a text in one's own first language about certain subjects in relation to the first-language context, one may have an experience of inseparability between language and discursive, thematic content and project this feeling out onto the idea of language at the systematic level. Something similar can occur if, as a bilingual speaker, e.g. Danish/German, one reads texts in each of one's languages and for each language experiences such an inseparability.

But this can happen only because at the same time one is subject to a first-language bias and therefore only considers each of the languages in its capacity of first language. If as an English speaker one reads a text about the USA, but in a language that is a *foreign language*, e.g. French, there is not necessarily a basis for experiencing a unity between French language and French 'content'.[7]

The relationship between language and culture when 'culture' is cultural content

If *the sociological point of view* is taken as the point of departure and linguistic/ languacultural/discursive practice is looked at, a distinction must be made between the textual micro-level and the textual macro-level. As far as the micro-level is concerned, one can on the one hand conclude that there is a clear connection between language and culture here, insofar as the lexicalisations that have been created in the course of time make it possible in some cases to make precise internal cultural references to elements in the first-language contexts of the language, references that are more precise than if one used other languages. On the other hand, one can also conclude that language and culture here can indeed be separated insofar as one can make cultural references to the given context with the aid of other languages, only not always as precisely and quickly. As far as the macro-level is concerned, one can conclude that there is no necessary connection insofar as any subject can be expressed with the aid of any language, via normal translation and/or via other forms of transmission or explanation.

If *the psychological point of view* is taken as the point of departure and linguistic/languacultural/discursive resources are looked at, the conclusion must be that there is inseparability between language and culture: the ontogenetic psychological and social process of development is a process of construction in which new linguistic and cultural experiences are added on and integrated with old ones.

If *the system-oriented point of view* is taken as the point of departure and language as a system is looked at, the conclusion must be that the potential that makes internal cultural references and representations possible constitutes the languaculture of a language, especially the semantic-pragmatic dimension. But to claim a unity between 'language' and 'culture', where culture is understood as a thematically defined, discursive content, makes no sense.

The Language–Culture Nexus

The basic unit for the link between language and culture is the communicative event – a concept which is central in linguistic anthropology, especially within the ethnography of communication. Saville-Troike defines a communicative event as follows:

> The *communicative event* is the basic unit for descriptive purposes. A single event is defined by a unified set of components throughout, beginning with the same general purpose of communication, the same general topic, and involving the same participants, generally using the same language variety, maintaining the same tone or key and the same rules for interaction, in the same setting. (Saville-Troike, 1989: 27, italics in the original)

This definition seeks to ensure an analytical demarcation of the object of study, focusing on the inner stability of the event: same general purpose, same general topic, etc. It has not been formulated in order to analyse the relationship between language and culture, so I intend to supplement it with the aid of the concept of language–culture nexus.

The language-culture nexus: A local integration

As was first argued in the companion volume (Risager, 2006), the communicative event must be seen in a larger perspective. It must be understood theoretically as a linkage of various flows coming from various sources: a language–culture nexus. The concept of *language–culture nexus* I would describe as follows (and here I am quoting from Risager, 2006: 186):

- it is a local integration of linguistic, languacultural, discursive and other cultural flows in more or less differing social networks;
- in written language it is normally divided into a production and a reception phase that can be more or less staggered in time and / or place;
- it takes place in a complex micro- and macro-context (or in several, in the case of written language);
- it is characterised by a discursive content of a more or less cohesive nature, possibly including cultural references and representations, internal or external;
- it can be multilingual, i.e. characterised by diverse forms of code-switching;
- it has a place in each of the entire life contexts of the participants (subs. producers and receivers) and is interpreted by each of them in the light of this life-context.

Local integration is a dialogical, possibly conflictual, process where the participants co-construct, negotiate or struggle for meanings and identities. There is always a power dimension involved.

The language–culture nexus: Convergent or divergent?

In the language–culture nexus, language and culture can blend in relatively convergent or divergent ways.

An example of a fairly convergent language–culture nexus would be a conversation in a pub in Aalborg (Aalborg is a city in Denmark). Those taking part were born in Aalborg and speak with a modern Aalborg accent and are characterised by modern Aalborg languaculture; the discussion is about local conditions in Aalborg. Another example could be a teaching sequence in Swedish as a second language. It takes place somewhere in Sweden, the teacher has Swedish as his/her first language, the students have various linguistic backgrounds but speak only Swedish in the class. The teaching is based on a novel written by a writer with Swedish as his first language, on a subject related to Swedish history: former labour conditions in the iron industry – an example in which the national framework of reference forms the entire language–culture nexus.

An example of a fairly divergent language–culture nexus would be a telephone conversation between an associate professor at the University of Copenhagen and a colleague at the University of Aix-Marseille. The person talking in Aix-Marseille speaks English with a tinge of Russian languaculture because this person is a Russian immigrant. The person talking in Copenhagen speaks English with some Danish languaculture. They discuss some plans for academic collaboration between their departments in the field of Iranian Studies.

As pointed out in the companion volume it is important to note the theoretical-methodological significance of this:

> if one investigates *only* convergent situations, one can easily come to the conclusion that there is, generally speaking, a close connection between language and culture. And one will perhaps generalise this assertion to talk about the unity between language and culture ('the marriage between language and culture'), possibly linked to an idea of national or ethnic identity. But if one turns one's gaze to divergent situations, such a conclusion is less likely. (Risager, 2006: 187–88)

This is perhaps an important reason why first-language bias dominates large sections of linguistics: linguistics has to a very large extent been looking at convergent situations only. And foreign-language teaching has almost 'specialised' in cultivating convergent situations.

Objective and subjective dimensions of the language–culture nexus

My description of the language–culture nexus emphasises the *empirical complexity*, both 'internally' in the communicative event, and 'externally' in the relation to the context. I have thus taken an 'objective' approach as my point of departure, but it would also be possible to adopt a more 'subjective' approach. So it is important to distinguish between two different approaches in the analysis, also in order to be able to examine the interaction between them: on the one hand an analytical approach that attempts to describe and analyse the empirical complexity in linguistic and cultural practice; on the other hand an analytical analysis that seeks to describe the language users' own *experiences and notions*, including their categorisations, identifications and narratives concerning the relationship between language and culture.

Language–culture nexuses at higher levels

The concept of language–culture nexus is primarily linked to the single communicative event, i.e. to the micro-level. But for analytical purposes an attempt can be made to define language–culture nexuses at higher levels, e.g. a teaching sequence.

Here we need to distinguish between lived and imagined communities. A small family unit (nuclear family, or something similar) forms the framework of a lived community, and there linguistic/languacultural practice develops in a dialectic with discursive and other cultural practice. Examples of other small-scale communities could be a kindergarten, a school staff, a small firm, a transnational team of managers, etc. In such cases it is possible to investigate language–culture nexuses empirically at both the micro-level and at a slightly higher level by using ethnographical methods: how does linguistic/languacultural practice in speech and writing take place in this (monolingual or multilingual) lived community? What themes and perspectives are verbalised by discursive practice? How is the rest of cultural practice included: buildings and objects, sounds and music, the use of the body, etc.? And how is this totality organised socially? At this level it is possible to investigate the interaction between language and culture empirically.

There is continuity from lived communities to imagined communities (Anderson, 1991 (1983)), where the 'members' are so many that they cannot know each other personally or act together in personal interaction. An imagined community is based only to a limited extent on an actual common network. It is, as the term implies, a community that first and foremost is only a construed one. Imagined communities can vary in extent and do not have to be defined in terms of territory. They can be a nation, a municipality, a generation, a trade union, a transnational school network, etc.

Even though one can define a lived community in, for example, a school class around certain activities that result in certain ways of using language and of verbalising certain subjects from certain angles, there is always some degree of difference as well as latent or open conflict between various interpretations and motives. And it will possible to trace this in breaks and clashes in linguistic and discursive practice (cf. Chouliaraki, 1998; Dendrinos, 1992). That one even so can call the class a community is because there is an extensive common understanding of the rules of the game and of the various perspectives of the situation on the part of those involved.

The core of the language–culture nexus: Reference to reality

In the language–culture nexus, language and culture are linked in a quite particular way. The core in this 'connection' is the meaning and reference potential of language. It is via its meaning and reference potential that language goes beyond itself and links up with (the rest of) physical, social and cultural reality.[8] Here it is once more useful to distinguish between language in a generic and a differential sense.

When we talk about human language in the generic sense, it is characteristic of language that it enables people to refer to the outside world in a very broad sense: both past, present and future, and both everyday reality and construed worlds. When we talk about a particular language, I have described how the languacultural accumulation through time has made precise, swift references possible to *first-language contexts*, among other things via borrowings from other languages and via lexicalisations. Thereby, a relatively high degree of semantic and pragmatic congruence[9] has developed between linguistic practice in a particular language and the first-language contexts. So *in general* it will be easier to make internal references than external references.

The main purpose of my entire argument concerning the relationship between language and culture is to draw attention to the ways in which language and culture can be separated – an argument that derives from my fundamentally critical attitude towards the national-romantic idea of the inseparability of language and culture at the national level. At the same time, however, I would also like to emphasise that if we look at in what respect there is the closest connection between language and culture in a differential sense, we have to look at the particular meaning and reference potential of the language involved, or – to talk in terms of practice – the exploitation by language users of their languacultural resources to refer to their outside world as precisely as is felt to be relevant.

Conclusion

Language and culture in a *generic* sense are always inseparable, for linguistic practice, no matter what language we are dealing with, always contains languaculture and is always embedded in some cultural context or other. But, understood in a *differential* sense, the question must always be asked: what forms of culture actually appear together with precisely this language – and under what circumstances?

In a differential sense, language and culture are both inseparable and separable. It is a question of the point of view: from the sociological point of view it can be confirmed that linguistic practice spreads over the whole world across cultural contexts and that linguistic practice can express discourses and subjects of every kind – even references and representations that are external to the target language, although more or less easily on account of the particular history of lexicalisation. It is also true that linguistic practice in a foreign language will typically show a blend of languaculture from both this language (the target language) and the learner's first language.

From the psychological point of view, however, language and culture have always developed together in the individual subject in a unique blend, the complexity of which I do not need to examine here.

From the system-oriented point of view, we are ultimately talking only about a construction of constructions: the idea of the linguistic (possibly national) community linked to the idea of the cultural (possibly national) community.

The general ideology of inseparability between language and culture seems to be attributable to two different, but related, factors. On the one hand the individual has a tendency to project his/her own subjective feeling of association between his/her personal language/languaculture and his/her personal culture and identity onto the community, for example the nation, and thus imagine an association at the system level for which there is no empirical basis. On the other hand this psychological tendency is used politically in national (or ethnic) propaganda, where an image is constructed of the nation state (or ethnic community) characterised by a common culture expressed in a common language.

Notes

1. The argument in this chapter is a development from that of the companion volume (Risager, 2006).
2. He has borrowed this term from Friedrich (1989) who called it 'linguaculture' (see also Risager, 2003: 363).
3. Instead of 'languaculture' the expression 'culture in language' might be used, but I think the term 'languaculture' is more flexible, making it possible to focus more clearly on the issue, and also to create an adjective and an adverb: languacultural, languaculturally.
4. In the following sections I will restrict myself to elaborating on the first (semantic and pragmatic) dimension.

5. It should be noted that the structuralist tradition has primarily focused (implicitly) on language as a first language.
6. See Berns (1990), who is also interested in the macro-contexts of foreign-language teaching.
7. On the other hand, it is possible to imagine that an experience of unity arises between French language and French *languaculture*, if the reading creates a French atmosphere (semantic-pragmatic dimension, identity dimension) via the experiences and connotations one has oneself.
8. When I write 'the rest of physical reality', it is so as to emphasise that language also has a physical side: sound waves, ink on paper, etc.
9. Here I am using Fishman's concept of congruence in a slightly extended sense. Fishman has used it in order to conceptualise the relationship between a social situation/a domain and the language use that is typically linked to it (Fishman, 1971).

Chapter 8
Towards a Transnational Language and Culture Pedagogy

Introduction

This chapter deals with the national paradigm and its possible replacement: a transnational paradigm. In connection with the transnational paradigm I will discuss some points of view and approaches that are already partly represented in certain areas of theoretical culture pedagogy and probably also in language-teaching practice here and there. The chapter is not conceived as a proposal for how language teaching can actually be organised. The main intention is to formulate a cohesive basis for the development of research within language and culture pedagogy in a transnational direction – a basis that can contribute to strengthening reflexivity regarding the global, the regional (e.g. the European dimension in Europe), the national and the local within all types of language teaching and in modern language studies in general.

With the contents of Chapter 7, on the relationship between language and culture, as my point of departure, I will now give a brief reinterpretation of the culture-pedagogical positions of which I provided an overview in Chapter 6 (Figure 6.1): There are a number of positions that focus solely on what I call languaculture (but without the social and idiolectic variability I am looking for): Vereščagin and Kostomarov (1973) (*Linguolandeskunde*), Galisson (1991) (*la culture dans la langue*) and Crozet and Liddicoat (2000) (culture in language). Other positions do not include languaculture at all, being solely interested in representations by texts/discourses of the world and in the formation of students' personalities: Fichou (1979), Zarate (1986), Melde (1987), Starkey (1991) and Guilherme (2002). Then there is an in-between group that is interested both in languaculture and in the representation by texts/discourses of the world and (in some cases) the formation of the personality: Seelye (1974), Byram (1989) and (1997), Kramsch (1993), Brøgger (1992) and Roberts *et al.* (2001). But this last group has not thematised what I stress in Risager (2003): that discourses can spread across the various language communities. If emphasis is placed on this interpretation of the concept of discourse, it is possible to question the traditional picture of a closed, self-referring universe of a language and its discourses that circulate without coming into contact with the world outside.

Once the idea of a closed universe – understood within a national or possibly an ethnic frame of reference – is abandoned, a very wide spectrum of possibilities opens up for language teaching. Language teaching is released from a constricting framework that has characterised it for more than a century – a process of emancipation that took its first steps in the 1990s and has since gathered speed.

In the following, I will contrast two paradigms for language and culture pedagogy: a national and a transnational. It must, however, be said from the very outset that these two paradigms do not have the same status: whereas the national paradigm can be derived from the tradition of international culture pedagogy, the transnational paradigm is my summary of tendencies since the 1980s and 1990s which, in one way or another, depart from the national paradigm. This summary has been made possible by the analysis of the relationship between language and culture in Chapter 7, with its emphasis on linguistic and cultural complexity and on transnational networks and processes. It could be said that my formulation of a possible transnational paradigm is an attempt to detect and systematise certain changes that characterise language subjects at present.

While my treatment of the history of culture pedagogy has been mainly descriptive-analytical and critical until now, the treatment in Chapters 8 and 9 cannot avoid taking an idealistic and programmatic turn. But my intention is really to contribute to the *realism* of culture pedagogy: to induce it to take the linguistic and cultural complexity of the world seriously. Only after that will I look at some of the pedagogical dilemmas this raises.

The transnational paradigm ought then to be the new anchorage for language and culture pedagogy. From this point it can, among other things, adopt a reflexive attitude to the national: it can treat the national language as a historical and discursive construction which – especially as far as the written language is concerned – is also a useful and necessary tool for communication in the language community. It can treat 'the national culture' as a construction that – if it is conceived inclusively – can have positive aspects since it can help support a feeling of community and solidarity in a population that transcends social and ethnic boundaries. It can treat the national political structures as the historical structures they are, yet recognise at the same time that if such concourses as the EU and the UN are ignored, then national political structures now constitute the only frameworks for representative democracy. As these frameworks are in the process of being undermined by neo-liberal globalism (Beck, 2000), it is important to concern oneself with democracy and its fate – and here the traditional national orientation of language subjects can actually be an asset.[1]

The National Paradigm

The national paradigm rests, as mentioned, on the fundamental and normally implicit conception of the national constituting the natural frame of reference for language teaching ('the target language' and 'the target-language countries'). The national paradigm as an ideal type comprises a number of organisational and discursive traits that mean that:

(1) The sole aim is a national standard norm of native-language use and a standardised languaculture.
(2) The teacher is a native speaker and uses the standard norm.
(3) Teaching is only in the target language and its standard norm.
(4) Subjects and discourses concentrate on cultural and social relations (incl. literature) in the country or one of the countries where the language is spoken as the first language, and then only 'the majority culture'.
(5) The subjects are contextualised nationally (e.g. 'this phenomenon is French)'.
(6) Teaching is only in one of the target-language countries.
(7) Student contacts outside the classroom are only with people who speak the language as a first language.

It is important to state that all these features can individually be well founded, and that they can also be found embedded in the transnational paradigm, under certain circumstances, in various phases. The indication that we are dealing with the national paradigm is the general, often implicit, approach to the national as something natural.

It must be remembered that the paradigms are meant as descriptive patterns for all forms of language teaching, not just foreign-language teaching. When, for example, in point 2 it says that the teacher is a native speaker, this does not of course normally apply to foreign-language teaching, but it can even so feature as an ideal. Something similar also applies to point (6). I will deal with this in more detail below.

The national paradigm can be described as a language–culture nexus that *focuses on the national level*. What forms of language teaching come closest to the national paradigm? In my opinion, more *traditional* first-language teaching in a majority language, e.g. Danish, can be characterised by such a paradigm: the aim is a Danish first-language standard norm (use of Danish dialects and Danish as a second language are sanctioned), the teacher speaks Danish as his or her first language (second-language speakers are not accepted as teachers), teaching takes place only in Danish, teaching deals with Denmark or is seen from a Danish perspective, teaching takes place in Denmark, and if students have contact outside the classroom as part of the teaching, it is assumed that such contact is with native speakers.

Foreign-language teaching within the framework of the national paradigm could, for example, be French teaching where the aim is French as a first-language standard form (in France); the teacher ideally speaks French at near-native level; teaching is only in French; teaching deals with the French majority community; teaching, however, for practical reasons takes place in the students' own residential area in Denmark, and students are possibly encouraged to have contact with French native speakers (e.g. penfriends). Some may want to accentuate the national paradigm further by, for example, preferring teachers who have French as their first language (an ideal that, for instance, is met within private-sector English schools), or by making efforts to ensure that students get a lengthy stay in France or some other French-speaking country (this is of course well motivated), and possibly by encouraging them to cultivate contacts with native speakers.

The national paradigm is not unambiguous. As I mentioned in Chapter 1, a distinction – in accordance with nationality research – must be made between two main variants of the national: a political variant (*Staatsnation*, or understood as a historical project: 'state-to-nation') and an ethnic variant (*Kulturnation*, or understood as a historical project: 'nation-to-state'). The latter variant occurs in many cases as linguistic-ethnic, i.e. the language is used as an important ethnicity marker and possibly as a legitimisation of the national project. These two understandings of the national have characterised language and culture pedagogy and created certain inner tensions between its different basic positions.

Those who represent the kind of culture pedagogy that is interested in societal relations and in social and political structures (Byram, Starkey, Doyé, Kramer, Poirier, Guilherme *et al.*) draw in particular on the political understanding, as they talk about countries and societies ('countries', *Landeskunde*, 'social studies', *civilisation*, etc.). The above definition of the national paradigm also draws on the political understanding ('countries'). Normally, advocates of this tendency place language (the target language) as the apparently only language in the country/society involved, i.e. other languages that happen to be spoken there are placed in brackets and ignored. France, for example, is dealt with as an exclusively French-speaking country and there is no mention of the existence of other languages in what in fact is a multilingual France. Equals signs are placed between France, the French language and French culture.

The cultural educationalists whose prime interest is the linguistic (Kramsch, Crozet and Liddicoat, Hinkel *et al.*) base themselves more on a linguistic-ethnic understanding, as they talk about (monolingual) language communities/language areas with their associated 'cultures' – and these cultures are sometimes referred to as ethnic. This may have something to do with the fact that these experts operate in immigrant countries with a long history of immigration (the USA/Australia), where it is more generally recognised that the target language in foreign-language teaching, e.g. German, is used both in the target-language countries such as Germany and Austria and in German-speaking immigrant communities in the USA/Australia themselves.

In general, then, there are two conflicting views of the world in present-day language subjects: a political conception of the world as consisting of national states/countries, each of which has its national language and its national culture (which may possibly be presented as diverse in itself); and a linguistic conception of the world as consisting of (monolingual) language areas each of which has its associated 'culture' (which may also possibly be presented as diverse in itself). The former conception clearly draws on the national paradigm, but the latter takes a more indirect and implicit stance.

A basic factor in this situation is the inherent monolingual self-understanding of the language subjects. Normally, the focus is on the target language with a concurrent exclusion of all other languages (with the possible exception of the students' first or second languages). This self-understanding has, of course, something to do with the central aim of the pedagogy of language subjects being linguistic development towards precisely the target language and no other languages. But this can easily lead to blindness as regards multilingualism and code-switching in society – including the learning space.

The Transnational Paradigm

The transnational paradigm rests on the recognition of linguistic and cultural complexity and on transnational flows, and is thus characterised by a view of language that operates with the three loci for language discussed in Chapter 7. The transnational paradigm as an ideal type comprises a number of organisational and discursive traits that mean that:

(1) The sole aim is not a national standard norm of native-language use and room is found for more inclusive language norms and various languacultures.

(2) The teacher does not need to be a native speaker in the standard language, so long as he/she has a high level of competence.

(3) Teaching is not only in the target language but, if necessary/possible, also in other languages, e.g. the students' first language.

(4) Subjects and discourses can be of any type whatsoever, as long as work is mainly done in the target language – assuming that the choice of subject can also be justified from a pedagogical point of view.

(5) The subjects are contextualised nationally only if this is necessary (e.g. conditions relating to the French national education system), and are otherwise sought to be contextualised transnationally (locally/globally, see below), e.g. 'this phenomenon is characteristic for towns on the coast of Brittany' or 'we also find this phenomenon elsewhere in the world'.

(6) Teaching does not have to take place in the country or countries in which the language is spoken as a first language, but can take place anywhere in the world if this can also be justified from a pedagogical point of view.

(7) Students can have contact with other people anywhere in the world, as long as this takes place mainly in the target language.

As with the national paradigm, we are dealing with a descriptive pattern for all forms of language teaching, and in the following sections I intend to comment on each of the points.

We are looking here at language–culture nexuses that are relatively divergent (cf. Chapter 7). The transnational paradigm is based on empirically demonstrable linguistic, discursive and cultural complexity, and it is interested in the target language as a first language, second language and foreign language – also in lingua franca use. It is also based on the separation I have made between language/languaculture on the one hand and discourse on the other: particular discourses do not necessarily come with the individual language.

The contours of a transnational[2] paradigm began to emerge in the course of the 1980s and 1990s. The general social background is the ambivalent status that the national acquired in connection with the processes of globalisation. States (most of which are constituted and legitimised as national states) are facing a decline in sovereignty – and at the same time there is a growth in national awareness and nationalism. Even though the transnational paradigm is called 'transnational', the national can still be an important focal point, but accompanied by an awareness of the contingent nature of the national.

The transnational paradigm grew out of various pedagogical tendencies, including wishes to connect language teaching with social movements that, in various ways, work for a better world (peace, environmental and human rights movements, etc.) (e.g. Guilherme, 2002; Risager, 1989a; Starkey, 1991a), or wishes to 'internationalise' language teaching in order to strengthen mobility and cooperation across EU borders, in countries of the Council of Europe, and more generally (e.g. Byram & Risager, 1999).

The transnational paradigm contains a number of openings in relation to the national. A recurrent rhetorical figure in the above list is: 'not only, but also'. It is important to underline here that my aim in defining the transnational paradigm is not to describe 'ideal language teaching'. That would also be impossible, considering the many different contexts in which language teaching takes place. The aim of defining the transnational paradigm is *to formulate a theoretically justified alternative* to the national paradigm, which can be used as a starting point for research and development in the various languages and in various types of language teaching: when the transnational paradigm is used as a point of departure, how much must teaching then be formed in national frameworks, what features must be preserved from the national paradigm, and what must – or can – be discarded and transcended?

In the next sections I will look a little more closely at what problem areas can lie hidden in the above seven points of the transnational paradigm. First, points 1–3: language and languaculture.

Language and Languaculture

Language norms and linguistic mediation

There can be no doubt that the central activity of language teaching is linguistic practice that can help the learner acquire a constantly improving mastery of a specific language, with a focus on more closely defined linguistic norms in writing and speech. Among the important discourses in this context are discourses ('awareness') to do with language and language acquisition/language learning. Here I would refer to Deborah Cameron's approach to language prescription, which emphasises the fact that linguistic practice always involves linguistic norms, and that every time one uses the language, these norms are reproduced and formed afresh. Linguistic prescription is part of social practice and negotiation about it is just like negotiation about other forms of social practice (Cameron, 1995).

The transnational paradigm involves awareness that variation and variability exist in linguistic practice and, correspondingly, that many local linguistic norms exist. The teacher needs not least to be able to act reflexively to both the (nationally) standardised written-language norm(s) and the numerous more regionally and socially specific spoken-language norms. As long as the basis of work – in traditional foreign-language teaching – was that all students in a class had roughly the same qualifications and future needs as regards use of the target language, it was logical to work in relation to one particular standard norm for the target language, more or less implicitly restricted to oral and written language use in adult well-educated native speakers in one of the central target-language countries (e.g. Great Britain, Germany, France).

But with increasing mobility such a standardised basis is even less defensible than it was before. Some students, even before entering the classroom, have various linguistic qualifications in relation to the target language: in the English class in Denmark, for example, there may be someone who has grown up in Kenya as the child of development workers and attended an English-language school there; someone who comes from a family where the mother is an English speaker and comes from Ireland; and someone who grew up in Sri Lanka in an English-speaking environment. In the German class there may be someone who grew up in Southern Jutland in local German- and Danish-speaking environments, and in the French class perhaps someone who has spent all her summer holidays in the South of France. If taking account of students' differing qualifications is to be taken seriously, it must in each case give rise to such questions as: what explicit spoken-language norm is it reasonable and realistic to operate with here? Should one adhere to a more traditional standard norm ('British English', 'French French', etc.), or should one broaden it with other possibly more local norms? Such a question cannot be answered generally, but in the concrete situation the various linguistic qualifications of the students must be taken into account as well as their possible future linguistic needs – which is of course highly hypothetical when it comes to teaching with a general purpose. The qualifications of the teacher must also be considered: what spoken language norms does he/she have sufficient knowledge of to be able to guide and assess the students in question?

Should 'the target language' be restricted to the varieties that characterise native-language speakers? Firstly, it must be said that it is not all that easy to define the concept of 'native speaker', cf. for example Skutnabb-Kangas (1981 and 2000), and Davies (1991). But, apart from that problem, a number of people have since the 1990s questioned 'the native-speaker model', e.g. Byram and Zarate (1994), Byram (1997a) and Kramsch (1998b). They argue in favour of an alternative model, called 'the intercultural speaker model'. It must be said that Byram's and Kramsch's conceptions of the intercultural speaker's competence differ quite a lot – and I will deal with this in the next chapter in connection with a discussion of the concept of intercultural communicative competence. But what unites them is their criticism of the traditional model for language teaching: 'the monolingual and monocultural native speaker'. Byram writes: 'I shall introduce the concept of the 'intercultural speaker' to describe interlocutors involved in intercultural communication and interaction' (Byram, 1997a: 32). And Kramsch writes the following about the competence of the intercultural speaker:

> not the ability to speak and write according to the rules of the academy and the social etiquette of one social group, but the adaptability to select those forms of accuracy and those forms of appropriateness that are called for in a given social context of use. This form of competence is precisely the competence of the 'intercultural' speaker, operating at the border between several languages or language varieties, manoeuvring his/her way through the troubled waters of cross-cultural misunderstandings. (Kramsch, 1998b: 27)

There are two sides to the concept of 'intercultural speaker' (in both Byram's and Kramsch's interpretations). One has to do with the target language. Some people seem to think that ongoing research projects on language (English) as a lingua franca will result in people beginning to *teach* English as a lingua franca, i.e. work with it as a goal for learning (cf. Seidlhofer, 2001). In my opinion, this is very problematic – and I suspect that Byram and Kramsch would agree with me here. As I have indicated earlier, it must be taken into consideration nowadays that students possibly come into contact with other people who speak the target language as a foreign language, and that they allow themselves to be influenced by the way these people speak the language. We are dealing here with beneficial linguistic experiences and temporary models. But the ultimate aim (the decisive model) for language learning must be a variety (or several) used by native speakers – or near-native speakers, i.e. normally people who have acquired the language as a second language early in life. This is because it is important that the ultimate goal for learning is a language that functions as an everyday language in a language community and which (therefore) is differentiated along social, regional, situational and poetical/stylistic lines.

Even so, there may be good reasons for other models featuring in the learning context, including the teacher as a foreign-language speaker with (ideally) a high level of competence.[3] And this is connected to the other side of the concept of 'intercultural speaker' – the ability to mediate between the two languages/languacultures and the ability to reflect on issues in connection with this. In developing as an intercultural speaker it is important to train in translation and interpreting in real or realistic situations. For that reason, it can be extremely well justified for the teacher to be bilingual, to possess a good knowledge both of the target language and of the first language/early second language of the students. And it is also well justified for the students to actively include their first language in their learning. An English class in Denmark, for example, can establish contact with a kindergarten and offer to translate an English children's book for them. Or a French class can invite a French-speaking guest teacher to take part in a conversation along with a group of Danes who do not know French, and the students can take turns in acting as interpreters. The teacher can take part and step in as a helper.

Critical awareness of language and language encounters

Transnational linguistic flows mix locally. This creates a whole series of language encounters in everyday life that most people have some experience of. The transnational exchange of commodities means, for example, a linguistic exchange of brands, advertising, slogans and lifestyle features from various language areas. This linguistic diversity can be observed in TV commercials and newspapers and advertising material delivered to households as well as in the local kiosk/video shop and in general in the streets in urban and shopping centres. The Internet has come to comprise many languages that anyone interested has direct access to.

The growing ethnic complexity of most countries will probably make an increasingly obvious impact on the media and, for example, in the goods and services on offer in the market with language designations that announce their more or less foreign cultural origins. Add to this the considerable amount of travel to many different destinations in the world, and it must be reasonable to assume that multilingualism and language encounters have a great significance for many people nowadays. This situation is the language-sociological context for eventual code-switching in (especially) foreign-language teaching.

The code-switching phenomenon is potentially of great interest for language and culture pedagogy, because it in most cases presumably has special pedagogical functions. On the part of the teacher, code-switching is probably most used to ensure understanding. On the part of students, code-switching can also be a learning strategy: by using a word from one's first language in a conversation that otherwise is in the target language, one invites the conversation partner to give information about the missing word if able (cf. Martin-Jones, 1995). Here we are talking about the semantic-pragmatic dimension of languaculture, but what about the poetic and identity-related dimension? Is code-switching with poetic value used in language teaching? And what identity-related implications lie in switching between languages? These questions still await illumination by research.

The multilingual reality that exists inside and outside the class should be considered by language subjects as the material they work with. Students should not, for example, be led to believe that India is simply an English-speaking country or Senegal French-speaking. It must be part of English and French teaching that students learn what languages English and French respectively are competing against in the various areas. An important aspect of language awareness is knowledge of such concepts as first language, second language and foreign language. This is a prerequisite for being able to deal with linguistic complexity in everyday life, including dealing with various ways of using languages. All these topics would be highly suitable for inclusion in cooperation between language subjects (Risager, 1993), not least so as to demonstrate that language subjects can cooperate on other linguistic topics than grammatical analysis.

The dimensions of languaculture

Language teaching is always languaculture teaching as well, no matter what discourses and topics are dealt with, but, as I have pointed out in Chapter 7, it is the single person who links languaculture to his or her linguistic practice, and this languaculture is idiolectal – uniquely composed for the individual subject. The languaculture that a person assigns to a language he or she is acquiring as a foreign language comes to a great extent from that person's own first language – partly its denotative core, and probably most of the connotations that branch out into the person's other knowledge of the world.

One of the important tasks of language teaching is to make students aware of languacultural variability and relationality, including the fact that everyone develops partially different languacultures as a result of their various biographies. Languaculture must be seen from a sociological point of view (linguistic practice), a psychological point of view (the individual's languacultural resources), and a system-oriented point of view (a language's broad and indefinable languacultural potential).

Kramsch is one of those who give some consideration to languacultural variability in practice, as she suggests working in the class with the various voices of literary texts and with the various receptions/interpretations of the text in the multicultural classroom (Kramsch, 1993). Such activities supplement the more cognitively oriented work on building up vocabulary and the use of words and idioms in relevant situations, and they focus on the differential and variable in the semantics and pragmatics of the target language, seen in relation to the students' specific first language and other languages they happen to know. Even if there are a number of first languages represented in the class, the teacher does not need to know them all for the class to be able to get something out of working with semantic and pragmatic differences; everyone can in principle include their first language as a resource and contrastive element in the class and learn to provide certain background information. Work with semantic and pragmatic languaculture will place special emphasis on the culturally dense parts of the vocabulary in a more absolute sense – the cultural words (Chapter 7). The cultural words can, for example, be discussed as part of text reading in a critical discourse analysis mode, where one looks at how words and phrases are linked together in particular subject areas and ideological perspectives (Fairclough, 1992a; Jäger, 1993). Proficiency in linguistic mediation, as I suggested earlier, presupposes work with semantic-pragmatic languaculture – as does the analysis of language encounters in a more general sense.

Work with the poetic dimension of languaculture can be seen as a continuation of work with semantics and pragmatics. While the latter deals more with registering regularities and patterns, the poetic has more to do with experiencing and making new and surprising linguistic products, playing with language and with the language encounter. There is no reason to ban such experiments from language teaching, for there is a need – with the postmodernist individualistic approach to the construction of identity – to cultivate 'linguistic leisurewear' as an alternative to 'linguistic working clothes', which one must be familiar with under all circumstances. 'Linguistic working clothes' refers to the conscious use of the language (the target language) in as close an accordance as possible with 'others' norms' (cf. Bülow-Møller, 2000), in contexts where one is dependent on other people's acceptance, e.g. at work. 'Linguistic leisurewear' is the freer use of language that one can amuse oneself with in other contexts, cf. the creative use of language in chat rooms and SMS messages. It may always be possible for one to get an opportunity later to develop this cultural work with language in professional careers.

Work with the identity-related dimension of languaculture can be seen as an extension of the two other dimensions: what does it mean when one (as a foreign-language speaker) expresses oneself as one does in the target language – what negotiations of identity does one carry out in the interaction (the sociological point of view)? What discourses or ideas are linked to the individual language, who has these ideas, how have they arisen, and how are they used (the system-oriented point of view)? And what do the discourses about the target language mean for one's own linguistic identities in the life-context, one's learning of the target language and one's possible future use of it? How does one feel when speaking and writing the target language (the psychological point of view)?

Topics and Discourses

We now turn to points 4–5 in the transnational paradigm, which deal with topics and their discursive construction in language teaching.

It is already possible to point to several tendencies towards a divergence of topic, so that they no longer point unequivocally to cultural and social relations in the central target-language countries. One tendency is for language teaching in general to have moved in an intercultural, culture-comparative direction. In connection with this, texts and themes have begun to be taken up that relate to the students' own society and the target language has been used in relation to these themes. In other words, external cultural references and representations have been used to a greater extent (e.g. English conditions have been talked about in French in French teaching in England).

A second tendency is linked to internationalisation (study trips, e-mail, etc.), especially in those instances where teachers and students have had contact with non-target-language countries and where they have used the target language as a language for international communication (Byram & Risager, 1999). Here, too, there is a need in the same way to make use of external references and representations.

A third tendency has been an increasing interest in taking up cross-cultural or more general topics in language teaching, such as human rights and the environment (Risager, 1989a) as well as an interest in including literature that has been translated into the target language from other languages.

Necessity and essentiality

So there are the beginnings of a radical spread on the content side in foreign languages, a spread that I believe to be positive in the sense that it can demonstrate the broad subject-related usability of the target language: it can be used for much more than internal cultural references and representations. But this spread brings up new questions: what should really be chosen with regard to topic and discourse?

The question of the necessary has to do with to what extent learning of the language involved presupposes working with particular cultural and social relations. Here there are two *linguistic* reasons for allowing parts of (but not all) teaching to have *first-language contexts* as their point of departure. I will deal more with this in the next section.

The question of the essential has to do with certain considerations that will naturally differ among the various people involved in planning the teaching. As might be surmised, I will argue in favour of using a transnational basis and a global orientation. I will return to this below.

First-language contexts

The most important linguistic reason for allowing parts of language teaching to focus on first-language contexts is of a practical nature: since the linguistic aim is ultimately a linguistic norm related to (near-)native speakers, the students must build up a constantly improving knowledge of native speakers' (expected) languaculture, first and foremost pragmatics and semantics (and their interaction with other cultural practices: material, visual, musical, etc.). Students ought, for example, to know something about (expected) connotations to do with frequently used cultural words that can be used for internal cultural references – and such cultural words are numerous and the result of a long process of semantic accumulation, the historical circumstances of which ought not to be completely unknown. For that reason, students ought to work in relation to the linguistic practice of native speakers in first-language contexts, to work with texts, simulations and tasks that can promote a feeling for first-language practice.

But which first-language contexts? There are networks of English, German and French speakers etc. throughout the world, as well as larger or smaller groups in all the countries that speak the languages involved as their first language. So a distinction must be made between majority and minority contexts.

It is perfectly possible to learn a language in a minority context. A child that grows up in a French-speaking family in Denmark and attends a French school will probably learn excellent French. So it is also possible to organise instruction in French as a foreign language with discourses about and representations of minority contexts as its starting point. But a possible disadvantage is that there are certain lexical areas that are less utilised, e.g. cultural words that can be used to refer to cultural and social relations that are specific to French-language majority communities, particularly political and legal institutions (in France, Belgium, Québec, etc.). As it is important to be able to formulate oneself within the political area as well (here I am talking about formal politics), one must prefer to focus on majority contexts as a starting point in teaching.

But which majority contexts? What reasons are there, for example, for choosing central target-language countries: Great Britain/the USA, Germany, France, etc.? It is possible to advance a reason that has to do with linguistic knowledge and awareness: students ought to have insight into the cultural/social history of the target language, to know where the intertextual chain in particular has developed, and in what historical contexts the language has become standardised. In French teaching, for example, it is relevant for students to know that the French language has not always been spoken in all of *la francophonie* (where considerable emphasis may be placed today), but that it has developed in the French-speaking area of Western Europe, has a social and regional prehistory in the upper class (aristocracy and bourgeoisie) of French absolutism concentrated in the area around Paris, and that it has been the subject of protracted standardisation on the part of the French state. This historical understanding does not of course have to be acquired in French – it can possibly be in the students' first language (or other languages) when the contexts are explained.

So there are language-historical reasons for choosing one of the central target-language countries as a majority context. But are there contemporary reasons for choosing them? There are, but they are not linguistic but political in the broad sense. The states in question play a large political and cultural role on the world stage (and some of them in Europe). It can therefore be a good idea to make use of the opportunity to deal with them, since one is anyway involved in teaching that cannot be implemented without subjects to talk about or act in relation to. In that way, language teaching has potentially an important role to play as a mediator of knowledge about some of the world's major powers and what goes on in them – also linguistically and culturally.

But there can also be good reasons for choosing other areas that can provide other perspectives on the world, such as postcolonial societies (where English, French, etc. also play an important economic, political and cultural role) and completely different areas, e.g. Japan, the Netherlands, arctic communities, Northern Africa. An important point is that any language can be used in cultural representations of all areas and contexts in the world, but with different languacultural potentials that can function as both possibilities and limitations. As a compensation for limitations, quote words – i.e. cultural words from the language area in question – can possibly be used that have been woven into the text for the situation (e.g. the word 'Folkeskole' in an English text about Danish education) – examples of temporary lexicalisations.

What geographical area is chosen as a point of departure in language teaching is, then, partially political and pedagogical. This can, for example, be seen from the fact that the *Common European Framework* (2001) has restricted itself to European countries[4] (Chapter 6). The implication is that English teaching in Europe is not assumed to deal with the USA.

Knowledge of the world

The above has dealt with geographical areas because I began with the problem area that has to do with which cultural contexts are most relevant when teaching a particular target language. But no matter the geographical area: what topics, issues and discourses are then essential?

The *Common European Framework* proposes a classification of subjects as a point of departure: (1) personal identification; (2) house and home, environment; (3) daily life; (4) free time, entertainment; (5) travel; (6) relations with other people; (7) health and body care; (8) education; (9) shopping; (10) food and drink; (11) services; (12) places; (13) language; (14) weather (*Common European Framework*, 2001: 52). Such a list is naturally more or less coincidental. It is possible to establish classsifications on the basis of many different criteria, and it is no coincidence that the editors have preferred to advance this overview rather than reproduce the more comprehensive classification that is to be found in the earliest precursor, van Ek (1975).[5] The list can help ensure that important areas of vocabulary are not forgotten, but it cannot of course be used for considerations of a more educative nature. In fact, it is not the subjects that are the important thing but the *context* in which they are discursively placed. A topic within the category 'food', for example, can be dealt with practically (how does one make a *bûche de Noël*?); it can be contextualised exclusively nationally (a *bûche de Noël* is something people eat at Christmas in France), or transnationally (where does the tradition come from, regionally and socially? In what sense is it a Christian tradition and does it have any corresponding tradition in Christian environments outside France?)

Language teaching – apart from promoting linguistic/communicative competence – must help students expand their knowledge of the world, which can be seen as a revitalisation of modernism in culture pedagogy, as I wrote in Chapter 6. But what does 'knowledge' mean here?

By 'knowledge' I mean both knowledge of facts and insight into societal contexts. There are (naturally) forms of knowledge that one can call factual knowledge, e.g. elementary geographical, historical and social knowledge: that Manchester is a city in England, that there are mountains and rivers in France, that Germany is divided into *Länder*, etc. But this knowledge will always be embedded in discourses (non-literary as well as literary) that articulate concepts and categories on the basis of particular points of view and positions. By knowledge of 'the world' I mean insight into 'the whole world', an insight that is also self-reflexive: who am I, and where do I stand in the global context – economically, politically, socially, culturally and linguistically? In what sense am I a world citizen, and what does that imply? And, in extension of that: in what sense am I a citizen in, for example, Denmark, and what does that imply?

This knowledge of the world is naturally not simply teaching material that is to be transmitted to passive students. Present-day more postmodernist conditions mean that students are considered as far as possible to be autonomous subjects who have different qualifications, motivations and life-perspectives. Like other subjects, language teaching must offer a knowledge of the world that students can use to develop their personal and cultural identity, via contact with many different discourses and cultural representations, fictive as well as non-fictive. By experimenting with openings in the transnational paradigm, language subjects can acquire a broader role as subjects that contribute to the development of students' identity as world citizens, including their ability to cut across national boundaries and catch sight of transnational connections.

Transnational connections

With the expression 'transnational connections' I am referring to the title of Hannerz's book *Transnational Connections*. Hannerz does not directly define the concept of 'transnational' in the book, but has the following comment on it in relation to the concept of globalisation – a comment that I find very apt:

> I am ... somewhat uncomfortable with the rather prodigious use of the term 'globalization' to describe just about any process or relationship that somehow crosses state boundaries. In themselves, many such processes and relationships obviously do not at all extend across the world. The term 'transnational' is in a way more humble, and often a more adequate label for phenomena which can be of quite

variable scale and distribution, even when they do share the characteristic of not being contained within a state. (Hannerz, 1996: 6)

In the following, I will clarify my use of the concept of transnational connections in relation to language and culture pedagogy. Naturally, there are many different types of transnational connection – I wish to focus on four of them, studies of:

- subnational localities;
- border regions and the border concept;
- issues of potentially global scope;
- images and narratives of the world as a whole.

It is possible to distinguish between two 'layers' in the above points: the two first disassociate themselves from or cut across the national – avoid the banal nationalistic contextualisation. The third, and especially the fourth, directly thematise the global level. While it can be said that the first two are characteristic of the transnational paradigm, the other two are of a transnational nature and in addition are more expressly orientated towards the global level – an orientation which I believe is necessary today, but which does not exclude focusing on other levels, e.g. the European.

Subnational localities

As early as the 1970s, culture pedagogy began to become interested in the local, mostly understood as the regional and its particular political and culture, possibly linguistic, issues, e.g. Brittany in France. But it was not until internationalisation and increased personal contact with people living in particular locations in the target-language countries that there has been a greater focusing on (subnational) local variation. In connection with this, certain people, especially Byram and Roberts, have sought to develop ethnographically oriented methods in language teaching, so that students partly practise doing home ethnographies in their own country/ area and partly carry out ethnographic studies in the locality visited abroad as part of an exchange trip or a study stay (Byram, 1997b; Morgan & Cain, 2000; Risager, 1996; Roberts *et al.*, 2001; Snow & Byram, 1997). The transnational connection is made up of the concrete cultural encounter between two or several locally anchored individuals, groups and contexts: e.g. a school class in the home country and one in the target-language country.

Ethnographic studies can be based on various understandings of culture. It is possible, for example, to distinguish between studies that focus on shared semantic systems in lived communities (e.g. Geertz, 1973; Roberts *et al.*, 2001), or studies that more directly have local cultural complexity as their point of departure (Barth, 1969; Hannerz, 1992a; Pratt, 1987). An example of the latter could be one of the study trips mentioned in Byram and Risager (1999: 131) where a Danish class studying French stayed with a number of families in Strasbourg, including immigrant families. This trip offered an opportunity to deal with various forms of the family on location, and also the local school attended by all the children in the families. The trip probably also made it possible to realise that some of the families spoke French as a second language and that this was signifi-cant in everyday life. And if the class had adopted an explicitly cultural complexity perspective, it could have analysed how the local linguistic and cultural complexity was the result of, among other things, transna-tional flows to France from many places, including Germany and North Africa (migration, use of media, etc.).

Issues relating to place and space are being studied a great deal at present, also within anthropology and Cultural Studies. Among the many publications that can provide inspiration for analysing culture, territoriality and place is *Siting Culture* edited by Olwig and Hastrup (1997). This is a collection of articles that deal with how it is possible to carry out cultural analyses which thematise the importance of place and space in people's creation of affiliation and identity in an everyday life that is characterised by comprehensive, non-territorial networks and transnational connections.

Border regions and the border concept

Culture pedagogy in Europe has long been interested in the border regions and cross-border cooperation – not least in connection with the border areas between France and (West) Germany (cf. Chapter 3). This subject can be dealt with on the basis of the national paradigm and can focus on binational differences, barriers to understanding and potential for cooperation. But it can also be considered from a transnational perspective, focusing on cultural complexity and the setting of boundaries and acts of inclusion and exclusion as are undertaken at many different levels. Since Barth (1969), many anthropologists have been of the opinion that a central element in culture and identity research is the study of how boundaries (national, ethnic, linguistic, etc.) are constructed and maintained (cf. also Byram, 1989: 92ff.). The French culture educationist Zarate has, for example, emphasised that the language teacher is a geopolitical player who finds himself or herself in a border position *(position frontalière)*, someone who can benefit from using work with maps and borders as a point of departure – political maps, historical maps, meteorological maps, etc. – in order to raise questions in class about what sort of a construction borders are, and what they can be used for (Zarate, 1998).

Issues of potentially global scope

In the course of the 1980s and 1990s, there has been a tendency in language teaching that culture pedagogy has not taken much interest in. Exceptions are Conner (1981) (mentioned in Chapter 4), Starkey (e.g. Starkey, 1991a) and myself (Risager, 1989a). During that period, a certain amount of teaching material has come on the scene that introduces topics that do not focus on the target-language countries as such but on cross-cultural or transnational issues of various types. In the 1980s, these were typically topics related to colonialism and imperialism, immigration, new technology, and the arms race and peace movements. Later, there has been growth in such areas as Islam, environmental issues, human rights and anti-racism (Osler & Starkey, 1996). Some people have supplemented more nationally oriented literature with various forms of transnational literature: postcolonial literature, travel literature, exile literature, etc., possibly in translation. Or the focus has been on forms and fusions of music from various parts of the world, e.g. Rastafari and reggae (see also Cates, 2000, on global education).

This tendency, which sometimes goes by the name of 'world studies' or 'global education', could draw support from UNESCO, which as early as the 1970s – during the Cold War – recommended that all education should have a global perspective (still strongly influenced by the national para-digm). In a recommendation from 1974, which still applies, the following guidelines are given for educational policy (not only language subjects):

- an international dimension and a global perspective in education at all levels and in all its forms;
- understanding and respect for all peoples, their cultures, civiliza-tions, values and ways of life, including domestic ethnic cultures and cultures of other nations;
- awareness of the increasing global interdependence between peoples and nations;
- abilities to communicate with others;
- awareness not only of the rights but also of the duties incumbent upon individuals, social groups and nations toward each other;
- understanding of the necessity for international solidarity and co-operation;

- readiness on the part of the individual to participate in solving the problems of his community, his country and the world at large. (Recommendation, 1974: 2)

This recommendation can still be a good input for developing language teaching, especially if it is conceived of as part of the transnational paradigm. As was not the position in the 1970s, it is now possible to say that language subjects are capable of fulfilling not only the recommendation to be *language studies*, and thus enable students to 'communicate with others', but also to be *culture studies* that can contribute to students' knowledge of the world and the formation of their identity, possibly in cooperation with other subjects.

It must be emphasised once more that work on these non-nationally defined topics does not mean a view of the target language that is 'culturally neutral'. There are always languacultural dimensions to take into account.

Images and narratives of the world as a whole

Language subjects (foreign-language subjects) are sometimes termed 'international subjects' – and it is also correct that in principle they extend beyond the national horizon. It is also possible to try to exploit the fact that the commonest 'foreign languages' are languages widely used across the world – especially English nowadays. Language teaching – and English teaching in particular – can be a place where one deals with where the world is heading, linguistically and culturally. What, for example, will the role of the English language be? Such issues can be approached by dealing with images and narratives of the world as a whole – both in the form of discussions of what globalisation is, and in the form of science fiction, cyberstories and other utopias and dystopias about this planet. It can involve other school subjects as well. In this connection, I would like to include the sociologist R. Robertson's thoughts about *images of the world*.[6]

Robertson is often cited for his brief definition of globalisation that emphasises both the objective and the subjective dimension and is to be found in his *Globalization. Social Theory and Global Culture* (1992: 8). The definition is as follows: 'Globalization as a concept refers both to the compression of the world and the intensification of consciousness of the world as a whole.' Robertson is therefore specially interested in how the world's population has to an increasing extent come to imagine the world as a whole.

In this connection, he describes four different *images of the world*: four ways of imagining the development of the world, in cultural and political terms (he does not himself deal with the linguistic). As can be seen, it is somewhat unclear to what extent these images are descriptive and to what extent they represent political projects. Here is the first[7] of Robertson's world images:[8]

> I *Global Gesellschaft 1*. This variant of the image of the world as a form of Gesellschaft involves seeing the global circumstance *as a series of open societies, with considerable sociocultural exchange among them*. The *symmetrical* version considers all societies as politically equal and of reciprocally beneficial material and cultural significance; while the *a*symmetrical version entails the view that there must be dominant or hegemonic societies which play strategically significant roles in sustaining the world and, indeed, that that is the primary mechanism of world order. In both cases national *societies* are regarded as necessarily constituting the central feature of the modern global circumstance. So the problem of globalization is to be confronted either by extensive societal collaboration or by a hierarchical pattern of inter-societal relationships. (Robertson, 1992: 79, italics in the original)

This image of the world as an aggregation of national states is of course well known, and it is also the one that best corresponds to the idea of banal nationalism. The image also corresponds to a certain extent with discourses in those sections of culture pedagogy that are interested in the institutional relations of the target language countries: the political system, the education system, etc. – i.e. the more socially and politically oriented version of the national paradigm.

The symmetrical version of *Global Gesellschaft 1* can be found in the idea of the equal relationship between the major foreign-language subjects: language subjects are seen as fairly equal in status, each with its parallel assignment. The asymmetrical version can perhaps be said to be reflected in the polarisation between English as the predominant language subject on the one hand, and the other language subjects on the other.

Robertson's second world image is described below:

> II *Global Gemeinschaft 1*. This conception of the global circumstance insists that *the world should and can be ordered only in the form of a series of relatively closed societal communities*. The *symmetrical* version of this image of world order sees societal communities as relatively equal to each other in terms of the worth of their cultural traditions, their institutions and the kinds of individual produced in them. The *a*symmetrical version, on the other hand, regards one or a small number of societal communities as necessarily being more important than

others. Those who advocate global 'relativism' based upon the 'sacredness' of all indigenous traditions fall into the symmetrical category; those who claim that theirs is 'the middle kingdom', 'the society of destiny' or 'the lead society' fall into the second category. In the late twentieth-century world both versions tend to seize upon the idea that *individuals* can only live satisfactory lives in clearly bounded societal communities. That does *not* mean that this image emphasizes individual*ism* or individual*ity*. Rather, it involves a particular concern with the problem of the 'homelessness' of individuals confronting the 'dangers' of globalization. (Robertson, 1992: 78, italics in the original)

This image views the world as a number of ethnic groups each of which constitutes a home for individuals who would otherwise become 'homeless' because of transnational migrations. This is a more ethnic-cultural and less political image. Robertson refers among other things to *the worldwide ethnic revival* as an illustration. In culture pedagogy the image can be linked to the schools of thought that focus on the language community and its particular culture. So we are dealing here with a national paradigm in its linguistic-ethnic variant.

The symmetrical version of *Global Gemeinschaft 1* can be found in the various more culturalist ambitions of language subjects, in those cases where the subjects are each seen as representing their separate cultural features: English: the British democratic institutions; German: the German philosophical and literary tradition; French: the French cultivated and aestheticised lifestyle, etc. The asymmetrical version can be reflected in conceptions of the subject English as representing the triumph of the modern life pattern, but also in the conception of the subject French as having a particular cultural mission as a counterweight to (Anglo-American) cultural dominance.

Robertson's third word image is as follows:

III *Global Gesellschaft 2.* This conception of world order claims that it can only be obtained *on the basis of formal, planned world organization.* The *centralized* version of *Gesellschaft 2* is committed to a strong supranatural (sic!) polity, while the *decentralized* form advocates something like a federation at the global level. Both variants take the *world-system* of societies as constituting the major unavoidable dimension of the contemporary global-human condition. They share the view that the only effective way of dealing with the dangers of globalization is by systematic organization of that process. (Robertson, 1992: 79, italics in the original)

This conception of a politically organised world order would seem to be far removed from the common self-understanding of language subjects. But the subject English, which generally speaking must be said to be further on the way towards a transnational paradigm than the other language subjects, is particularly interesting in this connection, because English may possibly acquire the role of 'official' global language and thus develop into a compulsory second language for everybody in their capacity of (also in a political sense) world citizens. This process is already under way at the European level in connection with the struggle for the official and unofficial status of the various languages involved. It is also evident in debates in Japan and Taiwan about making English the second official language. The problem areas in this world image thus relate to the transnational paradigm in a politically oriented understanding.

Robertson's fourth world image is described below:

> IV *Global Gemeinschaft 2*. This image of the world situation maintains that *only in terms of a fully globewide community per se can there be global order*. Corresponding to the distinction between symmetrical and asymmetrical versions of *Gemeinschaft I*, there are *centralized* and *de*centralized forms of this image of the world as almost literally a 'global village'. The first insists that there must be a globewide Durkheimian 'conscience collective', while the second maintains that a global community is possible on a much more pluralistic basis. Both versions of this second type of *Gemeinschaft* stress *mankind* as the pivotal ingredient of the world as a whole. Thus the dangers of globalization are to be overcome by commitments to the communal unity of the human species. (Robertson, 1992: 78ff., italics in the original)

This world image deals with the great community of humanity, understood more in a cultural than a political sense. Robertson names such examples as peace movements, ecofeminism and liberation theology. This image is not an extension of the way language teaching generally understands itself, as this is based on a differential concept of language and thus on a differential concept of culture. A transnational paradigm in language and culture pedagogy can, however, relate to this image via an interest in the linguistic, discursive and cultural flows in the world. Perhaps, parallel with the preceding more political image, it can be said that the subject English is sometimes based on a utopia of the English language as the future common language of communication for everyone, for use in international and transnational cooperation, in NGOs and the like?

These issues are not meant as questions that absolutely have to be raised in teaching itself, but they are fundamental for the linguistic and cultural self-understanding of language subjects at a more general level. Those who are involved in language subjects ought to be familiar with a holistic approach, one that tries to take a bird's eye view of the subject – sometimes referred to as 'the planetary perspective'. Even so, it is also important to retain a link with the local: the world images and the subject-related self-understandings are always seen from a certain perspective, a certain 'locus' – geographically, socially, culturally, etc. The self-understanding of the subject French, for example, will be different depending on whether the subject functions in Denmark, in Great Britain or in Vietnam – contexts that represent very different geopolitical and 'geocultural' positions in the world.[9]

Contexts and Contacts

This section deals with points 6–7 of the transnational paradigm, not with topics and discourses but with *how* learning takes place, and together with *whom*. It could be said that, whereas the transnational connections in points 4–5 are borne by discourse and contained in the way topics are selected and treated, the transnational connections in points 6–7 are some that have materialised in practice – no matter whether it is a question of purely physical mobility or of having contact with more or less reality-oriented chatrooms on the Internet.

Within the ideal-typical national paradigm, topics and discourses only deal with the target-language countries (implicitly: first-language contexts) and study and exchange trips also go only to the target-language countries, in order to experience 'authentic' cultural and social relations (what, among other things, is referred to as *erlebte Landeskunde*). But such trips always have to go to a particular location: a town, a region, etc., i.e. the national contextualisation can be difficult to maintain as the primary focus. We are dealing with individuals and their experiences and encounters, and therefore it is more difficult to interpret the cultural encounter as solely one between national cultures. The pedagogical task is rather to treat the encounter as a personal one, wherein many different identities can be made relevant and play a role – including, possibly, the national.[10]

At present, ethnographically inspired methods are being devised to study the here-and-now context that forms the framework for language use in the locality that is the destination for the trip. This ought also to include studies of the local sociolinguistic situation. When students travel to a particular locality in the target-language country, they will perhaps come into contact with people who have different social, ethnic and linguistic backgrounds from those they have previously experienced. In some localities, people will speak sociolects that differ considerably from more standard forms of pronunciation, or speak the language as a second language. So the students will come to experience the locality as both a first-language and a second-language context.

But there may also be good pedagogical reasons for allowing study trips to be made to foreign-language contexts: to places (countries) where the target language features as a foreign language by virtue of the fact that it is a language that is taught as a foreign language in the country's schools (cf. also Risager, 1998). This can, for example, take place in connection with a meeting between twinned towns. Danish students could, as part of an exchange trip, live in a Polish town and speak English with the Polish students. They can study the local cultural complexity – whose linguistic dimension can of course be difficult to relate to without previous knowledge (cf. Risager, 1996). Students experience the local language(s), first and foremost Polish, spoken and written around them, even though they do not understand it, or understand only snatches of it. It is under all circumstances an important contribution to their linguistic awareness – and it is the teachers' task to ensure that the students can upgrade their experiences via a certain knowledge of these languages (including Polish): how widespread are they, what other languages do they resemble, etc.? In other words, attempts must be made to transcend the monolingual tradition of language teaching and to try to avoid other languages becoming invisible.

Communication with people in foreign-language contexts (non-target-language countries) can also take place via e-mail and the Internet, where there are an infinite number of potential contacts throughout the world – and there are many examples in present-day foreign-language teaching of an interest in ICT.

One example could be as follows: a Danish German class makes use of the fact that the school is linked to the electronic network *'European Schools Project'*.[11] They gain inspiration from German-language material about 'The Image of the Other' and make e-mail contact with a German class in the Netherlands, corresponding in German with it about images of foreigners and national stereotypes for a particular nationality – possibly Germans. The Dutch and Danish students discover that they hardly have stereotypes about each other at all, which has to do with the fact that they know very little about each other. This cooperation is constructed nationally and focuses on a particular type of national representation. But it also encourages a discussion of the national in relation to European development, i.e. a treatment of the national level as something local that is placed within a larger context.

A second example of a European-oriented project might be the following: as part of French teaching, a Danish upper-secondary-level student takes part in a conference in 'The European Youth Parliament', which lasts a week and (in the year in question) is held in Strasbourg.[12] For a week, young people from many European countries discuss a whole series of political issues: democracy in the EU, the political situation in Eastern Europe, immigration and refugee problems, etc. A presentation is also given by a French member of the European Parliament. The student in question takes part in a broadly based multinational commission on environmental policy in Europe and helps draw up a resolution in French and English, which are the working languages of the conference. She brings the resolution home with her to the class in Denmark, where they work on the French version but also on the English, discussing such subjects as language differences and problems of translation. This project is also highly national in its composition, but it thematises trans-border subjects and problems of a more comprehensive (European) relevance.

Language teaching can also make use of other existing networks. It is possible, for example, to use contacts with the Turkish networks in various European countries. Turkish-speaking students in the class can be mediators to Turkish-speaking groups in such countries as Germany, so that the class, via Danish-German-Turkish mediation, can get to know something about other life forms and other images of Germany than they perhaps are accustomed to – either as a concrete experience in connection with a study trip, or mediated via e-mail communication or the like.

A more or less neglected, but potentially rewarding task for language teaching is to equip students to be able to enter into transnational cooperation of every type while using the target language. Here it is possible to point to a field that, broadly speaking, has remained unexploited in language teaching – cooperation with the increasingly numerous and important national and transnational NGOs (non-governmental organisations), i.e. all kinds of association and organisation, including some that operate across national borders: environmental organisations, sports organisations, political organisations and movements, developmental and aid organisations, business organisations, gender-political organisations, committees and associations related to the UN, UNESCO and UNICEF, etc., etc. If language teaching is to try to prepare students to be intercultural speakers, cooperation with NGOs must be able to contribute to this by strengthening students' competence to act and mediate in practice – linguistically, discursively and culturally. One of the possibilities would be to experiment with practice in such a context and possibly make use of ethnographic methods as described in the above-mentioned book by Roberts *et al.* (2001).

The National Dilemma: Between Complexity and Homogeneity

Language and languaculture

The transnational paradigm is based on an awareness of linguistic and cultural complexity, and of linguistic, languacultural and discursive flows. It is also based on an awareness that 'language', 'culture' and 'the nation' are historically constructed ideas each with its own conceptual history and its societal significance in the building of nation states in recent centuries. While the national paradigm contains a discourse that conceals the complexity, the transnational paradigm contains a discourse in which the acceptance of the complexity is a fundamental feature. For that reason, something arises that I intend to call 'the national dilemma' in language and culture pedagogy – especially for the teacher. The national dilemma consists of an impossible choice between two considerations.

On the one hand, we have the necessity for language teaching to be as realistic as possible and throughout to encourage contact with environments in which the target language is used, including first-language contexts – a consideration that in the more recent history of language pedagogy has been referred to by such terms as 'authentic language', 'authentic texts', 'authentic contexts'. Language teaching must, among other things, include (and it already does in some cases) the new ways of using language that are developed by written and oral communication via multimedia and the Internet in general.

On the other hand, there is the necessity for the aim of language teaching to be so clear-cut and unambiguous that learning is not complicated by sheer confusion about what is required. Homogeneity must be created that optimises learning. What this homogeneity is built up around is not the personal choice of those involved. It must be built up around the already existing norm expectations in society. Language teaching must be based on (one of) the existing (national) standard norms for the target language, especially as far as the written language is concerned. As a general rule, it must be based on what I referred to above as 'the norms of others' – knowing full well that these norms are discursively constructed and are, in principle, capable of being changed. At the same time, experiments can also be carried out with linguistic diversity and creativity – the poetic dimension of languaculture.

The teacher's dilemma arises in relation to the use of the target language in the classroom, on study trips, etc.: pronunciation, orthography, vocabulary, syntax, textual organisation, genres in the spoken and written language, etc. It is part of the teacher's job to occasionally intervene in the students' use of the target language and make decisions about what is right and what is wrong in their oral and written linguistic/ languacultural practice. In some cases, it is simply a matter of following directions that are already prescribed in the spelling dictionary, for example, but in other cases it is a matter of the teacher himself or herself making that decision – in correcting compositions, for example, and not least in connection with translations, where there are normally no 'rules' for a correct translation, once one has got beyond the near-equivalents (the Danish word *'hund'* corresponds to dog, *'flagermus'* corresponds to bat, etc.). If culturally specific connotations (cf. the dog's symbolic meaning in various cultural contexts) and genre conventions are to be taken into account, the complexity is considerable, and translation has very much to do with a personal weighting of the possible meanings. Here, the teacher cannot avoid having to make decisions from time to time when it comes to what 'weightings' are best.

The dilemma may also be connected with choice of language and attitudes to various languages and dialects. What varieties of the target language are chosen, for example, as a point of departure in language teaching? Here – as mentioned earlier – a distinction must be made between the language varieties the students are presented with for listening and reading comprehension, and the ones they learn to produce themselves. In English, for example, students may profit a great deal from trying to *understand* the target language as it is spoken by children in well-to-do families (many will become au-pair girls, perhaps) or the target language spoken as a foreign language by many different nationalities (many will perhaps become backpackers and need the target language in lingua franca situations).

The choice of the language the students are to learn to *produce* themselves is not something completely obvious. To stick to an upper-middle-class British English is only one of many possibilities – and one that is based more on notions than realities. In the subject English (in a country, for example, like Denmark – perhaps depending on the type of schooling) there is an intuitive consensus about what 'English' means in practice – a consensus that is supported by the teaching materials on the market – but what sort of English ought to be chosen has not been looked into enough by the profession, apart from the sporadic discussion of whether British or American English ought to be chosen.

When the class is on a study or exchange trip abroad, e.g. in Berlin, the students of German in most cases experience the local linguistic complexity. They meet the language in many guises – the language of men and women, social and professional varieties – and often meet the language as it is spoken by both first-language and second-language speakers. They listen to everyone, talk to them, and perhaps try to imitate their pronunciation. The question now is: are there language varieties the students ought to be warned against using? What criteria are relevant? Should students pronounce German as they can hear various language minorities do in Berlin, or should they exclusively try to imitate native speakers? Such decisions have languacultural implications for the students that have to do with their identity: the language choices that the students make when abroad must be expected to have certain consequences for how they are perceived – even though it may not necessarily be related to the same categories as for the native speakers.

This question of models has become topical in recent years in connection with criticism of 'the native-speaker model'. The most accessible model is in practice the teacher himself or herself – and in foreign-language teaching the teacher normally does not speak the target language as a first language but as a foreign language. So is it perhaps reasonable for students in, for example, English teaching to let themselves be influenced by people in England who talk English as a second language? Or why not people in Australia who speak English as a second language?

These difficult decisions actually demand a high degree of norm awareness and sociolinguistic insight on the part of teachers – an awareness they are rarely equipped with as a result of their own education.

The dilemma between linguistic complexity and homogeneity has always been at least implicitly present in language teaching. But it has been underexposed or completely repressed by a discourse about homogeneity, and in connection with the nationalisation of language subjects it has been repressed by a discourse about national linguistic homogeneity. It could be said that researchers and teachers via the national paradigm have ignored the complexity and thereby been unable to adopt a conscious attitude to the dilemma as such. This has meant that language subjects, especially at the more elementary levels of teaching, have been characteristic channels of banal nationalism, in Billig's sense of the term.

Within the transnational paradigm the dilemma is the opposite. Here the problem is not to glimpse the complexity but to retain a satisfactory notion of the homogeneous norm that is necessary in teaching contexts, especially at the more elementary levels. As a teacher, one is faced with the rhetorical challenge to *justify* the target-language norm and explain how it came about – and to what uses it can be put. In the pedagogical context, ways must be found to present spoken and written language norms as *pedagogically necessary simplifications*, especially in relation to the students' production of language.

Discourses and other dimensions of culture

The above is a matter of dilemmas concerning language and languaculture. When one turns to the discourses of language teaching and other cultural dimensions there are also many important choices that have to be made, some of which can be related to the linguistic/languacultural national dilemma.

When it comes to the choice of discourse, there are wide-ranging possibilities to demonstrate the usability of the target language in connection with many different types of topic and point of view – and right from the outset of teaching. An important question is whether to choose 'predictable' topics, e.g. fashion and gastronomy in French teaching, or Nazism in German teaching, or whether to choose more unusual topics, e.g. upset widespread national stereotypes about Germany and France respectively by choosing 'fashion' and 'gastronomy' in German teaching, and 'Nazism' in French teaching.[13] Clearly, such questions – if they can be asked at all – call for discussions in the class about what really are essential topics in language teaching.

The questions thematise the national dilemma in the sense that they deal with handling national-cultural representations and symbolisms. On the one hand, these must be taken seriously as telling cultural images; on the other hand, alternative (local/global) images and contextualisations must also be established. Here I have focused on discourses expressed in verbal language practice, but obviously quite parallel questions arise regarding practice that makes use of other sign systems: visual representations from various countries, musical expressions from various parts of the world, food, dress styles, etc., etc.

Discourses on language, culture and society will presumably adopt different attitudes towards the national, depending on whether teaching is oriented towards the past or the present in terms of content – or maybe the future. This can, among other things, affect the view of language. If teaching is mainly 'retrospective' in a literary or broadly cultural and social-historical sense, the role of the target language as national language and as part of the general formation of national identity will perhaps be emphasised. But if teaching is mainly oriented towards the present day and ongoing processes, the role of the target language as an international language will perhaps be emphasised. There may be a choice involved here that the individual teacher/individual class must make in the various phases of teaching. Is teaching to be retrospective and explore the historical roots of language, including the national ones – which may be important in maintaining a historical awareness – or is it to look forwards and explore possible uses of the language in a 'globalised' world – which may be important in relation to the students' own life-perspective?

Conclusion

In this chapter I have outlined certain basic differences between a national and a transnational paradigm for language and culture pedagogy and suggested what the latter could possibly contain.

When it comes to languaculture, I would maintain that language teaching is always to some extent languaculture teaching. This applies no matter what topics and discourses are involved. When it comes to topics and discourses in teaching, I would maintain that it is necessary in teaching that has a general aim to let part of the teaching have topics and discourses as its point of departure that related to first-language contexts (preferably majority contexts), and this is first and foremost in order to give the students the opportunity to acquire an understanding of cultural words in relation to their culture-historical context. But, in addition, the choice of topics and discourses is a question that is an independent – and language-independent – one, a question of what overall educative aim language teaching is to have.

To sum up, the transnational paradigm calls for increased reflexivity by those involved – not least the teacher. When the traditional content-based idea of culture pedagogy is abandoned – that 'language', 'cultural content' and 'cultural context' are inseparable – possibilities open up for other topics and discourses, other contexts and other contacts. There are even more choices to be made – and even more contexts to be explained.

Finally, I have looked at the 'national dilemma' language subjects are facing. This is a pedagogical dilemma that arises in connection with the transnational paradigm, a dilemma between, on the one hand, the linguistic and cultural complexity of the world and, on the other hand, the necessity of a certain homogeneity in the picture of the pedagogical aims for teaching – as regards both language and culture.

Notes

1. Which is also one of the points in my discussion of nationalism and internationalism in language subjects in Risager (1984).
2. Some people use the term 'transcultural', as I myself have done in Risager (1998). But I believe that the term 'transnational' is, theoretically speaking, more adequate in this context. The 'transnational' covers something that cuts across 'nations', i.e. partly national communities, partly national state structures. 'Transcultural' seems more to cover something that cuts across 'cultures', and this implies a holistic concept of culture that I do not share.

3. Lewis (1993) distinguishes between 'target language' and 'model language'. The former corresponds to what I call 'the decisive model' and the latter to 'a temporary model'.

4. These are not further defined, but presumably the countries of the Council of Europe are being thought of.

5. It is interesting to note the small but significant changes that have taken place to the list since it first featured in van Ek (1975). Then, the headings were: (1) personal identification; (2) house and home; (3) trade, profession, occupation; (4) free time, entertainment; (5) travel; (6) relations with other people; (7) health and welfare; (8) education; (9) shopping; (10) food and drink; (11) services; (12) places; (13) foreign language; (14) weather (van Ek, 1975: 22ff). There are changes to points (2), (3) and (13). It should however be remembered that van Ek (1975) was intended specifically for adult learners.

6. Implicitly: cultural world images – as opposed to the more physical world images that feature in astronomy, astrology and cosmology.

7. I have changed Robertson's original order in Robertson (1992).

8. Robertson in the following uses the terms *Gemeinschaft* and *Gesellschaft*, which are a classic pair of concepts in sociology, coined by the German sociologist Ferdinand Tönnies in the 1880s. He briefly characterises them as follows: 'Gemeinschaft … is a term for the internal links between people: family (the ties of kin), neighbourhood, ties of place based on custom, and friendship, the ties of disposition. The external forms of Gemeinschaft are house, village (common land) and borough town (die Stadt). Its general concepts are the people, united by inner ties, language, custom and belief as well as religious, in principle universal, community. As against this, Gesellschaft is a term for the external connections, where people meet as partners of interest and exchange. Gesellschaft is most concentrated in the metropolis, but is to be found in varying dosages everywhere in society. While the integrative aspect is strong in Gemeinschaft, the conflicting aspect is predominant in Gesellschaft' (Falk, 2000: 61).

9. Cf. maps of the world, that are also produced from a planetary perspective yet have to be depicted from a particular 'locus' out in space: there is always a particular focus, cf. the Europe-focused or 'Western'-focused world map.

10. A language-learning model that consistently utilises the personal encounter is tandem learning, where two people learn each other's language. But even this personal encounter can easily come to be viewed in banal-nationalism terms if those taking part are not trained to avoid this.

11. This example is based on Knudsen and Hagen (1996).

12. This example is based on Kornum (1999).

13. This does not, of course, mean that one should necessarily focus on *German* fashion and gastronomy or *French* Nazism.

Chapter 9

The Intercultural Competence of the World Citizen

Introduction

The previous chapter dealt with (the theory of) aims and content in language *teaching*, i.e. its point of departure was a sociological point of view. We now move on to the psychological point of view and take a look at (the theory of) the individual and his/her linguistic, languacultural and other cultural *competences* and *resources*. Let me underline that I will not deal specifically with psychological/cognitive processes but instead discuss the aims and content of personal development. In this connection, I am thinking of both primary learners (students) and teachers.

To begin with, let me return to the discussion of the concept of intercultural competence, which I left in Chapter 5 with the analysis of the relationship between language, culture and nation in Byram's book *Teaching and Assessing Intercultural Communicative Competence* (1997a). I now intend to reinterpret the understanding of intercultural communicative competence, using as my point of departure the analysis of the relationship between language and culture and the characterisation of the transnational paradigm.

One of the ingredients of this reinterpretation is the concept of world citizen identity. Every human being on this earth is in practice a world citizen in a linguistic, cultural and social sense, insofar as all of us are involved in certain structures and processes that, to an increasing extent, are worldwide. From this overall perspective, I will seek to describe the knowledge and insight that characterise the intercultural speaker who understands himself or herself as a world citizen – the long-term goal for general-purpose language teaching at all levels. So it is not 'the world citizen' in general this chapter deals with (here I would refer the reader to, in particular, Beck, 2002 and 2004) but 'the world citizen' seen *from the perspective of language and culture pedagogy.*

The Intercultural Speaker: Two Models

The concept of the 'intercultural speaker' came into being as a contrast to that of the 'native speaker' (and 'non-native speaker'). It directs attention to the role of negotiator and mediator that the language learner can cultivate through practice and conscious work on the negotiation of meaning: the forming of meaning in interaction. In my terminology, we are dealing here with languaculture, especially the first of the three dimensions – semantics and pragmatics.

There is, however, a major difference in how broadly this role of negotiator and mediator is conceived, and this is related to how one imagines the relationship between language and culture. On several occasions, I have mentioned the metaphors 'culture in language' and 'language in culture'. This can be described as a mutual meronymy, or part–whole relation, and I have attempted to resolve this paradoxical metaphorical structure by distinguishing between languaculture, discourse and the rest of culture. The two views of language connected to this pair of metaphors have led to two different models of intercultural competence and the intercultural speaker.

Those within language and culture pedagogy who mainly have a linguistic point of departure typically place cultural competence as a *subcomponent* of communicative competence. This we find most explicitly in van Ek (1987), but the presentation in Kramsch (1998) is also implicitly based on this idea. Kramsch focuses on the linguistic since, as already mentioned, she talks about 'the "intercultural" speaker, operating at the border between several languages or language varieties, manoeuvring his/her way through the troubled waters of cross-cultural misunderstandings' (Kramsch, 1998: 27, inverted commas in the original).[1]

Byram (and Zarate), who adopt an anthropological point of departure, have described a more comprehensive model, as they feel it is necessary to supplement the communicative, sociolinguistic competence with an intercultural competence that in principle is independent of language (although their prototype of an 'intercultural speaker' is still someone who develops and uses his or her intercultural competence as part of using a foreign language).[2] Communicative and intercultural competence are treated separately, and the relation between them is not further clarified. The model for intercultural competence is 'hitched onto' the model for communicative competence (cf. the discussion in Chapter 5).

So it can be said that we are dealing with two competing models of the intercultural speaker: one that operates with one integrated model (cf. 'culture in language' (van Ek and, indirectly, Kramsch), and one that operates with a two-part model consisting of a linguistic and a cultural part (an approximation of 'language in culture') (Byram and Zarate).[3] In my opinion, a more differentiated model should be developed that combines aspects of them both: the dichotomy between language and culture in Byram's model must be neutralised via the introduction of the concepts of languaculture and discourse, and it must be broadened with knowledge of language and critical language awareness. At the same time, Kramsch's poststructuralist and (signs of a) transnational approach is maintained and broadened to include the whole model. Byram's model in Byram (1997a) is still too ambivalent regarding the national paradigm: sometimes this paradigm is obvious, elsewhere he dissociates himself from it (cf. Chapter 5).

Intercultural Communicative Competence

To underpin the following discussion, I here briefly present the eight subcompetences of intercultural communicative competence described by Byram (Byram, 1997a). Byram defines the *linguistic* part of the intercultural speaker's competence in this way:

(1) *Linguistic competence*: the ability to apply knowledge of the rules of a standard version of the language to produce and interpret spoken and written language.

(2) *Sociolinguistic competence*: the ability to give to the language produced by an interlocutor – whether native speaker or not – meanings which are taken for granted by the interlocutor or which are negotiated and made explicit with the interlocutor.[4]

(3) *Discourse competence*: the ability to use, discover and negotiate strategies for the production and interpretation of monologue or dialogue texts which follow the conventions of the culture of an interlocutor or are negotiated as intercultural texts for particular purposes. (Byram, 1997a: 48, italics in the original)[5]

The *cultural* part of the intercultural speaker's competence contains the five *savoirs*, cf. Chapter 5:

(4) *Attitudes*: curiosity and openness, readiness to suspend disbelief about other cultures and belief about one's own *(savoir être)*.

(5) *Knowledge*: of social groups and their products and practices in one's own and in one's interlocutor's country, and of the general processes of societal and individual interaction *(savoirs)*.

(6) *Skills* of interpreting and relating: ability to interpret a document or event from another culture, to explain it and relate it to documents from one's own *(savoir comprendre)*.

(7) *Skills* of discovery and interaction: ability to acquire new knowledge of a culture and cultural practices and the ability to operate knowledge,

attitudes and skills under the constraints of real-time communication and interaction *(savoir apprendre/faire)*.

(8) *Critical cultural awareness/political education*: an ability to evaluate critically and on the basis of explicit criteria perspectives, practices and products in one's own and other cultures and countries *(savoir s'engager)*. (From Byram's summary in Roberts *et al.*, 2001: 231ff.)[6]

Byram emphasises that the five *savoirs* are not just minted for the person who acquires/learns a foreign language (or second language). Everyone, including monolinguals, can and ought to develop their intercultural competence.

Before embarking on a discussion of how the concepts of languaculture, discourse and (other forms of) culture can contribute to illuminating and developing Byram's subcompetences, I would like to comment on the concept of 'tertiary socialisation', which Byram uses in connection with intercultural competence.

Tertiary socialisation

Among other things, Byram describes intercultural communicative competence as the ability to cope with tertiary socialisation. He proposes, in accordance with the German cultural educationist Doyé, that the theory of primary and secondary socialisation (which comes from Berger and Luckmann, 1991, (1966)) should be enlarged to include a tertiary socialisation. While primary socialisation is what takes place in the close social and emotional environment of the family, and secondary socialisation takes place in school and subsequently the workplace and thus in more broadly oriented social professional/intellectual environments, tertiary socialisation is what one becomes involved in when one begins to learn foreign languages, e.g. at school age:

> When people learn a foreign language, many of the values, meanings, beliefs and behaviours they had acquired early in life and assumed to be natural and normal, are confronted by different interpretations... The values and beliefs they assume to be universal because they are dominant in the society in which they live, are found to be relative and different from one country to another. This is more than and different from an extension of experience into new social statuses in the same society, because it challenges the fundamental taken-for-granted norms acquired early in life. (Byram, 1995: 58ff.)

So Byram believes that in tertiary socialisation the individual is confronted with alternative ways of living and understanding the world, over and above those he / she has become accustomed to within the family, the national school system and the national labour market.

It is highly relevant to place foreign-language learning into a socialisation context, but Byram's presentation is based on the national paradigm and it tends to describe the three types of socialisation as relatively separate from each other. To take the last matter first, I believe the three types mesh much more with each other, keeping pace with the growth of linguistic and ethnic complexity in most societies.

Firstly, secondary socialisation meshes with primary socialisation: primary socialisation in the family is influenced by socialisation via children's institutions and the media. This means that small children gain certain experiences with social differences and contrasts – relations which, according to Berger and Luckmann, belong to secondary socialisation. Secondly, tertiary socialisation meshes with primary socialisation: primary socialisation in the family is influenced by socialisation in the possibly multi-ethnic children's institutions and transnational TV channels and programmes, which also give small children certain experiences with linguistic, ethnic and race-related differences. Thirdly, tertiary socialisation meshes with secondary socialisation: because of the processes of globalisation and internationalisation, the education system and business life – and parts of the youth and adult population – gain certain experiences with linguistic, ethnic, race-related and national differences (multicultural classes, multicultural workplaces, school trips abroad, etc.). Global development means, then, that many children and young people around the world get impulses and signals that contribute to a tertiary socialisation process from the early childhood years.

In addition, it is – as mentioned – problematic that the concept of tertiary socialisation is based on a national paradigm – in a politico-national sense (another society, another country) or in a linguistic-ethnic sense (another language and culture). Considering the increasing multiculturality in the world, it seems better to make do with a division into primary and secondary socialisation and not to operate with a tertiary socialisation: primary socialisation is the basic, personality-forming socialisation, which can quite well take place in a multilingual and multicultural environment (e.g. in a bilingual family). Secondary socialisation, which comes later, can also take place – and to an increasing extent will take place – in multilingual and multicultural environments (forms of education, workplaces, leisure activities).

Competences and Resources of the World Citizen

Let me begin by saying that I have used the competence concept in the title of this chapter because this concept has gradually gained wide acceptance. In fact, I believe the competence concept is problematic. Firstly, it has a positivist slant, as the concept of 'communicative competence' is related to the educational context and to assessment and testing in relation to labour-market requirements. Admittedly, there is nothing wrong with assessment as such, but the multilingual development of the individual comprises more than what can or ought to be assessed, e.g. the ability to use the English language's prestige in code-switching between Danish and English, or experiences of linguistic prejudices, e.g.: Arabic is inferior to Danish, German is an ugly language, etc. Secondly, the concept of competence is based on a concept of language that is too narrow: it does not include metalingual attitudes and conceptions, and it does not include private and inner speech. Moreover, it typically deals with only one (standard) language at a time and does not contain any sociolinguistic understanding of the multilingual individual. So in the following I will talk about *both* resources (the broader concept) *and* competences (the narrower concept). The concept of competence is used as a specialised subcategory of the concept of resources – a subcategory that contains the skill- and knowledge-related aspects that it seems relevant and possible to assess (Risager, 1999b).[7]

In the following, I will look at how Byram's model for intercultural communicative competence can be further developed with the aid of the concepts of languaculture and discourse. To begin with, here is an overview of the elements that comprise my interpretation:[8]

(1) Linguistic (languastructural) competence.
(2) Languacultural competences and resources: semantics and pragmatics.
(3) Languacultural competences and resources: poetics.
(4) Languacultural competences and resources: linguistic identity.
(5) Translation and interpretation.
(6) Interpreting texts (discourses) and media products in a broad sense.
(7) Use of ethnographic methods.
(8) Transnational cooperation.
(9) Knowledge of language and critical language awareness, also as a world citizen.
(10) Knowledge of culture and society and critical cultural awareness, also as a world citizen.

Although I do not deal with mental/cognitive development as such, I must nonetheless emphasise that competences and resources must always be seen in their life-historical context. The competences and resources of the individual subject develop on the basis of a psycho-social and psycho-dynamic basis that forms his/her fundamental trust in the world and other human beings, his/her feeling of self-worth and self-identity,[9] including sexual identity. This basis can be more or less challenging for attitudes that are important for the intercultural speaker: curiosity, openness, willingness to question prejudices, willingness to modify one's own identity. Life-historical breaks and traumas, e.g. in connection with political persecution and fleeing into exile, can also be of great importance for the individual's ability to further develop his/her competences and resources. In relation to Byram's model, these problem areas are mostly connected to no. 4: attitudes/*savoir-être*, but Byram does not have developmental psychology and socialisation theory as his point of departure here – he starts with social psychology and therefore *savoir-être* is mostly about attitudes and willingness to communicate and interact with others.

What are described in the following are the most important elements in the *long-term* goal for language teaching for general purposes. I do not distinguish between whether the target language is a foreign language, second language or community/heritage language, since I believe that the long-term goals for all forms of language learning are identical. In all cases, it is (in particular) the language teacher who actually decides what is relevant and possible for the students involved.

(1) Linguistic (languastructural) competence

The central thing about the acquisition/learning of a target language is the development of languastructural competence: the building-up of the mental lexicon and the increasing complexification of the morphology, syntax and textual structure of the interlanguage as regards both the content and the expression dimensions of language. This is related to both the building-up of the individual's own production capacity and his/her perception and comprehension capacity – also regarding other ways of using the language than the one he/she personally uses. This is closest to no. 1 in Byram's model: *linguistic competence*, but it should be emphasised that the acquisition of the target language must be seen in relation to the first language and any eventual other language the person in question might know. It is a matter of integrating certain competences with others already there. Furthermore, I think one ought to differentiate what Byram calls 'a standard version of the language', cf. the discussion of language norms in production and reception, and the relationship between written language norms and spoken language norms. In this process of acquisition/learning there are three languacultural dimensions that can be emphasised, as follows.

(2) Languacultural competences and resources: Semantics and pragmatics

As the languastructural competence develops, so do the languacultural competences and resources within the semantic and pragmatic areas. The person involved practises relating dialogically to language,[10] negotiating meaning, distinguishing between semantics/pragmatics in spoken and written language genres respectively, using paralanguage and kinesics to accompany personal linguistic expression and utilising his or her private and inner speech (probably in the first language) to solve problems and aid memory. He or she learns to deal with linguistic complexity, also by communicating with people who speak the target language as their first language, second language or foreign language and with various linguistic backgrounds. This is close to no. 2 in Byram's model: *sociolinguistic competence*, but formulated in languacultural terms.

(3) Languacultural competences and resources: Poetics

The second dimension of languaculture, the poetic use of language, can theoretically develop alongside the above. Here we are dealing more with resources than with competences, and this aspect is not included in Byram's model. In language pedagogy there is actually considerable use of poetic methods (normally as a tool, not a goal), but I feel there can be reasons for upgrading linguistic creativity in the form of, for example, creative writing or conscious code-switching and code-mixing, and thus to incorporate the poetic use of language into the competences worth assessing.

(4) Languacultural competences and resources: Linguistic identity

The third dimension (which is not included in Byram's model) also develops in parallel with the above, more or less consciously or explicitly. As the speaker of a foreign language one faces a particular problem of identity, as the way one uses the language is not automatically included in the social categorisations of first language speakers. How is one to guarantee optimum reception and recognition by native speakers, no matter what the level of competence one has attained (in both speech and writing)? This question is central to the identity-related dimension of languaculture.

(5) Translation and interpretation

The kinds of competence and resource that it is important for the intercultural speaker to have are familiarity and certain practice with translation and interpretation (especially simultaneous interpretation in small groups) – where these activities are not viewed as being 'purely linguistic' but as something that involves both languacultural issues and more general ones that have to do with cultural translation and intercultural communication. This aspect is connected to no. 3 in Byram's model: discourse competence: intercultural texts.

(6) Interpretation of texts (discourses) and media products in a broad sense

The intercultural speaker needs to be able to do some discourse analysis of texts in the target language. An important element here are the products of the culture industry, including media and Internet products of a discursive but also a visual and a musical nature. For this reason, the speaker involved needs to develop competences and resources with the aim of interpreting such products and relating them to his or her own and others' perspectives, knowledge and experiences. We find this in no. 6 in Byram's model: *savoir comprendre*, but here I have indicated more clearly that we are dealing, among other things, with proficiencies in relation to one of the important areas within 'the rest of culture' (which is not linguistically formed): the cultural flow of visual and musical products in the national and transnational mass media and on the Internet.

(7) Use of ethnographic methods

Another important field is everyday life and its both discursive and material, silent sides. Here, the intercultural speaker needs to be able to use ethnographic methods to seek out, examine, understand and relate to the life of lived communities where there is a greater or lesser degree of linguistic and cultural complexity. Here we have no. 7 in Byram's model: *savoir apprendre/faire*. This proficiency I have made quite a lot out of in connection with considerations to do with studying subnational localities, in Chapter 8.

(8) Transnational cooperation

As I argued in the previous chapter, I believe it would be highly beneficial to establish cooperation with the many different forms of transnational organisation and association, which also contain linguistic challenges in their internal communication. These could be sports associations, twinned-town associations or more activist movements such as Amnesty International. Such cooperation (which Byram does not mention in his model) gives the individual learner competences and resources that are action-oriented and which contribute at the same time to building up a knowledge of the world and the possibility of making personal attachments to people in other language areas.

(9) Knowledge of language and critical language awareness, also as a world citizen

A task for language subjects that Byram does not include in his model (or perhaps it is there implicitly in no. 5: *Savoirs*) is the contribution to the students' knowledge of language and their language awareness. I am thinking of knowledge (discourses) of the relationship between language and identity, of differences between knowing a language as a first language, second language and foreign language, and of how (generally speaking) languages can be acquired. I am also thinking of what Fairclough, among others, refers to as critical language awareness (Fairclough, 1992b), i.e. knowledge and awareness of the relationship between language and power, first and foremost to do with the issue of language norms and the differences between spoken and written language norms, but also language policies, e.g. favouring certain languages at the expense of others.

The global perspective must also be added: as mentioned earlier, all people are in a certain sense world citizens. This is not so much to be understood in formal political terms, for as yet there are no worldwide representative political structures, apart from the UN. But we are world citizens in an economic, social, cultural, linguistic and ethical sense. We are involved in comprehensive, transcontinental processes and face a common responsibility for the continued sustainability of the earth and the future of humanity. In Chapter 8, I have tried to outline how this common human condition can come to influence the traditionally nationally limited basis of language and culture pedagogy.

The global perspective is not least justified by the fact that the actual object of language teaching, the target language, has a global nature – and that applies of course not least to the major foreign and second languages: English, French, German, Spanish, Portuguese, Arabic, Chinese, Japanese, etc. These languages are spoken in more or less worldwide networks, both actual and virtual, and are taught in many places in the world.

So critical language awareness also comprises knowledge of the languages of the world and an awareness of linguistic hierarchies and their interaction with social hierarchies (critical multilingual awareness) (see, for example, Lund & Risager, 2001).

(10) Knowledge of culture and society and critical cultural awareness, also as a world citizen

Byram's no. 5: knowledge/*savoirs* deals mainly with knowledge of non-linguistic relations. As the reader will recall, I believe that the knowledge component is important, and that the tendency to downgrade it in post-modernist approaches to language and culture pedagogy must be resisted (cf. Chapter 8). Part of the necessary knowledge is knowledge of relevant first-language contexts for the target language: e.g. cultural and social relations in French-speaking majority communities, as well as experience with relevant cultural words, cultural references and cultural representations.

Added to which, there is the global perspective: the world citizen's knowledge of the world and his/her identity as a participant in processes and issues of potentially global scope. This perspective means that teacher and students together seek to establish (the rudiments of) a relevant and as far as possible cohesive knowledge of the world. This work can have one or more groups of topic as its point of departure, such as human rights, cultural diversity, the global environment, social inequality in the world, the peace issue, terrorism, etc. As the German educational philosopher Wolfgang Klafki says:

> It is possible very early on in individual development to form the basis for the development of points of view, the observation of problems and attitudes – to limit, for example, the horizon of children's thoughts and interests to comprise the immediate environment or the frameworks for one's own culture, nation, state – or conversely, to open up wider, international, humane perspectives. We are neglecting not only vital *possibilities* but also something that is *necessary* if we do not very early on commence the development of an in principle *international problem awareness*... (Klafki, 2001 (1985): 100, italics in the original)

It is also possible to build such a foundation in language teaching, even at the lower levels, where linguistic competence is not yet all that developed. It will, for example, always be possible to use visual material to illustrate and initiate activities, and as a rule it will – at least in foreign-language teaching – be possible to make oneself understood via use of the first language.

In a book about the world citizen as an educational ideal, written by the Danish educational philosopher Peter Kemp (Kemp, 2005) three major themes are formulated towards which all education ought to be oriented: financial globalisation, the sustainability of the globe for future genera- tions, and the relationship between nations and cultures. Here, foreign- language teaching will naturally be particularly well able to contribute as regards the third theme – but not only there.

Byram places critical cultural awareness and political education centrally in no. 8 of his model, defining critical cultural awareness as an ability to assess and discuss cultural relations on the basis of explicit crite- ria. While Byram writes from within the national perspective, namely about the world citizen in a particular state,[11] I believe that this must be supplemented by the global perspective, as do, for example, Starkey and Guilherme. A central element of critical cultural awareness is an aware- ness of banal nationalism (Risager, 2000).

Hannerz has dealt with cultural competence in connection with the concept of cosmopolitanism. He describes cosmopolitanism as 'a perspec- tive, a state of mind, or – to take a more processual view – a mode of managing meaning' (Hannerz, 1990: 238). Cosmopolitanism is first and foremost 'an orientation, a willingness to engage with the Other' (Hannerz, 1990: 239). Next, there is a general competence: 'a state of readi- ness, a personal ability to make one's way into other cultures, through listening, looking, intuiting and reflecting' (Hannerz, 1990: 239). And, furthermore, there is a cultural competence in the stricter sense: 'a built-up skill in manoeuvring more or less expertly with a particular system of meanings and meaningful forms' (Hannerz, 1990: 239). Hannerz is of the opinion that it is possible to have a more or less cosmopolitan attitude, and he also says that cosmopolitanism has a tinge of narcissism, in the sense that the self is constructed in the space where cultures mirror them- selves in each other.[12]

'Cosmopolitans' possibly travel around the world and empathise with the places they visit. They investigate things and ask people questions; they are interested in cultural differences. They despise ordinary tourists, who for them are people who, despite their eagerness to travel, are 'locals at heart' (Hannerz, 1990: 241). Perhaps it is not even necessary to travel in order to be a cosmopolitan. Hannerz raises the question at any rate of whether it is equally possible to develop into a cosmopolitan without leaving home, whether cosmopolitanism is in fact a matter of an intellec- tual attitude that involves one's reflecting on life and on oneself.

Hannerz's description of cosmopolitanism is generally speaking remi- niscent of Byram's description of intercultural competence. It would seem that both Hannerz and Byram have a particular prototype in mind when they describe the cosmopolitan and the intercultural speaker respectively:

the ethnographer who attempts to empathise with the cultural practices in particular environments – possibly also by acquiring a certain competence in the local language.

At the same time, both of them lack a more explicit sociological perspective of competences of the cosmopolitan and intercultural speaker – and here an approach such as that of Bourdieu is valuable. As John Gullov Christensen writes (see also Chapter 5) concerning teaching about language and culture in Europe: 'The cultural encounter takes place... not between independent individuals but between people who are part of fields and have various social and cultural possessions. The different positions of the fields in relation to each other therefore have consequences for the possibilities for the individuals to understand and integrate' (translated from Christensen, 1994: 39). This sociological understanding is important, and I would say that, no matter what the long-term (and necessary) aim of foreign-language teaching is, the various participants will already have formed early on a habitus and have developed certain symbolic forms of capital that dispose them to, or orientate them towards, particular positions in the cultural encounter. Since there is probably no doubt that the educational elite would itself consider the cosmopolitan attitude to be the more valuable one, this social distinction (Bourdieu, 1979) may be one of the things that provokes nationalist or racist reactions in certain groups – which makes the conflict-laden content of the cultural encounter visible.

The intercultural speaker as mediator

Byram's model deals with the individual and personal development of intercultural communicative competence. The focus is on the relationship between this person and the outside world, 'the other' – an I–You relationship.

It is possible to contrast this with a different, more social understanding of the intercultural speaker as a *mediator between different people or groups* in his or her outside world – an I–You–You relationship. In such an interpretation, the intercultural speaker is an interpreter, an intermediary,[13] a catalyst. This role is more oriented towards social, cultural and linguistic complexity, involving the person relating to the identities of different people or groups and their conceptions of each other. It could be said here that the intercultural speaker relates to the (more or less different) intercultural competences of *the others*. This is the typical role of the teacher, but it can be relevant for everybody, and when I emphasise training in both interpretation and translation, it is in order to point to this social understanding of the intercultural speaker.

The implicated intercultural speakers are thus players in a social space, their competences and resources influencing each other and developing together. The languastructural, languacultural and discursive resources do not necessarily have to be seen only as individual but also as collective resources, i.e. resources that are distributed between various persons in a group, e.g. in a language class. This conception supports the use of collective forms of learning in language teaching, e.g. various forms of project work, possible in conjunction with interdisciplinary cooperation and/or transnational cooperation with NGOs, etc.

The world citizen and national identity

As a rule, language teaching is something one experiences only for quite a short period of one's life – normally within a fairly brief span of years. Even so, it can prove to be significant for the entire life and identity of the individual student. This naturally particularly applies to second-language teaching, for better or worse,[14] although it also applies to foreign-language teaching.

A topic that has been researched only to a very small extent is the significance of foreign-language teaching for students' identity – especially national identity – as it is constantly reformulated and reinterpreted in relation to the wider political context. In the international project on teacher identity (Byram & Risager, 1999), we spoke with the teachers about their students' national and European identities, but we did not ask the students themselves – or former students. Within the framework of a transnational paradigm it will be interesting to see how one can contribute to a fruitful dialogue about identities at a national, (possibly) European and global level. And, here, national identity occupies a central position, because the entire framework for language subjects and language teaching is shaped nationally and rests on a national tradition. Even though a transnational paradigm can be used as orientation in the actual didactics, the national framework is the point of departure – especially when teaching takes place in national institutions such as the Danish Folkeskole.

Here we touch on another aspect of the national dilemma discussed in the previous chapter – the question of how 'complexity' and 'homogeneity' are to be dealt with at the personal, socialisation-related level. On the one hand, the transnational paradigm provides an opportunity for an understanding of identity as a complex and in many ways changeable entity, where the national dimension is only one of many possible ones. On the other hand, the participants, no matter what country they come from, are put together in a pedagogical situation where national identities also inevitably end up being centre stage, as a result of the national framework mentioned above. This aspect of the national dilemma should not be underestimated, for here we are touching on a dimension of personal and cultural identity that for many people is highly emotionally charged and is felt to be fundamental.

As Christensen emphasises, there can be differences between students' understanding of their present/future identity. Some are perhaps more likely to develop a transnational form of intercultural competence than others (cf. Hannerz's idea of the cosmopolitan). Some are perhaps moving towards more nationalistic identities. Some wish to identify themselves with 'the world citizen' in one of his/her many manifestations; others identify themselves more locally. The challenge of the transnational paradigm is, among other things, to show that national identities do not have to be exclusive; they can be *in*clusive. By working with images of France, Belgium, Ireland, the USA, Germany, Austria, Denmark, etc., which contain a social, religious, ethnic and linguistic complexity, it can be demonstrated that it is possible to understand national identities and national cultural communities as being inclusive.

Such an inclusive conception of national identity relates to one of the two conceptions of the nation – the political (as opposed to the ethnic or cultural, cf. Chapter 8). In the analysis of the history of culture pedagogy I referred to a (European) tradition for dealing with social relations also at the political level (Melde, Zarate, Byram, Doyé, Kramer, Starkey, Guilherme), and this tradition is interested in developing the students' understanding of themselves as citizens, as political players in a democratic society – an important part of what in Chapter 8 I called critical cultural awareness. Here I am thinking of the citizen of an individual state, the European citizen (if relevant) and – in a more informal political sense – the world citizen.

Conclusion

The following statements summarise the fundamentals of a transnational understanding of language and culture pedagogy:

(1) The target-language community is not confined to a nationally defined language area but exists in a linguistic network with a potentially global range, mainly as a result of transnational migration and communication.

The target language may be spoken in all corners of the earth. This demands that education authorities, language teachers, and editors and authors of teaching materials seriously consider their image of the world and remain open to the diversity of contexts that might be relevant and interesting for learners. Focusing on conditions in Spain in the teaching of Spanish, for example, is not a 'natural' choice; it is a decision that has to be specifically motivated and justified.

(2) The target language is never isolated but always exists in a local interplay with other languages.

All languages, even those of the most isolated tribes, are part of larger linguistic landscapes. Though it does not fall within the aim of the teaching of a specific language to *teach* these other languages, it does fall within the aim of language teaching to make students aware of the multilingual contexts of use of the target language. They should be aware that the status of the target language is a result of language policies, historical or contemporary, formal or informal – for example in the teaching of French they should be told something about the status of the French language in multilingual settings such as France and Canada.

(3) The target language is associated with an infinite range of socioculturally different, personal languacultures.

The target language is not just a code, it is a means of expression and understanding of living people (and not only native speakers). Linguistic practice is meaningful, and meaning-producing, practice. Language and culture teaching should from the very first lessons give students an idea of semantic and pragmatic variability in language, both in their first language(s) and in the target language – by including, for example, discussions of possible meanings of words like 'work' or 'friend' or 'no'.

(4) The target language is not associated with definite discourses and topics.

As mentioned earlier, there are perhaps certain topics and discourses that circulate within a language community without ever 'coming out' via translation to other languages. But, apart from that, topics and discourses normally flow from language to language. Thus there are no 'natural' topics in the teaching of a specific language. The thematic content of language teaching, including the choice of texts and text genres, thus has to have an independent, pedagogical justification, not derived from the language in question.

Here lies one of the main reasons for writing this book, namely the wish to make fully visible the two-sided nature of language teaching: on the one hand the learning and teaching of the target language in a global context, and, and on the other hand, the work with *contents*, also seen in a global context. In parallel with learning the language and its languacultures, one cannot avoid also dealing with contents or, in other words, representations of reality, fictional or non-fictional: topics, discourses, texts, images, etc. In most language teaching, especially at the elementary and intermediate levels, there is generally a deplorable lack of awareness of the choices of content and thus the choices of areas of insight and interest for all participants.

It is my hope that the analysis of the international history of culture pedagogy in a transnational perspective may contribute to the awareness of the importance of the cultural dimension of language learning and teaching in the modern world, both as regards languaculture and as regards cultural content in a broader sense. Language and culture learning and teaching is, after all, not concerned with codes, but with tools for the production and interchange of meaning.

Notes

1. Liddicoat and Crozet (2000) (Chapter 7) agree with Kramsch in this respect.
2. Byram explicitly says (in Byram, 1997a) that he is not going to deal with the particular issues linked to the development of intercultural competence in connection with second-language acquisition and learning.
3. Guilherme implicitly operates with a two-part model insofar as she does not deal with the linguistic competence of the intercultural speaker.
4. All three instances of 'interlocutor' refer to the same (imagined) person.
5. The three linguistic subcomponents are reformulations of subcomponents in van Ek (1987) (see Chapter 4; van Ek's model presupposes 'the native speaker' as the goal). In relation to van Ek, Byram's target language description is a trifle more sociolinguistic in orientation, as Byram talks about a standard version of the language, which implies that there can be a number of possible standard versions, and that there are also versions that are not standard. He does not distinguish here between writing and speech. It is also important to notice that Byram has shifted the formation of meaning away from linguistic to sociolinguistic competence: understanding is formed because of negotiation processes in social situations. Finally, it should be noted that Byram (like van Ek) uses the purely linguistic concept of discourse which deals with production and understanding of oral and written texts. And under discourse competence Byram emphasises the intercultural aspects: proficiency at working with 'intercultural texts' (which can, for example, be translations).
6. The five *savoirs* and complete reformulations of van Ek's strategic, sociocultural and social competence.
7. It should be noted that I do not address assessment and assessment criteria in this book.
8. This overview is not really a 'model', for it is only a listing of relevant ingredients in a particular order. The same can be said about van Ek's overview, and one can also question whether Byram's model really is one as it is only loosely structured. Ideally, there would be an integrated dynamic model, but such a

model can only be constructed when the ingredients are connected to each other within the framework of a more general theory of personal development, which I am not doing in the present context.

9. I am thinking here of Giddens' concepts of 'self-identity' and 'ontological security' (Giddens, 1991).
10. As described in, for example, Morgan and Cain (2000).
11. Byram has, however, dealt in other contexts with the European dimension of political education.
12. Hannerz contrasts the 'cosmopolitan' with 'the local', but in a polarisation that goes too far and does not take account of the cultural complexity he otherwise emphasises.
13. Zarate also talks about *l'intermédiaire culturel* or *le médiateur culturel*.
14. Cf. e.g. Norton (2000).

References

Adaskou, K., Britten, D. and Fahsi, B. (1990) Design decisions on the cultural content of a secondary English course for Morocco. in: *ELT Journal* 44 (1), pp. 3–10.

Agar, Michael (1994) *Language Shock. Understanding the Culture of Conversation*. New York: William Morrow.

Aktor, Leon and Risager, Karen (2001) Cultural understanding in Danish schools. In Michael Byram, Adam Nichols and David Stevens (eds) *Developing Intercultural Competence in Practice*. Clevedon: Multilingual Matters, pp. 219–235.

Alix, Christian *et al.* (1988) *Vivre l'école. Unterrichtskonzepte mit Schülermaterialien*. Paderborn: Schöningh.

Allen, Wendy W. (1985) Toward cultural proficiency. In Alice C. Omaggio (ed.) *Proficiency, Curriculum, Articulation: The Ties that Bind*. Middlebury, VT: Northeast Conference on the Teaching of Foreign Languages, pp. 137–166.

Alred, Geof, Byram, Mike and Fleming, Mike (eds) (2003) *Intercultural Experience and Education*. Clevedon: Multilingual Matters.

Altmayer, Claus (1997) Zum Kulturbegriff des Faches Deutsch als Fremdsprache. In *Zeitschrift für interkulturellen Fremdsprachenunterricht* 2 (2), 24 pp. (on line)

American Council on the Teaching of Foreign Languages (ACTFL) (2006) President Bush brings languages front and center. www.actfl.org/i4a/pages/Index.cfm?pageID=4249

Ammon, Günther *et al.* (1987) *Le Languedoc-Roussillon. Une région face à l'Europe*. Paderborn: Schöningh.

Andersen, Hanne L., Lund, Karen and Risager, Karen (eds) (2006) *Culture in Language Learning*. Aarhus: Aarhus University Press.

Andersen, Helga and Risager, Karen (1977) Samfunds- og kultur-formidling. In Esther Glahn m.fl. (red.) *Fremmedsprogspædagogik*. Copenhagen: Gyldendal, pp. 27–55.

Anderson, Benedict (1991) *Imagined Communities* (2nd edn). London: Verso (1983).

André, Jean-Claude and Galisson, Robert (1999) *Dictionnaire des noms de marques courants: Essai de lexiculture ordinaire*. Paris: Didier-Erudition.

Apelt, W. (1967) *Die Kulturkundliche Bewegung im Unterricht der neueren Sprachen in Deutschland in den Jahren 1886 bis 1945*. Berlin: Volk und Wissen.

Aplin, Richard, Miller, Ann and Starkey, Hugh (1985) *Orientations*. London: Hodder and Stoughton.

Appadurai, Arjun (1996) *Modernity at Large. Cultural Dimensions of Globalization*. Minneapolis etc.: University of Minnesota Press.

Armour, William (2000) Identity slippage: A consequence of learning Japanese as an additional language. *Japanese Studies* 20 (3), pp. 255–268.

Arndt, Horst and Weller, Franz-Rudolf (eds) (1978) *Landeskunde und Fremdsprachenunterricht*. Frankfurt a. M.: Diesterweg.

Bakhtin, Mikhail M. (1981) *The Dialogic Imagination*. Austin: University of Texas Press.

Barrera-Vidal, Albert (1972) Pour une nouvelle conception de l'enseignement de la civilisation française. *Praxis des neusprachlichen Unterrichts* 19, pp. 85–90.

Barth, Fredrik (1969) *Ethnic Groups and Boundaries*. Oslo: Universitetsforlaget.

Baumgratz, Gisela and Picht, Robert (eds) (1978) *Perspektiven der Frankreichkunde II. Arbeitsansätze für Forschung und Unterricht*. Tübingen: Max Niemeyer Verlag.

Baumgratz, Gisela, Melde, Wilma and Schüle, Klaus (1980) Landeskunde im Fremdsprachenunterricht – das Beispiel der Frankreichkunde. *Englisch-amerikanische Studien* 1, Köln, pp. 76–94.

Baumgratz, Gisela *et al.* (1982) *Fremdsprachenunterricht und Internationale Beziehungen: Stuttgarter Thesen zur Rolle der Landeskunde im Französischunterricht*. Stuttgart: Robert Bosch Stiftung Gmbh., und Ludwigsburg: Deutsch-Französisches Institut.

Baumgratz-Gangl, Gisela (1990) *Persönlichkeitsentwicklung und Fremdsprachenerwerb. Transnationale und transkulturelle Kommunikationsfähigkeit im Französischunterricht*. Paderborn: Ferdinand Schöningh.

Baur-Langenbucher, Wilfried (1972) Frankreichkunde und Sprachunterricht. *Französisch Heute* 1, pp. 7–20.

Beck, Ulrich (2000) *What is Globalization?* Cambridge: Polity Press. (German ed. 1997).

Beck, Ulrich (2002) *Macht und Gegenmacht im globalen Zeitalter. Neue weltpolitische Ökonomie*. Frankfurt a. M.: Suhrkamp.

Beck, Ulrich (2004) *Der kosmopolitische Blick, oder: Krieg ist Frieden*. Frankfurt a. M.: Suhrkamp.

Bekendtgørelse af 24. september 1975 om formålet med undervisningen i folkeskolens fag. København: Undervisningsministeriet.

Benadava, S. (1990) Enseignement de la civilisation et objectifs linguistiques. In *Culture et enseignement du français. Colloque international*. Louisiana State University, Baton Rouge, Louisiana, pp. 77–88.

Berger, Peter and Luckmann, Thomas (1991) (1966) *The Social Construction of Reality. A Treatise in the Sociology of Knowledge*. Harmondsworth: Penguin.

Berns, Margie (1990) *Contexts of Competence. Social and Cultural Considerations in Communicative Language Teaching*. New York and London: Plenum Press.

Best, Steven and Kellner, Douglas (1991) *Postmodern Theory. Critical Interrogations*. New York: The Guilford Press.

Billig, Michael (1995) *Banal Nationalism*. London: Sage Publications.

Bishop, G. Reginald (ed.) (1960) *Culture in Language. Northeast Conference on the Teaching of Foreign Languages 1960*. Reports of the working committees. New Brunswick, N.J.: Rutgers. The State University.

Blinkenberg, A. and Svanholt, O. (1932) *Frankrig. Tekster af kulturelt og socialt indhold*. Copenhagen: Det Schønbergske Forlag.

Bodelsen, C.A. (1942) *A Survey of English Institutions*. Copenhagen: Hagerups Forlag.

Börsch, Sabine (ed.) (1987) *Die Rolle der Psychologie in der Sprachlehrforschung*. Tübingen: Gunter Narr Verlag.

Bona, K. (1938) Die Sprachenfolge Englisch-Latein. *Neuphilologische Monatsschrift*, pp. 353–365.

Bourdieu, Pierre (1979) *La distinction*. Paris: Les Editions de Minuit.

Bredella, Lothar and Delanoy, Werner (eds) (1999) *Interkultureller Fremdsprachenunterricht*. Tübingen: Gunter Narr Verlag.

Bredella, Lothar and Burwitz-Melzer, Eva (eds) (2004) *Rezeptionsästhetische Literaturdidaktik mit Beispielen aus dem Fremsprachenunterricht Englisch*. Tübingen: Gunter Narr.

Brinton, Donna M. and Master, Peter (eds) (1997) *New Ways in Content-Based Instruction*. Alexandria VA: Teachers of English to Speakers of Other Languages, Inc.

Brislin, R.W. *et al.* (eds) (1971) *Cross-Cultural Perspectives on Learning*. New York: John Wiley.

Brodow, Ulla (2005) *Lära över gränser. Om internationella kontakter i skolan*. Lund: Studentlitteratur.

Brooks, Nelson (1960) *Language and Language Learning. Theory and Practice*. New York etc.: Harcourt, Brace and World, Inc.

Brooks, Nelson (1968) Teaching culture in the foreign language classroom. *Foreign Language Annals* 1, pp. 204–217.

Brøgger, Fredrik Chr. (1979) For at kommunisere må man forstå andres tankesett: Kulturkunnskapen i engelskundervisningen i den videregående skolen. *Språk og språkundervisning* 12, pp. 39–44.

Brøgger, Fredrik Chr. (1980) A cultural approach to American Studies. *American Studies in Scandinavia* 12, pp. 1–15.

Brøgger, Fredrik Chr. (1992) *Culture, Language, Text: Culture Studies within the Study of English as a Foreign Language.* Oslo: Scandinavian University Press.

Bülow-Møller, Anne Marie (2000) Andre folks normer. *Sprogforum* 17, pp. 11–15.

Burwitz-Melzer, Eva (2001) Teaching intercultural communicative competence through literature. In Michael Byram, Adam Nichols and David Stevens (eds) *Developing Intercultural Competence in Practice.* Clevedon: Multilingual Matters, pp. 29–43.

Burwitz-Melzer, Eva (2003) *Allmähliche Annäherungen: Fiktionale Texte im interkulturellen Fremdsprachenunterricht der Sekundarstufe 1.* Tübingen: Gunter Narr.

Buttjes, Dieter and Kane, Lawrence (1978) Theorie und Zielsetzung der Landeskunde im Fremdsprachenstudium. *Anglistik und Englischunterricht* 4, pp. 51–61.

Buttjes, Dieter (ed.) (1981) *Landeskundliches Lernen im Englischunterricht.* Paderborn: Schöningh.

Buttjes, Dieter (1982) Landeskunde im Fremdsprachenunterricht. Zwischenbilanz und Arbeitsansätze. *Neusprachliche Mitteilungen* 35, pp. 3–16.

Buttjes, Dieter (1986) Literarische und andere Texte in der Landeskunde. In Franz Kuna and Heinz Tschachler (eds) *Dialog der Texte: Literatur und Landeskunde. Beiträge zu Problemen einer integrativen Landes- und Kulturkunde des englischsprachigen Auslands.* Tübingen: Gunther Narr Verlag, pp. 65–95.

Buttjes, Dieter and Byram, Michael (eds) (1991) *Mediating Languages and Cultures. Towards an Intercultural Theory of Foreign Language Education.* Clevedon: Multilingual Matters.

Buttjes, Dieter (1991) Culture in German foreign language teaching: Making use of an ambiguous past. In Dieter Buttjes and Michael Byram (eds) *Mediating Languages and Cultures.* Clevedon: Multilingual Matters, pp. 47–62.

Byram, Michael (1989) *Cultural Studies in Foreign Language Education.* Clevedon: Multilingual Matters.

Byram, Michael and Esarte-Sarries, Veronica (1991) *Investigating Cultural Studies in Foreign Language Teaching.* Clevedon: Multilingual Matters.

Byram, Michael, Esarte-Sarries, Veronica and Taylor, Susan (1991) *Cultural Studies and Language Learning*. Clevedon: Multilingual Matters.

Byram, Michael (ed.) (1993) *Germany: Its Representation in Textbooks for Teaching German in Great Britain*. Frankfurt a. M.: Diesterweg.

Byram, Michael, Morgan, Carol and colleagues (1994) *Teaching-and-Learning Language-and-Culture*. Clevedon: Multilingual Matters.

Byram, Michael and Zarate, Geneviève (1994) *Definitions, Objectives and Assessment of Socio-cultural Competence*. The Council of Europe, CC-LANG (94) 1.

Byram, Michael (1995) Acquiring intercultural competence. In Lies Sercu (ed.) *Intercultural Competence. A New Challenge for Language Teachers and Trainers in Europe*. Aalborg: Aalborg University Press, pp. 53–69.

Byram, Michael (ed.) (1996) Education for European Citizenship. Special issue of *Evaluation. Research in Education* 10 (2&3).

Byram, Michael (1997a) *Teaching and Assessing Intercultural Communicative Competence*. Clevedon: Multilingual Matters.

Byram, Michael (ed.) (1997b) *Face to Face. Learning 'Language-and-culture' Through Visits and Exchanges*. London: Centre for Information on Language Teaching and Research (CILT).

Byram, Michael and Fleming, Michael (eds) (1998) *Language Learning in Intercultural Perspective. Approaches through Drama and Ethnography*. Cambridge: Cambridge University Press.

Byram, Michael and Risager, Karen (1999) *Language Teachers, Politics and Cultures*. Clevedon: Multilingual Matters.

Byram, Michael (ed.) (2000a) *Routledge Encyclopedia of Language Teaching and Learning*. London and New York: Routledge.

Byram, Michael (2000b) Learning language without a culture? The case of English as a lingua franca? In L. Bredella *et al.* (eds) *Wie ist Fremdverstehen lehr- und lernbar?* Tübingen: Gunter Narr, pp. 1–17.

Byram, Michael, Nichols, Adam and Stevens, David (eds) (2001) *Developing Intercultural Competence in Practice*. Clevedon: Multilingual Matters.

Byram, Mike and Grundy, Peter (eds) (2002) *Context and Culture in Language Teaching and Learning*. Clevedon: Multilingual Matters.

Cain, Albane and Briane, Claudine (1994) *Comment collégiens et lycéens voient les pays dont ils apprennent la langue. Représentations et stéréotypes*. Paris: Institut National de Recherche Pédagogique.

Cain, Albane and Zarate, Geneviève (1996) The role of training courses in developing openness to otherness: from tourism to ethnography. In Geneviève Zarate *et al.* (eds) *Cultural Representation in Language Learning and Teacher Training*. Special issue of *Language, Culture and Curriculum* 9 (1), pp. 66–83.

Cameron, Deborah (1995) *Verbal Hygiene.* London and New York: Routledge.

Canagarajah, A. Suresh (1999) *Resisting Linguistic Imperialism in English Teaching.* Oxford etc.: Oxford University Press.

Canale, M. and Swain, M. (1980) Theoretical bases of communicative approaches to second language teaching and testing. *Applied Linguistics* 1, pp. 1–47.

Candlin, E. Frank (1962) *Present Day English for Foreign Students, Book 1.* London: University of London Press.

Carroll, John B. (ed.) (1956) *Language, Thought and Reality. Selected Writings of Benjamin Lee Whorf.* Cambridge, Mass.: The MIT Press.

Cates, Kip A. (2000) Global education. In Michael Byram (ed.) *Routledge Encyclopedia of Language Teaching and Learning.* London and New York: Routledge, pp. 241–243.

Chouliaraki, Lilie (1998) Regulation in 'progessivist' pedagogic discourse: Individualized teacher-pupil talk. *Discourse and Society* 9, 1, pp. 5–32.

Christensen, John Gulløv (1994) Sprog og kultur i europæisk integration. In John Liep and Karen Fog Olwig (eds) *Komplekse liv. Kulturel mangfoldighed i Danmark.* Copenhagen: Akademisk Forlag, pp. 23–42.

Cohen, Robin (1997) *Global Diasporas. An Introduction.* London: UCL Press.

Comenius, J.A. (1649) *Ianua lingvarum reserata.* Amsterdam: Apud Ludovicum Elzevirium.

Common European Framework of Reference for Languages: Learning, Teaching, Assessment (2001) Council of Europe. Cambridge: Cambridge University Press.

Conner, Maurice W. (1981) *A Global Approach to Foreign Language Education.* Skokie, Ill.: National Textbook Company.

Corbett, John (2003) *An Intercultural Approach to English Language Teaching.* Clevedon: Multilingual Matters.

Coste, Daniel *et al.* (1976) *Un niveau-seuil.* Strasbourg: Conseil de l'Europe, Conseil de la Coopération Culturelle.

Crawford-Lange, Linda M. and Lange, Dale L. (1984) Doing the unthinkable in the second language classroom: A process for the integration of language and culture. In Theodore V. Higgs (ed.) *Teaching for Proficiency, the Organizing Principle.* Lincolnwood, Ill.: National Textbook Company, pp. 139–177.

Crozet, Chantal and Liddicoat, Anthony J. (2000) Teaching culture as an integrated part of language: Implications for the aims, approaches and pedagogies of language teaching. In Anthony J. Liddicoat and Chantal Crozet (eds) *Teaching Languages, Teaching Cultures.* Applied Linguistics Association of Australia, Melbourne, Vic.: Language Australia, pp. 1–18.

Damen, Louise (1987) *Culture Learning: The Fifth Dimension in the Language Classroom*. Reading, Mass.: Addison-Wesley Publishing Company.

Darbelnet, Jean (1971) Sémantique et civilisation. *Le français dans le monde* 81, pp. 15–19.

Davies, Alan (1991) *The Native Speaker in Applied Linguistics*. Edinburgh: Edinburgh University Press.

Debyser, Francis (1973) Le rapport langue/civilisation et l'enseignement de la civilisation aux débutants. In André Reboullet (dir.) *L'enseignement de la civilisation française*. Paris: Hachette, pp. 58–75.

Delanoy, Werner (2005) A Dialogic Model for Literature Teaching. *ABAC Journal* 25 (1), pp. 53–66.

Dendrinos, Bessie (1992) *The EFL Textbook and Ideology*. Athens: N.C. Grivas Publications.

Dobrynine, Olivier (1991) Les mots 'porteurs de civilisation' dans les manuels de russe pour débutants. *Les langues modernes* 85, pp. 84–88.

Doyé, Peter (1966) Politische Erziehung im neusprachlichen Unterricht. *Westermanns Pädagogische Beiträge* 6, pp. 270ff.

Doyé, Peter (ed.) (1991) *Grossbritannien. Seine Darstellung in deutschen Schulbüchern für den Englischunterricht*. Frankfurt: Verlag Moritz Diesterweg.

Doyé, Peter (1996) Foreign language teaching and education for intercultural and international understanding. *Evaluation and Research in Education* 10, (2) and (3), pp. 104–12. Special issue of *Education for European Citizenship*. Guest editor: Michael Byram.

Edmondson, Willis and House, Juliane (1998) Interkulturelles Lernen: Ein überflüssiger Begriff. *Zeitschrift für Fremdsprachenforschung* 9 (2), pp. 161–188.

Ek, J.A. van (1975) *Systems Development in Adult Language Learning. The Threshold Level*. Strasbourg: Council of Europe, Council for Cultural Cooperation.

Ek, J.A. van (1986) *Objectives for Foreign Language Learning. Volume I: Scope*. Strasbourg: Council of Europe, Council for Cultural Co-operation.

Ek, J.A. van (1987) *Objectives for Foreign Language Learning. Volume II: Levels*. Strasbourg: Council of Europe, Council for Cultural Co-operation.

Ek, J.A. van and Trim, J.L.M. (1991) *Threshold Level 1990*. Strasbourg: Council of Europe, Council for Cultural Co-operation.

Elbeshausen, Hans and Wagner, Johannes (1985) Kontrastiver Alltag – Die Rolle von Alltagsbegriffen in der interkulturellen Kommunikation. Rehbein 1985, pp. 42–59.

Emmerich, Wolfgang (1971) *Zur Kritik der Volkstumsideologie*. Frankfurt a. M.: Suhrkamp.

Engel, Ulrich *et al.* (1979) *Mannheimer Gutachten zu ausgewählten Lehrwerken Deutsch als Fremdsprache, Band 2.* Heidelberg: Julius Groos Verlag.

Erdmenger, Manfred and Istel, Hans-Wolf (1973) *Didaktik der Landeskunde.* Tübingen: Max Hueber Verlag.

Erdmenger, Manfred (1996) *Landeskunde im Fremdsprachenunterricht.* Ismaning: Hueber.

Fairclough, Norman (1989) *Language and Power.* London and New York: Longman.

Fairclough, Norman (1992a) *Discourse and Social Change.* Cambridge: Polity Press.

Fairclough, Norman (ed.) (1992b) *Critical Language Awareness.* London and New York: Longman.

Falk, Jørn (2000) Ferdinand Tönnies. In Heine Andersen and Lars Bo Kaspersen (eds) *Klassisk og moderne samfundsteori. 2.* Reviderede udgave. Copenhagen: Reitzels Forlag, pp. 57–68.

Fichou, Jean-Pierre (1979) *Enseigner les civilisations.* Paris: Presses Universitaires de France.

Firges, Jean and Melenk, Hartmut (1982) Landeskunde als Alltagswissen. *Praxis des neusprachlichen Unterrichts* 29, pp. 115–123.

Fischer, Gudrun (1979) Sprache und Kultur – Linguolandeskunde in Deutsch als Fremdsprache. *Deutsch als Fremdsprache* 16 (1), pp. 42–48.

Fishman, Joshua A. (1971) The sociology of language: An interdisciplinary social science approach to language in society. In Fishman, Joshua A. (ed.) *Advances in the Sociology of Language I.* The Hague and Paris: Mouton, pp. 217–404.

Fishman, Joshua A. (1982) Whorfianism of the third kind: Ethnolinguistic diversity as a worldwide societal asset. *Language in Society* 11, pp. 1–14.

Freudenstein, Reinhold (ed.) (1978) *The Role of Women in Foreign Language Textbooks.* Bruxelles: AIMAV.

Friedrich, Paul (1989) Language, ideology, and political economy. *American Anthropologist*, Vol. 91, pp. 295–312.

Friz, Susanne (1991) *Das Bild von England, Amerika und Deutschland bei Fremdsprachenlerners und in Fremdsprachenlehrwerken. Ein Beitrag zur komparativen Landeskunde.* München: Tuduv-Verlagsgesellschaft.

Furnham, A. and Bochner, S. (1986) *Culture Shock. Psychological Reactions to Unfamiliar Environments.* London: Methuen.

Gagel, W. (1983) *Einführung in die Didaktik des politischen Unterrichts.* Opladen: Leske und Budrich.

Gagnestam, Eva (2003) *Kultur i Språkundervisning – med fokus på engelska.* Karlstad: Karlstad University Studies.

Galisson, Robert (1991) *De la langue à la culture par les mots*. Paris: CLE International.

Galisson, Robert (1992) Etrange outil pour étrangers: Un dictionnaire des noms de marques courants. *Etudes de Linguistique Appliquées* 85–86, pp. 191–227.

Galisson, Robert (1994) *D'hier à demain, l'interculturel à l'école. Actes du colloque international: Enseignement des langues et intercompréhension européenne* (17–18 déc. 1993, Athens, pp. 91–104).

Gardner, Robert C. (1985) *Social Psychology and Second Language Learning: The Role of Attitudes and Motivation*. London: Edward Arnold.

Gauvenet, H. *et al.* (1960) *Voix et images de la France*. Paris: CREDIF.

Geertz, Clifford (1973) Thick description: Toward an interpretive theory of culture. In Cl. Geertz: *The Interpretation of Cultures. Selected Essays by Clifford Geertz*. New York: Basic Books, pp. 3–30.

Geertz, Clifford (1988) *Works and Lives. The Anthropologist as Author*. Cambridge: Polity Press.

Gellner, Ernest (1983) *Nations and Nationalism*. London: Blackwell.

Giddens, Anthony (1991) *Modernity and Self-Identity. Self and Society in the Late Modern Age*. Cambridge: Polity Press.

Goodenough, Ward H. (1964 (1957) Cultural anthropology and linguistics. In Dell Hymes (ed.) *Language in Culture and Society*. New York: Harper and Row Publishers, pp. 36–39.

Gougenheim, Georges (1964) *L'élaboration du français fondamental (1er degré)*. Paris: Didier.

Gougenheim, Georges (1966) *Les mots français dans l'histoire et dans la vie. Tome I et II*. Paris: Picard.

Gudykunst, William B. and Kim, Y.Y. (1984) *Communicating with Strangers. An Approach to Intercultural Communication*. New York: McGraw-Hill.

Guilherme, Manuela (2002) *Critical Citizens for an Intercultural World. Foreign Language Education as Cultural Politics*. Clevedon: Multilingual Matters.

Gulliksen, Øyvind (1978) Kulturkunnskapens plass i engelskfaget. *Språk og språkundervisning* 4, pp. 56–69.

Gumperz, John J. (1992) Contextualization and understanding. In Charles Goodwin and Alessandro Duranti (eds) *Rethinking Context. Language as an Interactive Phenomenon*. Cambridge: Cambridge University Press, pp. 229–252.

Haastrup, Niels (1988) On phrasebooks. In Karl Hyldgaard-Jensen and Arne Zettersten (eds) *Symposium on Lexicography III*. Tübingen: Max Niemeyer Verlag, pp. 389–409.

Habermas, Jürgen (1981) *Theorie des kommunikativen Handelns*. Vol. 1. Frankfurt: Suhrkamp.

Hall, Edward T. (1959) *The Silent Language*. Garden City, N.Y.: Doubleday.

Hall, Edward T. (1966) *The Hidden Dimension*. Garden City, N.Y.: Doubleday.

Hallig, Rudolf and von Wartburg, Walther (1963) (1952) *Begriffssystem als Grundlage für die Lexikographie*. Berlin: Akademie-Verlag.

Hannerz, Ulf (1990) Cosmopolitans and locals in world culture. *Theory, Culture and Society* 7 (2–3), pp. 237–251.

Hannerz, Ulf (1992a) *Cultural Complexity. Studies in the Social Organization of Meaning*. New York: Columbia University Press.

Hannerz, Ulf (1992b) The global ecumene as a network of networks. In Adam Kuper (ed.) *Conceptualizing Society*. London and New York: Routledge, pp. 34–56.

Hannerz, Ulf (1996) *Transnational Connections. Culture, People, Places*. London and New York: Routledge.

Hansen, Hans Lauge (ed.) (2002) *Changing Philologies. Contributions to the Redefinition of Foreign Language Studies in the Age of Globalisation*. Copenhagen: Museum Tusculanum Press.

Hansen, Hans Lauge (ed.) (2004) *Disciplines and Interdisciplinarity in Foreign Language Studies*. Copenhagen: Museum Tusculanum Press.

Hermann, Jesper and Gregersen, Frans (1978) *Gennem sproget. Om undersøgelse af sprogbrug i samfundet*. Copenhagen: Gyldendals sprogbibliotek.

Herrde, Dietrich, Grimm, H.J. and Petzschler, H. (1975) Review of: Vereščagin und Kostomarov: Jazyk i kul'tura 1973. *Deutsch als Fremdsprache* 12, pp. 241–249.

Hinkel, Eli (ed.) (1999) *Culture in Second Language Teaching and Learning*. Cambridge UK: Cambridge University Press.

Hjort, Peter (1852) *Den danske Børneven. En Læsebog for Borger- og Almue-Skoler*. Copenhagen: Gyldendal (6th impression).

Hobsbawm, E.J. (1990) *Nations and Nationalism Since 1780. Programme, Myth, Reality*. Cambridge: Cambridge University Press (1990).

Hoijer, Harry (ed.) (1954) *Language in Culture. Conference on the Interrelations of Language and Other Aspects of Culture*. Chicago: Chicago University Press.

Holmen, Anne and Risager, Karen (2003) Language and culture teaching. Foreign languages and Danish as a second language. *International Journal of the Sociology of Language* 159, pp. 93–108.

Hosokawa, Hideo, n.d. (2003 or later) Reconsideration of the 'culture of individuals' theory: The meaning and problem of the linguistic and cultural education in the field of the Japanese language education. Unpubl. ms.

Hu, Adelheid (1999) Interkulturelles Lernen. Eine Auseinandersetzung mit der Kritik an einem umstrittenen Konzept. *Zeitschrift für Fremdsprachenforschung* 10 (2), pp. 277–303.

Hüllen, Werner (2005) *Kleine Geschichte des Fremdsprachenlernens*. Berlin: Erich Schmidt Verlag.

Jäger, Siegfried (1993) *Kritische Diskursanalyse. Eine Einführung*. Duisburg: Duisburger Institut für Sprach- und Sozialforschung (DISS).

Jakobsen, Karen Sonne, Risager, Karen and Kristiansen, Marianne (1984) Mellem tradition og modernisering – om fremmedsprogenes historie og funktion i gymnasiet. In Marianne Kristiansen, Karen Risager and Karen Sonne Jakobsen (eds) *Umoderne Sprog? Om fremmedsprog i gymnasiet*. Copenhagen: Gyldendal, pp. 9–52.

Jakobson, Roman (1960) Closing statement: Linguistics and poetics. In Thomas Sebeok (ed.) *Style in Language*. Cambridge, Mass.: The Bellknap Press of Harvard University Press, pp. 428–435.

Jespersen, Otto (1901) *Sprogundervisning*. Copenhagen: Det Schubotheske Forlag.

Jespersen, Otto (1904) *How to Teach a Foreign Language*. London: Allen and Unwin.

Jonas, Kurt and Rosenbohm, Hans-Otto (1994) (2nd edn) *Kleines Wörterbuch zur Landeskunde. Schweiz, Österreich, Deutschland*. Holbæk: Forlaget Sprogbøger.

Kaikkonen, Pauli (1991) *Erlebte Kultur- und Landeskunde*. Tampere: Universität Tampere.

Kaikkonen, Pauli (2001) Intercultural learning through foreign language education. In Viljo Kohonen, Riitta Jaatinen, Pauli Kaikkonen and Jorma Lehtovaara. *Experiential Learning in Foreign Language Education*. Harlow: Longman, pp. 61–105.

Keller, Gottfried (1970) Grundlegung einer neuen Kulturkunde. *Zeitnahe Schularbeit 7*, Stuttgart, pp. 1–21.

Keller, Gottfried (1983) Grundlegung einer neuen Kulturkunde als Orientierungsrahmen für Lehrerausbildung und Unterrichtspraxis. *Neusprachliche Mitteilungen 4*, pp. 200–209.

Keller, Gottfried (1987) Werden Vorurteile durch einen Schüleraustausch abgebaut? In Horst Arndt und Franz-Rudolf Weller (Hrsg.) *Landeskunde und Fremdsprachenunterricht*. Diesterweg, pp. 130–150.

Keller, Gottfried (1996) Zehn Thesen zur Neuorientierung des interkulturellen Lernens. *Praxis des neusprachlichen Unterrichts 3*, pp. 227–236.

Kelly, Louis G. (1969) *25 Centuries of Language Teaching. 500 BC–1969*. Rowley, Mass.: Newbury House.

Kemp, Peter (2005) *Verdensborgeren som pædagogisk ideal*. Copenhagen: Hans Reitzels Forlag.

Klafki, Wolfgang (2001) (1985) *Dannelsesteori og didaktik – nye studier*. Aarhus: Forlaget Klim.

Knudsen, Annie Ring and Hagen, Lone (1996) 'Das Bild der Anderen'. Begynderundervisning med anvendelse af e-mail. *Sprogforum* 5, pp. 58–60.

Koefoed, Oleg (1967) *Le français sans soucis. Fransk for begyndere.* Copenhagen: Schultz Forlag.

Kornum, Lis (1999) Eksempler på europæiske initiativer inden for undervisning. *Sprogforum* 13, pp. 17–19.

Kramer, Jürgen (ed.) (1976a) *Bestandsaufnahme Fremdsprachenunterricht.* Stuttgart: J.B. Metzler.

Kramer, Jürgen (1976b) Cultural Studies versus Landes-/Kulturkunde. In Jürgen Kramer (Hrsg.) *Bestandsaufnahme Fremdsprachenunterricht.* Stuttgart: J.B. Metzler, pp. 139–150.

Kramer, Jürgen (1990) *Cultural and Intercultural Studies.* Frankfurt a. M.: Peter Lang.

Kramer, Jürgen (1992) Der Krieg um die Falkland Islands/Islas Malvinas. *Der fremdsprachliche Unterricht* 26 (7), pp. 22–29.

Kramer, Jürgen (1997) *British Cultural Studies.* München: Wilhelm Fink Verlag.

Kramsch, Claire (1989) New directions in the teaching of language and culture. In *NFLC Occasional Papers*, Washington DC (National Foreign Language Center at the Johns Hopkins University, pp. 1–13.

Kramsch, Claire (1991) Culture in language learning: A view from the States. In Kees de Bot, R.B. Ginsberg and Claire Kramsch (eds) *Foreign Language Research in Cross-Cultural Perspective.* Amsterdam: John Benjamins, pp. 217–240.

Kramsch, Claire (1993) *Context and Culture in Language Teaching.* Oxford: Oxford University Press.

Kramsch, Claire (1998a) *Language and Culture.* Oxford: Oxford University Press.

Kramsch, Claire (1998b) The privilege of the intercultural speaker. In Michael Byram and Michael Fleming (eds) *Language Learning in Intercultural Perspective. Approaches through Drama and Ethnography.* Cambridge: Cambridge University Press, pp. 16–31.

Kramsch, Claire (2002) Introduction: How can we tell the dancer from the dance? In Claire Kramsch (ed.) *Language Acquisition and Language Socialization: Ecological Perspectives.* London: Continuum, pp. 1–30.

Kramsch, Claire (2004) Language, thought, and culture. In Alan Davies and Catherine Elder (eds) *The Handbook of Applied Linguistics.* Malden, MA etc.: Blackwell, pp. 235–261.

Kramsch, Claire (2006) Culture in language teaching. In Hanne Leth Andersen, Karen Lund and Karen Risager (eds) *Culture in Language Learning.* Aarhus: Aarhus University Press.

Kramsch, Claire (forthcoming) The multilingual subject. In I. de Florio Hansen und A. Hu (eds) *Mehrsprachigkeit und multikulturelle Identität.* Tübingen: Stauffenberg Verlag.

Krauskopf, Jürgen (1985) *Das Deutschland- und Frankreichbild in Schulbüchern.* Frankfurt a. M.: Gunter Narr Verlag.

Kroeber, A.L. and Kluckhohn, Clyde (1952) *Culture – A Critical Review of Concepts and Definitions.* New York: Vintage Books.

Kroymann, Maren and Ostermann, Dorothea (1977) Beitrag zur Untersuchung des Französischunterrichts von 1914–1945. In *Kritik der Frankreichforschung. Argument Sonderband* 13, pp. 144–167.

Krueger, Merle and Ryan, Frank (eds) (1993) *Language and Content. Discipline- and Content-Based Approaches to Language Study.* Lexington, Mass.: D.C. Heath and Company.

Lado, Robert (1957) *Linguistics Across Cultures: Applied Linguistics for Language Teachers.* Ann Arbor: University of Michigan Press.

Lafayette, Robert C. (ed.) (1975) *The Cultural Revolution in Foreign Language Teaching. A Guide for Building the Modern Curriculum.* Skokie, Ill.: National Textbook Company.

Lahbabi, M. (1961) *Du clos à l'ouvert.* Casablanca: Comité du Maghreb pour la Publication, la Traduction et l'Edition.

Langer, Jürgen and Schurig, Manfred (1972) Politik im Fremdsprachenunterricht. *Praxis des neusprachlichen Unterrichts* 19, pp. 5–13.

Lantolf, James P. (1999) Second culture acquisition. Cognitive considerations. In Eli Hinkel (ed.) *Culture in Second Language Teaching and Learning.* Cambridge: Cambridge University Press, pp. 28–46.

Leathes Report (1918) *Modern Studies, Being a Report of the Committee on the Position of Modern Languages in the Educational System of Great Britain.* London: HMSO.

Le Page, R. and Tabouret-Keller, A. (1985) *Acts of Identity: Creole-based Approaches to Language and Ethnicity.* Cambridge: Cambridge University Press.

Lessard-Clouston, Michael (1997) Towards an Understanding of culture in L2/FL education. *The Internet TESL Journal* 3, 5. 11 pp. (on line)

Lewis, Michael (1993) *The Lexical Approach. The State of ELT and a Way Forward.* Hove: Language Teaching Publications.

Liddicoat, Anthony J. and Crozet, Chantal (eds) (2000) *Teaching Languages, Teaching Cultures.* Applied Linguistics Association of Australia, Melbourne, Vic.: Language Australia.

Lo Bianco, Joseph, Liddicoat, Anthony J. and Crozet, Chantal (eds) (1999) *Striving for the Third Place. Intercultural Competence through Language Education.* Melbourne, Vic.: Language Australia.

Lo Bianco, Joseph and Crozet, Chantal (eds) (2003) *Teaching Invisible Culture. Classroom Practive and Theory.* Melbourne: Language Australia Ltd.

Lo Bianco, Joseph (2004) *Resources for Cultural Language Learning.* Melbourne: CAE Press.

Löschmann, Martin and Stroinska, Magda (eds) (1998) *Stereotype im Fremdsprachenunterricht.* Frankfurt a. M.: Peter Lang.

Lund, Karen and Risager, Karen (2001) Dansk i midten. *Sprogforum* 19, pp. 4–8.

Lundgren, Ulla (1995) Från realia till interkulturell förståelse – engelskämnet i Lgr 80 och Lpo 94. *LMS-Lingua* 2, pp. 24–26.

Lundgren, Ulla (2001) *Att utbilda för interkulturell förståelse. En studie av styrande texter för grundskolans engelskundervisning.* Malmö Högskola, Institutionen för pedagogik.

Lyons, John (1995) *Linguistic Semantics. An Introduction.* Cambridge: Cambridge University Press.

Mailhac, Jean-Pierre (1996) The formulation of translation strategies for cultural references. In Charlotte Hoffman (ed.) *Language, Culture and Communication in Contemporary Europe.* Clevedon: Multilingual Matters, pp. 132–151.

Martin-Jones, Marilyn (1995) Code-switching in the classroom: Two decades of research. In Lesley Milroy and Pieter Muysken (eds) *One Speaker, Two Languages. Cross-disciplinary Perspectives on Code-switching.* Cambridge: Cambridge University Press, pp. 344–355.

Maslow, A.H. (1954) *Motivation and Personality.* New York: Harper.

Mauger, G. (1953) *Cours de langue et civilisation françaises.* Paris: Hachette.

Melde, Wilma (1987) *Zur Integration von Landeskunde und Kommunikation im Fremdsprachenunterricht.* Tübingen: Gunter Narr Verlag.

Mennecke, Arnim (1992) Nicht-linguistische Inhalte in Lehrwerken und interpretative Lehrwerkkritik. In Manfred Erdmenger (ed.) *Interkulturelle Bildung und Sprachen. Festschrift für Peter Doyé.* Abt. Schulpädagogik des Seminars für Unterrichtswissenschaft des technischen Universität Braunschweig, pp. 183–192.

Meyer, Meinert (1986) *Shakespeare oder Fremdsprachenkorrespondenz? Zur Reform des Fremdsprachenunterrichts in der Sekundarstufe II.* Wetzlar: Büchse der Pandora.

Michaud, Guy and Marc, Edmond (1981) *Vers une science des civilisations?* Bruxelles: Editions Complexe.

Milroy, Leslie (1980) *Language and Social Networks.* Oxford: Blackwell.

Modern Languages: Learning, Teaching, Assessment. A Common European Framework of Reference (1996) Strasbourg: Council of Europe, Council for Cultural Co-operation.

Morain, Genelle (1983) Commitment to the teaching of foreign cultures. *The Modern Language Journal* 67, pp. 403–412.

Morgan, Carol and Cain, Albane (2000) *Foreign Language and Culture Learning from a Dialogic Perspective*. Clevedon: Multilingual Matters.

Müller, Bernd-Dietrich (ed.) (1981) *Konfrontative Semantik*. Tübingen: Gunther Narr.

Müller-Jacquier, Bernd (2000) Interkulturelle Didaktik. In Michael Byram (ed.) *Routledge Encyclopedia of Language Teaching and Learning*, pp. 303–307.

Munck, Maria (1988a) Indledning til temahæfte for russisklærere, kulturundervisning. *Tværsproglige Blade*, Danish University of Education, Copenhagen.

Munck, Maria (1988b) Sprog, samfund og kultur i fremmedsprogsundervisningen: En sociolingvistisk skitse. In *Tværsproglige Blade* 8 (1), pp. 37–58.

Murphy, Elizabeth (1988) The cultural dimension in foreign language teaching: Four models. *Language, Culture and Curriculum* 1 (2), pp. 147–162.

Musumeci, Diane (1997) *Breaking Tradition. An Exploration of the Historical Relationship between Theory and Practice in Second Language Teaching*. New York etc.: The McGraw-Hill Companies, Inc.

Neuner, Gerhard (1994) *The Role of Sociocultural Competence in Foreign Language Teaching and Learning*. Strasbourg: Council of Europe, Council for Cultural Co-operation.

Newmark, Peter (1988) *A Textbook of Translation*. New York etc.: Prentice Hall.

Norton, Bonny (2000) *Identity and Language Learning. Gender, Ethnicity and Educational Change*. Harlow, England etc.: Pearson Education.

Nostrand, Howard Lee (1966) Describing and teaching the sociocultural context of a foreign language and literature. In A. Valdman (ed.) *Trends in Language Teaching*. McGraw-Hill Company, pp. 1–25.

Nostrand, Howard Lee (1967) *Background Data for the Teaching of French*. Seattle: University of Washington.

Oakland, John (1984) British Civilisation: Institutions, units and problems at Grunnfag Level. *Språk og språkundervisning* 3, pp. 15–19.

Ochs, Elinor (1988) *Culture and Language Development. Language Acquisition and Language Socialisation in a Samoan Village*. Cambridge: Cambridge University Press.

Ogden, C.K. (1930) *Basic English. A General Introduction with Rules and Grammar*. London: Kegan Paul, Trench, Trubner and Co.

Olbert, Jürgen (ed.) (1977) *Gesammelte Aufsätze zur Frankreichkunde*. Berlin: Diesterweg.

Olwig, Karen Fog and Hastrup, Kirsten (eds) (1997) *Siting Culture. The Shifting Anthropological Object*. London and New York: Routledge.

Osler, Audry and Starkey, Hugh (1996) *Teacher Education and Human Rights*. London: David Fulton Publishers.

Oxford, Rebecca L. (1994) Teaching culture in the language classroom: Toward a new philosophy. In James E. Alatis (ed.) *Educational Linguistics, Crosscultural Communication and Global Interdependence*. Georgetown University Press, pp. 27–45.

Palmer, Gary B. (1996) *Toward a Theory of Cultural Linguistics*. Austin: University of Texas Press.

Papademetre, Leo (2000) Developing pathways for conceptualising the integration of culture-and-language. In Anthony J. Liddicoat and Chantal Crozet (eds) *Teaching Languages, Teaching Cultures*. Applied Linguistics Association of Australia, Melbourne, Vic.: Language Australia.

Papademetre, Leo with Scarino, Angela (2000) *Integrating Culture Learning in the Languages Classroom. A Multi-perspective Conceptual Journey for Teachers*. With video. Melbourne, Vic.: Language Australia.

Pavlenko, Anita (2003) 'Language of the enemy': Foreign language education and national identity. *International Journal of Bilingual Education and Bilingualism* 6 (5), pp. 313–331.

Pennycook, Alastair (1994) *The Cultural Politics of English as an International Language*. London and New York: Longman.

Pennycook, Alastair (1998) *English and the Discourses of Colonialism*. London and New York: Routledge.

Phipps, Alison and Guilherme, Manuela (eds) (2004) *Critical Pedagogy. Political Approaches to Language and Intercultural Communication*. Clevedon: Multilingual Matters.

Picht, Robert (Hrsg.) (1974) *Perspektiven der Frankreichkunde. Ansätze zu einer interdisziplinär orientierten Romanistik*. Tübingen: Niemeyer Verlag.

Pike, Kenneth L. (1967) (1954) *Language in Relation to a Unified Theory of the Structure of Human Behavior*. The Hague and Paris: Mouton et Co.

Poirier, François (1983) L'objet civilisation. *Les langues modernes* 77, pp. 157–173.

Porcher, Louis (1982) L'enseignement de la civilisation en questions. *Etudes de Linguistique Appliquée* 47, pp. 39–49.

Porcher, Louis *et al.* (eds) (1986) *La civilisation*. Paris: Cle International.

Porcher, Louis (1994) Paysage de langues. *Zielsprache Französisch* 26 (4), pp. 194–198.

Pratt, Mary Louise (1987) Linguistic utopias. In Nigel Fabb *et al.* (eds) *The Linguistics of Writing*. Manchester: Manchester University Press, pp. 48–66.

Puren, Christian (1998) La culture en classe de langue: 'Enseigner quoi?' et quelques autres questions non subsidiaires. *Les langues modernes* 4, pp. 40–46.

Puren, Christian (1999) La didactique des langues-cultures étrangères entre méthodologie et didactologie. *Les langues modernes* 3, pp. 26–41.

Raasch, Albert, Hüllen, Werner and Zapp, Franz Josef (Hrsg.) (1983) *Beiträge zur Landeskunde im Fremdsprachenunterricht*. Frankfurt a. M.: Verlag Moritz Diesterweg.

Rampton, Ben (1995) *Crossing: Language and Ethnicity Among Adolescents*. London and New York: Longman.

Reboullet, André (éd.) (1973) *L'enseignement de la civilisation française*. Paris: Hachette.

Recommendation Concerning Education for International Understanding, Co-operation and Peace and Education Relating to Human Rights and Fundamental Freedoms. Adopted by the General Conference of UNESCO at its 18th session on 19 November 1974 (www.unesco.org).

Rehbein, Jochen (Hrsg.) (1985) *Interkulturelle Kommunikation*. Tübingen: Gunther Narr.

Renan, Ernest (1882) *Qu'est-ce qu'une nation?* Conférence faite en Sorbonne le 11 mars 1882. Paris. English translation: John Hutchinson and Anthony D. Smith (eds) (1994) *Nationalism*. Oxford and New York: Oxford University Press, pp. 17–18.

Richards, J. and Rodgers, T. (1986) *Approaches and Methods in Language Teaching*. Cambridge: Cambridge University Press.

Ring Hansen, H. and Mouridsen, F.T. (eds) (1955) *On England and the English*. Copenhagen: Gyldendal.

Risager, Karen and Andersen, Helga (1980) Basale ordforråd. *TRUC* 6, pp. 35–78.

Risager, Karen (1984) Sprogfagene mellem nationalisme og internationalisme. In Marianne Kristiansen, Karen Risager and Karen Sonne Jakobsen (eds) *Umoderne Sprog? Om fremmedsprog i gymnasiet*. Copenhagen: Gyldendal, pp. 112–128.

Risager, Karen (1987a) Cultural studies and foreign language teaching in Denmark. *ROLIG-papir* 41, Roskilde University.

Risager, Karen (1989a) World studies and foreign language teaching: A perspective from Denmark. *World Studies Journal* 7 (2), pp. 28–31.

Risager, Karen (1989b) Kulturformidling. En idehistorisk oversigt over kulturbegrebet i fremmedsprogsfagene. In Gabriele Kasper and Johannes Wagner (eds) *Grundbog i fremmedsprogspædagogik*. Copenhagen: Gyldendal, pp. 254–267.

Risager, Karen (1991a) Cultural studies and foreign language teaching after World War II: The international debate as received in the Scandinavian countries. In Dieter Buttjes and Michael Byram (eds) *Mediating Languages and Cultures*. Clevedon: Multilingual Matters, pp. 36–46.

Risager, Karen (1991b) Cultural references in European foreign language teaching textbooks: An evaluation of recent tendencies. In Dieter Buttjes and Michael Byram (eds) *Mediating Languages and Cultures*. Clevedon: Multilingual Matters, pp. 181–192.

Risager, Karen (1993) Buy some petit souvenir aus Dänemark! Viden og bevidsthed om sprogmødet. In Karen Risager, Anne Holmen and Anna Trosborg (eds) *Sproglig mangfoldighed – om sproglig viden og bevidsthed*. Association Danoise de Linguistique Appliquée, Roskilde University, pp. 30–42.

Risager, Karen (1994) Forskning i den kulturelle dimension af fremmedsprogsundervisningen. *Sprog og Kulturmøde* 6, Aalborg University, pp. 75–83.

Risager, Karen (1996) Eleven som etnograf. *Sprogforum* 4, pp. 49–54.

Risager, Karen (1998) Language teaching and the process of European integration. In Michael Byram and Michael Fleming (eds) *Language Learning in Intercultural Perspective. Approaches through Drama and Ethnography*. Cambridge: Cambridge University Press, pp. 242–254.

Risager, Karen and Aktor, Leon (eds) (1999) *Kulturforståelse i folkeskolens sprogundervisning*. Albertslund: Malling Beck.

Risager, Karen (1999a) Critique of textbook criticism. In Dorthe Albrechtsen *et al.* (eds) *Perspectives on Foreign and Second Language Pedagogy*. Odense: Odense University Press, pp. 53–62.

Risager, Karen (1999b) Kulturtilegnelse og kulturundervisning. In Anne Holmen and Karen Lund (eds), *Studier i dansk som andetsprog*. Copenhagen: Akademisk Forlag, pp. 207–236.

Risager, Karen (2000) Cultural awareness. In Michael Byram (ed.) *Routledge Encyclopedia of Language Teaching and Learning*. London and New York: Routledge, pp. 159–162.

Risager, Karen (2003) *Det nationale dilemma i sprog- og kulturpædagogikken. Et studie i forholdet mellem sprog og kultur*. Copenhagen: Akademisk Forlag.

Risager, Karen (2004) A social and cultural view of language. In Hans Lauge Hansen (ed.) *Disciplines and Interdisciplinarity in Foreign Language Studies*. Copenhagen: Museum Tusculanum Press, pp. 21–34.

Risager, Karen (2005) Cross- and intercultural communication. In Ulrich Ammon *et al.* (eds) *Sociolinguistics/Soziolinguistik*. Berlin and New York: Walter de Gruyter.

Risager, Karen (2006) *Language and Culture: Global Flows and Local Complexity*. Clevedon: Multilingual Matters.

Roberts, Celia *et al.* (2001) *Language Learners as Ethnographers*. Clevedon: Multilingual Matters.

Robertson, Roland (1992) *Globalization. Social Theory and Global Culture.*
London: Sage Publications.

Robinson, Gail L. Nemetz (1985) *Crosscultural Understanding. Processes and
Approaches for Foreign Language, English as a Second Language and
Bilingual Educators.* New York: Pergamon Press.

Rülcker, T. (1969) *Der Neusprachenunterricht an höheren Schulen.* Frankfurt
a. M.: Diesterweg.

Ryan, Phyllis (1996) Sociolinguistic goals for foreign language teaching
and teachers' metaphorical images of culture. *Foreign Language Annals*
29 (4), pp. 571–586.

Sauvageot, A. (1964) *Portrait du vocabulaire français.* Paris: Larousse.

Saville-Troike, Muriel (1989) (2nd edn) *The Ethnography of Communication.
An Introduction.* Oxford: Blackwell.

Schieffelin, Bambi B., Woolard, Kathryn A. and Kroskrity, Paul V. (eds)
(1998) *Language Ideologies. Practice and Theory.* New York and Oxford:
Oxford University Press.

Schumann, Adelheid (1986) *Etre Français – Rester Breton.* Paderborn:
Schöningh.

Schüttler, A. (1964) *Unser Nachbar Frankreich.* Gütersloh.

Seelye, H. Ned (1974) *Teaching Culture. Strategies for Foreign Language
Educators.* Skokie, Ill.: National Textbook Company.

Seidlhofer, Barbara (2001) Brave new English? *The European English
Messenger* X (1), pp. 42–48.

Sercu, Lies (2000) *Acquiring Intercultural Communicative Competence from
Textbooks. The Case of Flemish Adolescents Learning German.* Leuven:
Leuven University Press.

Sercu, Lies *et al.* (2005) *Foreign Language Teachers and Intercultural Competence.*
Clevedon: Multilingual Matters.

Sevaldsen, Jørgen and Thorsen, Niels (1994) *Samfundsvidenskab for
sprogstuderende. Vejledning i opgaveskrivning, især for engelskstuderende.*
Copenhagen: Akademisk Forlag.

Sigtryggsson, S. (ed.) (1933) *Deutsche Kultur- und Characterbilder.*
Aschehoug Dansk Forlag.

Skutnabb-Kangas, Tove (1981) *Tvåspråkighet.* Lund: Liber Läromedel.

Skutnabb-Kangas, Tove (2000) *Linguistic Genocide in Education or
Worldwide Diversity?* Mahwah, N.J.: Lawrence Erlbaum.

Skårdal, Dorothy Burton (1979) Kulturkunnskapens plass i engelskfaget.
Språk og språkundervisning 3, pp. 36–40.

Smith, Anthony D. (1986) *The Ethnic Origins of Nations.* London: Blackwell.

Snow, David and Byram, Michael (1997) *Crossing Frontiers. The School
Study Visit Abroad.* London: Centre for Information on Language
Teaching and Research (CILT).

Snow, Marguerite Ann and Brinton, Donna M. (eds) (1997) *The Content-Based Classroom. Perspectives on Integrating Language and Content*. White Plains, N.Y.: Longman.

Sörensen, Christer and Thunander, Rodolf (1980) Das Deutschlandbild in schwedischen Deutschlehrwerken. *LMS-Lingua* 2, pp. 78–87.

Sohlberg, Anna-Liisa (1957) *Ranskankielen Alkeiskirja*. Helsinki: Kustannusosakeyhtiö Otava.

Spantzel, Claudia (2001) *Die Landeskunde-Diskussion im Rahmen des Fremdsprachenunterrichts in der DDR*. Frankfurt a.M.: Peter Lang Verlag.

Spranger, E. (1925) *Der gegenwärtige Stand der Geisteswissenschaften und die Schule*. Leipzig/Berlin.

Standards for Foreign Language Learning. Preparing for the 21st Century (1996) ISBN: 0–935868–85–2.

Starkey, Hugh (1988) Foreign languages. In Graham Pike and David Selby *Global Teacher, Global Learner*. London: Hodder and Stoughton, pp. 239–241.

Starkey, Hugh (ed.) (1989) *World Studies and Foreign Languages*. Special issue of *World Studies Journal* 7 (2).

Starkey, Hugh (1991a) World Studies and foreign language teaching: Converging approaches in textbook writing. In Dieter Buttjes and Michael Byram (eds) *Mediating Languages and Cultures*. Clevedon: Multilingual Matters, pp. 209–227.

Starkey, Hugh (ed.) (1991b) *The Challenge of Human Rights Education*. London: Cassell Education Limited (The Council of Europe).

Starkey, Hugh (1996) Intercultural education through foreign language learning: A human rights approach. In A. Osler, H.F. Rathenow and H. Starkey (eds) *Teaching for Citizenship in Europe*. Stoke-on-Trent: Trentham Books, pp. 103–116.

Starkey, Hugh (1999) Foreign language teaching to adults: Implicit end explicit political education. *Oxford Review of Education*, 25 (1–2), pp. 155–169.

Steele, Ross and Suozzi, Andrew (1994) *Teaching French Culture. Theory and Practice*. Lincolnwood, Ill.: National Textbook Company.

Stern, H.H. (1983) *Fundamental Concepts of Language Teaching*. Oxford: Oxford University Press.

Stern, H.H. (1992) *Issues and Options in Language Teaching* (ed. by Patrick Allen and Birgit Harley). Oxford: Oxford University Press.

Stevenson, Patrick (1993) The German language and the construction of national identities. In John L. Flood *et al.* (eds) *'Das unsichtbare Band der Sprache'. Studies in German Language and Linguistic History. In Memory of Leslie Seiffert*. Stuttgart: Verlag Hans-Dieter Heinz, Akademischer Verlag, pp. 333–356.

Strasheim, Lorraine A. (1975) We're *all* ethnics: In Hyphenated Americans, professional ethnics, and ethnics by attraction. In Robert C. Lafayette (ed.) *The Cultural Revolution in Foreign Language Teaching.* Skokie, Ill.: National Textbook Company, pp. 1–18.

Strength Through Wisdom: A Critique of U.S. Capability (Nov. 1979) *Modern Language Journal* 64, 1980.

Summers, Della (ed.) (1992) *Longman Dictionary of English Language and Culture.* Harlow, Essex: Longman.

Süss, J. (1961) Stellung und Aufgaben der Auslands- und Kulturkunde im deutschen Fremdsprachenunterricht mit besonderer Rücksichtigung der Sowjetkunde als eines Mittels der sozialistischen Bildung und Erziehung auf der Elementar- und Mittelstufe in der allgemeinbildenen polytechnischen Oberschule der Deutschen Demokratischen Republik. Dresden.

Svanholt, O. (1968) *Bøger og metoder i dansk fremmedsprogsundervisning. En historisk fremstilling.* Copenhagen: Det Schønbergske Forlag.

Thürmann, Eike (1994) Fremdsprachenunterricht, Landeskunde und interkulturelle Erziehung. *Die neueren Sprachen* 93 (4), pp. 316–334.

Tomalin, B. and Stempleski, S. (1993) *Cultural Awareness.* Oxford: Oxford University Press.

Tornberg, Ulrika (2000) *Om språkundervisning i mellanrummet.* Uppsala: Uppsala University.

Vereščagin, E.M. and Kostomarov, V.G. (1972) Bemerkungen zu einer sprachlich orientierten landeskundlichen Methodik im Fremdsprachenunterricht. *Deutsch als Fremdsprache* 9, pp. 70–77.

Vereščagin, E.M. and Kostomarov, V.G. (1973) *Jazyk i kul'tura.* Moskva: Izsatel'stvo moskovskogo universiteta.

Vereščagin, E.M. and Kostomarov, V.G. (1974) Sprachbezogene Landeskunde. Versuch einer methodischen Begriffsbestimmung am Beispiel des Russischen. *Praxis des neusprachlichen Unterrichts* 21, pp. 308–315.

Verlée, Léon (1973) *Enseignement des langues et information culturelle.* Bruxelles: Labor (1st edn, 1969, Paris: Nathan.)

Wagner, Johannes (1999) Faglig identitet og faglig udvikling i dansk som andetsprog. In Anne Holmen og Karen Lund (eds) *Studier i dansk som andetsprog.* Copenhagen: Akademisk Forlag, pp. 167–193.

Weber, Horst (ed.) (1976) *Landeskunde im Fremdsprachenunterricht.* Kösel-Verlag.

Wegner, Anke (1999) *100 Jahre Deutsch als Fremdsprache in Frankreich und England. Eine vergleichende Studie von Methoden, Inhalten und Zielen.* München: Iudicium Verlag.

Widdowson, H.G. (1988) Aspects of the relationship between culture and language. In *Interkulturelle Kommunikation und Fremdsprachenlernen* (= *Triangle* 7). AUPELF/The British Council/Goethe Institut, Paris: Didier Erudition, pp. 13–22.

Wilkins, D.A. (1976) *Notional Syllabuses. A Taxonomy and its Relevance to Foreign Language Curriculum Development.* Oxford: Oxford University Press.

Zarate, Geneviève (1986) *Enseigner une culture étrangère.* Paris: Hachette.

Zarate, Geneviève (1993) *Représentations de l'étranger et didactique des langues.* Paris: Didier.

Zarate, Geneviève (1998) Pourquoi faut-il expliciter les frontières culturelles? *Les langues modernes* 1, pp. 8–15.

Author Index

Subject Index

aesthetic, 8, 52, 84, 110, 136
Alltagswissen, 78
America, 55, 64, 123, 140
American, 20, 29, 33, 34, 35, 36, 40, 41, 42,
    63, 64, 69, 72, 75, 92, 93, 100, 101, 102,
    103, 106, 107, 112, 113, 115, 127, 130, 131,
    134, 135, 142, 148, 151, 156, 162, 170, 211,
    217
antiquities, 37
Arabic, 12, 118, 136, 142, 175, 227, 231
audio-visual, 26, 34, 62, 87
Australia, 76, 136, 137, 141, 155, 193, 218
Australian, 13, 148, 155, 162
Austria, 76, 146, 193, 236

background studies, 5
banal nationalism, 13, 14, 16, 17, 76, 87, 124,
    153, 159, 210, 218, 233
banal nationalist, 206
Belgian, 26, 29
Belgium, 76, 150, 203, 236
Bildung, 56, 78, 117
border concept, 206, 207
Britain, 37, 39, 46, 52, 66, 92, 93, 119, 120,
    127, 131, 135, 136, 143, 196, 203, 213
British, 13, 37, 38, 49, 65, 75, 94, 107, 120,
    131, 134, 135, 148, 162, 196, 211, 217
Brötchen-Gretchen model, 28, 40, 70

Canada, 22, 76, 106, 113, 136, 237
Chinese, 118, 142, 173, 231
civilisation, 5, 22, 37, 52, 59, 63, 64, 65, 66, 67,
    69, 71, 75, 84, 85, 86, 101, 107, 135, 179,
    192
code-mixing, 17, 130, 229
code-switching, 17, 193, 198, 199, 227, 229
collaboration, 57, 120, 140, 184, 210
Common European Framework, 115, 143,
    204
communicative event, 167, 174, 175, 177,
    182, 184, 185
community, 1, 6, 14, 32, 88, 89, 110, 138, 154,
    156, 174, 177, 185, 186, 187, 190, 192, 197,
    209, 211, 212, 221, 228, 236, 237

complex commentary, 61, 62, 71
complexity, 16, 17, 66, 147, 148, 153, 166,
    184, 185, 187, 190, 193, 194, 198, 199, 207,
    214, 216, 217, 218, 220, 226, 229, 230, 234,
    235, 236, 239
connotation, 89
construction, 46, 77, 82, 128, 133, 138, 139,
    169, 173, 177, 182, 187, 190, 200, 201, 208
contact, 12, 17, 48, 54, 115, 116, 124, 149, 154,
    156, 167, 168, 190, 192, 194, 197, 198, 201,
    205, 206, 213, 214, 216
content dimension, 8, 9, 30, 70, 138, 158,
    159, 163, 164
content-based, 22, 220
context dimension, 8, 159, 160
contextualisation, 206, 213
convergent, 183, 184
cooperation, 1, 8, 56, 113, 115, 118, 120, 121,
    128, 129, 143, 144, 162, 195, 199, 207, 209,
    212, 214, 215, 227, 230, 231, 235
cosmopolitan, 233, 234, 236, 239
Council of Europe, 10, 46, 47, 50, 71, 76, 77,
    78, 84, 113, 114, 115, 118, 119, 120, 127,
    139, 143, 195
cultural content, 36, 39, 50, 70, 76, 88, 94, 99,
    116, 118, 136, 155, 182, 220, 238
cultural context, 10, 47, 96, 108, 109, 110,
    111, 113, 128, 132, 136, 138, 154, 155, 159,
    167, 175, 176, 177, 187, 204, 217, 220
cultural flow, 16, 17, 135, 153, 183, 212, 230
cultural learning, 6, 74, 102, 114, 122, 145,
    164
cultural load, 88, 89, 90, 91
cultural reference, 178, 179, 182, 183, 201,
    202
cultural representation, 118, 158, 164, 180,
    181, 203, 205, 219, 232
Cultural Studies, 7, 49, 73, 75, 92, 93, 101,
    106, 116, 117, 132, 145, 152, 160, 207
cultural word, 59, 64, 179, 200, 202, 203, 204,
    232
culturally neutral, 137, 140, 145, 159, 166
culture assimilator, 42
culture capsule, 41